Divine Order

Abundant Overflow

CARRIE PICKETT

Published by Harrison House Publishers

Shippensburg, PA 17257

ISBN 13 TP: 978-1-6675-1511-3

ISBN 13 eBook: 978-1-6675-1512-0

For Worldwide Distribution, Printed in the USA

1 2 3 4 5 6 / 29 28 27 26

Dedication

This book is dedicated to the many missionaries I journeyed with as a young missionary—those who took the time to pull me aside and lovingly counsel me that my calling was a marathon, not a sprint. They taught me practical ways to prioritize my relationship with God, to value rest, and to prepare for the future marriage and family the Lord desired for me. Even today, I draw daily from those lessons, and I continue to carry with me the deep care and love shown to an immature yet passionate and eager young woman discovering the call of God on her life. I am profoundly grateful.

This book is also dedicated to my husband, Mike, who believes in me and in the calling and gifts on my life like no one else. He consistently creates space for rest and creativity and supports the home we are building together—a place where our relationship and our family are rooted in serving the Lord. His strength, encouragement, and partnership are a constant gift.

Acknowledgment

I would also like to acknowledge Shirley Pound, whose insight and skill were instrumental in helping shape my teaching voice into words on the page—words that will impact more lives than we could imagine. Thank you so much!

Contents

Preface

I'm excited to bring this book into the body of Christ and grateful that you're taking the opportunity to let these principles transform your life. I believe each of us can relate to those days when we feel focused, productive, and deeply aligned with our divine purpose. Our goals are clear, our path is sure, and we can sense that we're walking in step with God's plan.

But I also know many believers who struggle—not only in discovering their divine destiny, but in maintaining strength and focus in the face of constant busyness. Life can become a relentless cycle of striving, and in the process, many lose sight of the order, peace, and rest God designed for them to walk in.

My own story is one marked by seasons of being a workaholic—driven by performance, unable to rest, and eventually burned out more times than I care to admit. Yet through every valley, God was faithful. He met me in the exhaustion and taught me priceless spiritual lessons that didn't just bring healing—they completely transformed the direction of my life.

The principles the Lord showed me about surrendering my time were deeply intertwined with surrendering my destiny. This was a key discovery: that surrender is the only pathway to true promotion and alignment. And surrender is not a one-time prayer; it is a lifestyle, one that must be revisited again and again in each new season of our lives as we learn to walk submitted to Christ.

The Lord had to dismantle my old ways of thinking and rebuild my understanding of what divine order truly looks like. He showed me that rest is not weakness, that margin is not laziness, and that productivity divorced from His presence is not fruitfulness. This book is a testimony of that journey—a roadmap for anyone longing to trade chaos for clarity, strife for peace, and human effort for Spirit-led effectiveness.

My prayer is that, as you read these pages, you won't just gain principles but encounter the God of order Himself—and that His divine design will begin to shape every part of your life.

Believing that you're entering a new season of Divine Order and Abundant Overflow!

Carrie Pickett

Chapter One

Surrendered Time, Surrendered Vision, Surrendered Life

Introduction

There's something truly powerful about surrender, but it's not always what we think. Surrender isn't weakness. It isn't giving up. Surrender is trust. It's the confident handing over of what we hold onto so tightly, our time, our plans, our expectations, and saying, "God, I believe You can do more with this than I ever could." For many believers, the frustration they feel in their walk with God often stems from this very area: they're trying to serve God without first surrendering the details of their everyday life to Him.

I remember when the Lord first started challenging me on how I viewed my time. I was in ministry, constantly busy, feeling like I was doing good things for God. But somewhere in the noise, I had stopped asking Him what He actually wanted me to do. I had created a schedule and asked Him to bless it. That moment of realization was so convicting, but also so freeing. I remember sitting with my planner and saying, "God, this calendar is Yours." That one simple act shifted everything.

In this chapter, we're going to explore how divine order begins with surrender, specifically surrendering your time, your vision, and ultimately your life. These three areas are deeply connected. When you learn to give God your time, you create space to hear His voice. As you hear His voice, you begin to walk in the unique vision He's placed inside of you. And when you begin walking in that vision, rooted in relationship, you step into a life of supernatural abundance, not just financial, but abundant joy, clarity, peace, fruitfulness, and purpose.

This isn't a chapter about doing more. It's about doing what matters most, what God has designed specifically for you. It's about pulling away from the world's definitions of productivity and success and anchoring yourself in kingdom reality. Because when your time is surrendered, your vision becomes clear. And when your vision is from Him, your life begins to overflow.

Fix Your Focus

At the heart of this chapter are three divine themes, intricately woven together to lead you into a lifestyle of clarity, peace, and fruitfulness:

- Surrendered Time: Time management isn't about packing more into your day; it's about handing your day over to the One who designed it. When God is the master of your time, your life becomes ordered, peaceful, and productive in ways you could never achieve on your own.
- Surrendered Vision: Vision isn't a career path or five-year goal; it's letting the life of God lead you into what He already planned for you. True vision flows from intimacy. It's discovered when we stop trying to be great and start letting God be great in us.
- Surrendered Life: Abundance isn't found in striving; it's found in trusting. When you surrender your life to the Shepherd, you begin

to live from a place of rest, provision, and supernatural increase. The surrendered life is the abundant life.

These three are not separate chapters of your story; they are pages turning together. When you surrender your time, your heart becomes available to hear God's voice. When you hear His voice, your steps are ordered by His vision. And when you walk in His vision, you experience the overflow of His abundance.

God Doesn't Want to Fit into Your Schedule; He Wants to Lead It

One of the greatest lies the enemy sells to believers is that we don't have time. I hear it so often, even in Bible school settings: "I'm too busy to pray," "I wish I had more time to get into the Word," or "Once this season settles down, I'll really press into God." But what if I told you that the problem isn't the time; it's the ownership!

I'll never forget sitting with my planner one day, stressed out and overwhelmed. I was in ministry, I was serving God, and yet I felt dry and tired. And in that moment, the Holy Spirit spoke something so clearly to my heart: "I don't want to be part of your schedule. I want to lead it." That statement changed my life.

You see, we often invite God to bless our plans instead of surrendering our plans to His leadership. But when we do that, we rob ourselves of the divine order He wants to bring into our daily lives. Proverbs 16:9 says, "*A man's heart plans his way, But the Lord directs his steps.*" When you let the Lord direct your steps, it's not about doing less; it's about doing what matters most. That's where divine order begins: not with efficiency, but with surrender.

Time isn't something we own; it's something we steward. And that stewardship starts when we hand over the calendar. The enemy knows how powerful a focused, Spirit-led believer is. That's why he keeps so many people bound in distraction and busyness. John 10:10 reminds us, "*The thief does not come except to steal, and to kill, and to destroy. I have come that they may have life, and that they may have it more abundantly.*" One of the first things the enemy steals is time because he knows it's where intimacy grows.

When we allow the Holy Spirit to lead our time, He begins to identify the things that are stealing from us. It might be too many commitments, unhealthy relationships, or simply the pressure to keep up with the world's idea of productivity. But when you begin asking the Lord, "What do You want to do with this day?" He'll show you how to cut out the noise and walk in clarity.

There was a full-time mom, working part-time, trying to juggle it all while attending classes online. She felt like she was failing in every area. But after one class session on surrendered time, she told me, "I realized I've been making plans and asking God to bless them instead of asking Him what He wants. I went home, and I physically handed Him my planner. And it's like peace walked into my living room." Her life didn't suddenly slow down, but her heart did. And that made all the difference.

The surrendered calendar is the beginning of supernatural order. God doesn't just want your quiet time; He wants your timeline. When He leads your schedule, He fills your life.

When You Make Room for God in Your Time, You Make Room for His Vision in Your Heart

There's a reason the enemy fights our time so intensely. It's not just to keep us tired or busy, it's to keep us disconnected from the voice of God. Because if he can clutter your time, he can cloud your vision.

When your time is surrendered, your heart becomes quiet. And when your heart is quiet, you can actually hear God speak. Psalm 46:10 says, "*Be still, and know that I* am *God.*" Stillness isn't inactivity; it's intimacy. It's choosing to be present with the Lord so you can receive His direction, not just His correction.

The surrendered calendar is the beginning of supernatural order. God doesn't just want your quiet time; He wants your timeline. When He leads your schedule, He fills your life.

I remember a season in my life when I was running from one thing to the next, always busy, always "productive," but I felt like I was missing something. And it was during a quiet moment in prayer that the Lord said to me, "Carrie, you've been moving, but not progressing." That hit me hard. I was doing a lot for Him, but not with Him. I had filled my schedule with good things, but not always *God* things.

That's when I learned the value of guarding my mornings. I began to treat my time with God not as an appointment, but as my foundation. It was in those moments that vision came. Ideas, direction, strategy, all flowed from simply being with Him.

Jeremiah 29:11–13 says, "'*For I know the thoughts that I think toward you,' says the Lord, 'thoughts of peace and not of evil, to give you a future and a hope. Then you will call upon Me and go and pray to Me, and I will listen to you. And you will seek Me and find* Me, *when you search for Me with all your heart.*'" Vision doesn't come through striving; it comes through seeking.

Vision isn't about climbing a ladder or chasing success; it's about relationship. When you surrender your time to God, you position yourself to receive His thoughts, His desires, and His creative strategies for your life. That's how vision is born—not out of ambition, but out of abiding.

One young woman came to me after a teaching session and said, "I've always felt like I didn't have a calling because I didn't have a specific career goal. But after hearing that vision comes from relationship, I realized I've had vision all along, I just didn't know that being faithful with my kids, with my home, and with the people in my life *was* part of the calling." That testimony stuck with me, because it's so true. Vision isn't always big and dramatic. Sometimes it looks like faithfulness in what's already in your hand.

Proverbs 29:18 (*King James Version*) tells us, "*Where* there is *no vision, the people perish.*" The *New King James Version* says, "*The people cast off restraint.*" When we don't have God's vision guiding our lives, we drift. We say "yes" to everything, hoping something will fulfill us. But when His vision anchors us, we can say "no" with confidence and yes with joy. That's how divine order begins to take shape.

So let me encourage you: the next time you sit down with your calendar, bring your Bible. Invite the Holy Spirit into your week. Ask Him not just what to do, but how to do it with His grace. Because surrendered time makes space for eternal vision. And once you see what God sees, you'll never want to go back to busyness again.

Vision Is Not Discovered Through Striving but Through Surrender

One of the most freeing revelations I've ever received is this: you don't have to figure it all out. You don't have to manufacture vision. You don't have to map out your destiny or try to impress God with your five-year plan. That's not how vision works in the kingdom.

Vision begins in surrender.

Ephesians 2:10 tells us, "*For we are His workmanship, created in Christ Jesus for good works, which God prepared beforehand that we should walk in them.*" Your calling was prepared before you were born. God isn't waiting for you to create it—He's inviting you to walk in what He's already authored.

In the early days of ministry, I wrestled with insecurity. I felt the weight of expectation, especially stepping into full-time missions. *What if I miss it? What if I'm not enough? What if I fail?* But one morning in prayer, the Lord spoke to my heart, "Carrie, I'm not asking you to figure out the plan. I'm asking you to follow Me." That truth settled something deep inside me. My job wasn't to *build* the vision; it was to *trust* the One who held it.

True vision flows out of intimacy with God. It's not a task list or job title; it's the expression of His life through you. When you surrender your life to Him, His dreams begin to unfold naturally. Psalm 37:4–5 says, "*Delight yourself also in the Lord, And He shall give you the desires of your heart. Commit your way to the Lord, Trust also in Him, and He shall bring it to pass.*" When your delight is in Him, your desires begin to align with His.

A woman once came to me feeling disqualified. She had grown up in a broken home, made choices she regretted, and believed that her past had disqualified her from anything significant. But as she spent time in the Word, something shifted. She stopped striving to prove herself and began abiding in the Father's love. And over time, vision began to stir—quietly at first, but powerfully. Today, she's walking in a beautiful, fruitful ministry of healing and restoration for women who've walked through the same pain she once carried. That's what surrender does; it redeems and redirects everything.

You can't mess up the call of God when you're surrendered to His voice. He's not looking for perfect execution; He's looking for yielded hearts.

Romans 8:14 says, "*For as many as are led by the Spirit of God, these are sons of God.*" Vision isn't about climbing a ladder; it's about following a

Shepherd. He leads you step by step. And with each step, your confidence grows, not in yourself, but in His faithfulness.

If you've been trying to "figure out" your purpose, let me encourage you to stop striving. The more you focus on intimacy with God, the more clearly you'll see your vision. Because when you know Him, you begin to see as He sees. And what He sees in you is powerful, fruitful, and full of impact.

God's Abundance Is Found in His Presence

When we think about abundance, it's easy to picture excess, overflowing bank accounts, opportunities, or possessions. But kingdom abundance is very different from the world's definition. In the kingdom, abundance begins with alignment. It's not about how much you have; it's about how closely your heart is aligned with the One who is your source.

True prosperity isn't just external; it's internal. Third John 1:2 says, "*Beloved, I pray that you may prosper in all things and be in health, just as your soul prospers.*" The condition of your soul determines how you carry blessing. Without alignment to God's heart, abundance can actually become a distraction. But when you're surrendered, prosperity becomes a tool for impact, not identity.

I remember first stepping into full-time ministry. I had very little by the world's standards. No savings. No guarantees. But what I had was a word from the Lord, and I clung to it. That year, I saw God's provision in ways that still bring tears to my eyes. A check would come in the mail right when a bill was due. Groceries would show up on our porch without me telling a soul. Opportunities opened that I never pursued. But even greater than the physical provision was the peace that settled into our hearts. I knew I was aligned with His will, and that's what abundance really is, rest in the certainty that God is faithful.

Matthew 6:33 says, "*But seek first the kingdom of God and His righteousness, and all these things shall be added to you.*" That's divine order: you don't chase the "things", you seek the King. And when your life aligns with His purposes, abundance flows freely.

A woman once shared with me that she used to stress constantly about finances. She grew up in poverty and carried a scarcity mindset into adulthood, even after she came to know Christ. But after one teaching on abundance as a reflection of alignment, she went home and repented. She told the Lord, "I trust You. I'm done making fear-based decisions." She began tithing, even when it felt risky. She started praying over her bills and inviting the Holy Spirit into her budget planning. Within months, not only were her needs met, but she began sowing into others and with joy! That's the shift that happens when alignment replaces anxiety.

Psalm 23:1–3 says, "*The Lord is my shepherd; I shall not want. He makes me to lie down in green pastures; He leads me beside the still waters. He restores my soul.*" You weren't made to live in a constant state of hustle. You were made to follow the Shepherd. And where He leads, provision is waiting.

Abundance isn't just about receiving; it's about becoming. When you're aligned with God's heart, you become a river of blessing. Your words carry life. Your giving becomes seed. Your joy is contagious. The fruit of the Spirit overflows in your daily life, and that's the kind of prosperity that transforms generations.

If you've been chasing abundance, pause and ask yourself: *Am I aligned with the heart of God in this area?* Because when your spirit, soul, and schedule align with the voice of the Holy Spirit, you stop living paycheck to paycheck spiritually, and you start living from overflow.

Your Time Is a Seed That Determines Your Harvest

Everything in the kingdom operates on seedtime and harvest. And one of the most overlooked seeds we have is our time. How we invest it determines the kind of fruit we'll see in our lives.

We often think of giving in terms of money, but time is one of the most valuable things you can offer God. Unlike money, once it's spent, you can't get it back. That's why surrendering your time is such a powerful act of worship. It's saying, "God, I trust that what You can do in one hour is more fruitful than what I could do in ten."

Galatians 6:7–8 says, "*Do not be deceived, God is not mocked; for whatever a man sows, that he will also reap. For he who sows to his flesh will of the flesh reap corruption, but he who sows to the Spirit will of the Spirit reap everlasting life.*" When you sow your time into the Spirit, into relationship with the Lord, into the Word, and into listening, you reap spiritual clarity, purpose, and direction.

I've watched this unfold countless times in students. One man in his 60s came to me feeling like it was too late for him. He had a successful career, raised a family, and had already "lived life," so to speak. But as he began dedicating time to study, prayer, and relationship with God, a completely new season of ministry opened up. He's now leading a men's ministry and mentoring young leaders with a fire he never had in his 30s. Why? Because he began sowing his time into the kingdom, and the harvest was explosive.

Jesus Himself modeled this. He would often withdraw from the crowds to pray, even when people were demanding His time. Luke 5:15–16 says, "*However, the report went around concerning Him all the more; and great multitudes came together to hear, and to be healed by Him of their infirmities. So, He Himself* often *withdrew into the wilderness and prayed.*" Jesus understood the power of sowing time into intimacy. If He needed that, how much more do we?

Your calendar reveals your convictions. If we say God is our priority but give Him no time, then we're sowing to something else. The good news is, it's never too late to change the seed. You can start today, this very hour, by giving God the first portion of your day and asking, "Lord, what matters to You?"

I remember a time when the ministry was exploding with opportunities. I had meetings scheduled back-to-back, travel plans every weekend, and students needing my attention. And in the middle of that, the Holy Spirit prompted me to block out an entire morning each week for just Him. No meetings. No phone calls. Just time in the Word and prayer. That one act of obedience transformed everything. I received more direction in those quiet mornings than I did in any boardroom.

Ecclesiastes 3:1 says, "*To everything there is a season, a time for every purpose under heaven.*" If you'll trust the Lord with your time, He'll help you discern the season. And when you know the season, you'll know what to sow and what to stop sowing.

Time is a seed. Sow it into the Spirit. Sow it into your calling. Sow it into people. Sow it into rest. And watch God multiply it in ways you never imagined.

Clarity Comes When You Eliminate the Distractions That Compete with Your Destiny

One of the greatest challenges we face in walking out divine order is not choosing between good and evil; it's choosing between the good and the God-appointed.

Distraction is one of the enemy's most effective weapons, not because it's obvious, but because it's subtle. It disguises itself in busyness, in the pressure to please people, or in doing "all the things" so that we feel productive. But activity isn't the same as fruitfulness.

If the enemy can't get you to sin, he'll try to get you to commit to everything. And in doing so, you slowly move off the path of God's best. You start missing appointments you didn't even know were divine, because your time is no longer surrendered to the Spirit; it's consumed by the urgent.

Hebrews 12:1–2 tells us, "*Therefore we also, since we are surrounded by so great a cloud of witnesses, let us lay aside every weight, and the sin which so easily ensnares* us, *and let us run with endurance the race that is set before us, looking unto Jesus....*" Not every weight is a sin. Some things are just weights, things that slow you down from running your race with clarity and joy.

One of the greatest challenges we face in walking out divine order is not choosing between good and evil; it's choosing between the good and the God-appointed.

I remember a season when I was involved in too many projects. Every one of them was good. They helped people, made an impact, and seemed important. But I was feeling overwhelmed and distant from the Lord. During a quiet time, the Lord gently said, "I didn't ask you to do all of this." That broke something in me. I realized I had taken on assignments He never gave me. So, I began a process of pruning, letting go of what was good to make room for what was *God*.

When we let the Spirit lead our time and decisions, clarity begins to replace chaos. Suddenly, you're not stretched thin. You're focused, fruitful, and present in the places that matter most.

First Corinthians 10:23 says, "*All things are lawful for me, but not all things are helpful; all things are lawful for me, but not all things edify.*" Just because something is permissible doesn't mean it's profitable. You have to ask, "Is this building what God called me to build?"

A woman once shared how she used to say yes to every ministry request, nursery duty, worship team, and outreach event, until she had nothing left to give. Her heart was for the Lord, but her yes was undisciplined. Through a teaching on priorities, she learned that saying no doesn't mean disobedience; it means alignment. She began prayerfully considering her commitments and the result. She became far more effective in fewer things, and her joy returned.

Distraction will always be knocking. It doesn't go away because you're in ministry or "doing the right thing." That's why divine order is a daily decision. It means you ask the Lord, "What's Your assignment for this day, this week, this season?" And then you obey, even if it means laying down something you love.

Luke 10:41–42 captures this beautifully: "*And Jesus answered and said to her, 'Martha, Martha, you are worried and troubled about many things. But one thing is needed, and Mary has chosen that good part, which will not be taken away from her.'*" Mary chose what couldn't be taken: intimacy over obligation, presence over productivity. And that's still the better choice today.

Clarity doesn't come from doing more. It comes from pruning more. When your life is simplified by the Spirit, your vision sharpens, your peace increases, and your fruit multiplies.

When You Prioritize Presence, You Begin to Walk in Purpose

So often, we search for purpose like it's some far-off destination. We think, "Once I arrive, once I get the job, the title, the ministry, then I'll be walking in my purpose." But in the kingdom, purpose is not a location. It's a Person. And when you make presence your priority, purpose unfolds naturally.

That relationship is the birthplace of calling. That means you don't discover your purpose by reading a self-help book or climbing a corporate ladder. You discover it by sitting at the feet of Jesus and saying, "Here I am, Lord." The more you know Him, the more you begin to know who you are.

Acts 17:28 says, "*For in Him we live and move and have our being.*" Your movement in life, your vision, your mission, your purpose, it all flows from being in Him. You were never meant to create your purpose outside of God's presence. It doesn't work that way. When you dwell with Him, purpose becomes a byproduct.

There was a woman who shared with me how she had spent years chasing various ministry ideas, trying to figure out what "her thing" was. She felt frustrated, confused, and discouraged. But when she began carving out consistent time in the Word and letting her identity be shaped in the secret place, the striving stopped. Purpose started showing up in her everyday life, in her family, her job, her words. What changed? She stopped pursuing the *what* and started embracing the *who*.

John 15:4–5 says, "*Abide in Me, and I in you. As the branch cannot bear fruit of itself, unless it abides in the vine, neither can you, unless you abide in Me. I am the vine, you* are *the branches. He who abides in Me, and I in him, bears much fruit; for without Me you can do nothing.*" Abiding is not passive; it's the most productive thing you can do. Because it is from abiding that true fruit emerges.

I remember one particularly busy season when I was overwhelmed with the demands of leadership, motherhood, and ministry. I found myself pouring out constantly but feeling spiritually dry. One day, during a teaching, I shared about abiding and realized I was preaching something I hadn't been living. That night, I repented. I returned to my secret place with God, not out of duty, but out of deep hunger. The presence of the Lord flooded that room, and tears rolled down my face. I wasn't failing, I had just become disconnected. But as I reconnected to the Vine, clarity and joy returned.

> *When you prioritize presence, you walk in purpose without even realizing it.*

Psalm 16:11 reminds us, "*You will show me the path of life; In Your presence* is *fullness of joy; At Your right hand* are *pleasures forevermore.*" The path of life is not revealed through stress or striving. It's shown in the presence of God. That's where your purpose is birthed, protected, and clarified.

Divine order isn't just about time slots and task lists; it's about choosing presence first. When you choose to meet with Him, before you meet your deadlines, you begin to experience the joy of living from His agenda rather than your own. And in that place, purpose doesn't feel like pressure; it feels like overflow.

So, if you're unsure of your next step, don't try to figure it out. Just get into His presence. Sit with the Word. Worship Him. Let Him speak. Because when you prioritize presence, you walk in purpose without even realizing it. You're not chasing your calling; you're walking with the One who already wrote it.

Rest Is Not Inactivity; It Is Divine Strategy

For many believers, rest feels like a reward after obedience, but in the kingdom, rest is often the first step. It's not what you do after the battle; it's how you win the battle. Rest is how you access God's wisdom, direction, and strength. It's not inactivity, it's trust in action.

Many Christians burn out trying to do good things, thinking that hustle equals holiness. But that's not how God designed us. He didn't create us to strive. He created us to abide. True rest is not laziness or escape; it's the confident posture of someone who knows their Father is in control.

Isaiah 30:15 says, "*In returning and rest you shall be saved; in quietness and confidence shall be your strength.*" There is a strength that only comes when we slow down long enough to hear what heaven is saying. When we don't rest, we risk running ahead of God. We start doing things in our own strength, and even if the activity is good, the fruit won't last.

I met a woman who came to me exhausted. She was juggling classes, a job, ministry outreach, and leading a small group. She said, "I love it all, but I'm drowning." I asked her, "When was the last time you sat with God just to be with Him, not to get a word or prepare a lesson?" She teared up. It had been months. That week, she cleared her calendar and scheduled an entire day with the Lord. She came back radiant. She had direction, clarity, and peace. Nothing external had changed—but rest changed *her*.

True rest is not laziness or escape; it's the confident posture of someone who knows their Father is in control.

Matthew 11:28–30 gives this invitation straight from Jesus: "*Come to Me, all* you *who labor and are heavy laden, and I will give you rest. Take My yoke upon you and learn from Me ... and you will find rest for your souls. For My yoke* is *easy and My burden is light.*" Rest is found in His presence, not in finishing your checklist.

There was a time in our ministry when we were facing multiple major decisions at once, building projects, leadership transitions, and financial commitments. It was tempting to rush into action, gather every team, and brainstorm solutions. But instead, we paused. We fasted, we prayed, and we worshipped. And in that space of rest, God began to speak with clarity.

Some of the clearest strategies we've ever received came during that time of divine rest, not from pressure, but from presence.

Hebrews 4:9–11 speaks of a promised rest for the people of God. Verse 11 says, "*Let us therefore be diligent to enter that rest ....*" Isn't that beautiful? Diligent to rest. It almost sounds contradictory. But in reality, rest takes intentionality. It's choosing to pause and prioritize the voice of God over the noise of life.

You will never experience true divine order without the rhythm of rest. It's in rest that you hear the next step. It's in rest that your soul is aligned. It's in rest that you remember who's really in control. And that's where supernatural strategy flows.

Rest doesn't mean you stop living. It means you stop carrying the weight of your life by yourself. You surrender the timeline, the vision, the outcome, and you say, "God, I trust You more than I trust my own effort."

So, take the invitation: step into divine rest. You'll be amazed at what God can do when you stop long enough to let Him lead.

You Discover Vision When You Stop Trying to Create It

One of the most liberating truths in walking with God is this: you don't have to invent your purpose; you inherit it. Vision isn't something you force; it's something you receive. And you receive it through relationship, not striving.

Words like "calling" and "purpose" can intimidate people because we often think we have to build our identity from the ground up. But real vision begins when we surrender our ideas of what success should look like and let God breathe His perspective into our lives.

Jeremiah 29:11 says, "'*For I know the thoughts that I think toward you,' says the Lord, 'thoughts of peace and not of evil, to give you a future and a hope.*'" Notice, it doesn't say, "You know the thoughts." It says, "*I know the thoughts.*" Vision is not born from what you can see; it's born from what He already sees.

You will never experience true divine order without the rhythm of rest.

I remember when I was fresh out of Bible school. I had all these dreams, big, bold, exciting plans for what I wanted to do for the kingdom. But the Lord asked me to do something that felt small. He asked me to serve behind the scenes, out of the spotlight. And in that place of hidden obedience, He began to whisper a vision I never could have come up with on my own. The nations, the teaching, the influence, it didn't come because I planned it. It came because I laid down my own plan.

Proverbs 19:21 reminds us, "*There are many plans in a man's heart, Nevertheless the* Lord*'s counsel—that will stand.*" You may have ideas. You may have ambition. But only God's counsel is eternal. If your plans have crumbled, maybe it's because He's trying to hand you something better, something eternal.

A lady once told me, "I'm so afraid I'll miss God's will. What if I choose the wrong path?" I told her, "You're not powerful enough to mess up God's plan when your heart is surrendered." He is a good Shepherd, and He knows how to lead His sheep. You don't have to have all the answers; you just need to stay close to the One who does.

Psalm 32:8 says, "*I will instruct you and teach you in the way you should go; I will guide you with My eye.*" He doesn't bark directions from a distance. He leads with His eye, which means proximity. When you walk close with God, vision becomes clear.

One of the most powerful things I've learned is this: when you stop trying to prove yourself, God can position you. When you stop striving to be "somebody," you're finally ready to be led. And in that humility, vision comes alive, not because you fought for it, but because you yielded to it.

This kind of surrendered vision produces joy, not pressure. You're no longer performing, you're partnering. You're not racing others, you're running with God. You're not building a name; you're building the kingdom.

Stop trying to create vision. Just be with Him. And watch as He begins to reveal what's been in His heart for you all along. You don't have to force your future; you just have to follow His voice.

Abundance Flows from Alignment, Not Accumulation

Abundance isn't about how much you have; it's about how aligned your heart is with God's truth. You can have a packed bank account, a full schedule, and a long list of accomplishments and still feel empty. That's because true abundance doesn't begin in your wallet; it begins in your spirit.

Abundance is the nature of God. It's who He is. And when you align your thinking, priorities, and time with His kingdom, you tap into that supernatural flow. It's not something you chase; it's something you live from.

Real vision begins when we surrender our ideas of what success should look like and let God breathe His perspective into our lives.

John 10:10 says, "*The thief does not come except to steal, and to kill, and to destroy. I have come that they may have life, and that they may have it more abundantly.*" The abundant life Jesus promised isn't just about material blessing; it's a life full of purpose, peace, clarity, joy, and divine provision.

One of the lies the enemy uses to steal that abundance is comparison. When we start looking at someone else's life, ministry, or financial status and think, "Why don't I have that?" we shift from alignment to striving. We stop listening to the Holy Spirit and start listening to social pressure. That's when abundance starts to feel distant. But the truth is, God's provision follows your obedience, not your image.

I've seen this over and over in my own life. I remember a season when my husband and I had to make a tough financial decision. The natural choice was to say yes to something that promised more income. But as we prayed, we both sensed the Lord saying, "Trust Me, I'm your source." We said no to that opportunity, and in the months that followed, God opened doors that were *better*, more fruitful, and full of peace. He multiplied what we needed because we chose alignment over accumulation.

Deuteronomy 28:2 says, "*And all these blessings shall come upon you and overtake you, because you obey the voice of the* Lord *your God.*" Did you catch that? The blessings overtake you, not because you chase them, but because you obey. Alignment causes abundance to pursue you.

The blessings overtake you, not because you chase them, but because you obey. Alignment causes abundance to pursue you.

I met another woman who had been working three jobs and barely making it. She came into class one day, tears in her eyes, and said, "I've been trying to provide for myself, and I've left no space for God to show up." That week, she made the radical decision to drop one of the jobs and dedicate that time to being in the Word and seeking God for direction. Within three weeks, unexpected income came in, and her remaining jobs were more fruitful than before. She said, "I stopped striving, and God started multiplying."

Matthew 6:33 is the anchor for this kind of life: "*But seek first the kingdom of God and His righteousness, and all these things shall be added to you.*"

When the kingdom becomes your priority, your time, your energy, your thoughts, and your budget, abundance becomes a lifestyle.

You see, abundance isn't something you earn. It's something you align with. When your heart, your time, and your vision are surrendered to the Lord, you create the conditions for overflow. And that overflow isn't just for you; it's so you can bless others, fund kingdom work, speak life into broken places, and reveal the nature of God to a world in lack.

You weren't created to just get by. You were created to walk in the fullness of who God is. And that fullness flows not from what you own, but from the One who owns you.

The Holy Spirit Is Your Time Manager, Vision Keeper, and Abundance Guide

We often try to compartmentalize our walk with God, inviting Him into our spiritual growth but leaving Him out of the practical rhythms of life. But the Holy Spirit isn't just your comforter; He's your counselor, your teacher, your organizer, your guide, your divine scheduler. He knows not only your purpose but the *pace* you're called to walk in. He helps manage your time, guard your vision, and release abundance into your life.

God can be the master of your time. That means you don't have to live stressed, overscheduled, and burned out. You can walk in divine rhythm. When you hand your calendar to the Holy Spirit, you make room for supernatural efficiency and wisdom beyond your own capacity.

When your heart, your time, and your vision are surrendered to the Lord, you create the conditions for overflow.

Proverbs 3:5–6 reminds us, "*Trust in the* L*ORD* *with all your heart, and lean not on your* *own understanding; In all your ways acknowledge Him, And He shall direct your paths.*" It's not just your big life decisions that need His direction; it's your daily schedule, your yeses and nos, your quiet times, and your commitments. When you acknowledge Him in everything, He directs everything.

I remember one time when I had two speaking opportunities presented to me in the same week. Both were good. Both were aligned with what I love to do. But as I prayed, the Holy Spirit gave me a clear check in my spirit about one of them. It didn't make sense in the natural; it looked like the more influential choice. But I obeyed His nudge. The opportunity I said yes to ended up being one of the most powerful weekends of ministry I've ever experienced. Divine alignment brings divine fruit.

Holy Spirit is also the One who reveals God's vision in a way that's personal, not generic. He doesn't just call you "into ministry" or "into business." He shapes the exact assignment, people, and timing that are unique to your life. That's why staying in tune with Him is key.

When you acknowledge Him in everything, He directs everything.

First Corinthians 2:10–12 says, "*But God has revealed* them *to us through His Spirit. For the Spirit searches all things, yes, the deep things of God ... that we might know the things that have been freely given to us by God.*" The Holy Spirit searches the deep things of God, things we can't access with our natural minds. That includes the deep strategies for your calling and provision.

I once spoke with a lady who was wrestling with how to run her business God's way. She felt torn between what the market demanded and what she sensed in prayer. I encouraged her to ask the Holy Spirit to be her business partner, not in theory, but in every decision. Weeks later, she came back saying, "The moment I surrendered the leadership of my company to the Holy Spirit, things shifted. He gave me insight I never would've considered." Her profits increased, but more importantly, her peace returned.

The Holy Spirit is the One who brings to remembrance everything Jesus has given us. He teaches us how to walk in what we already have. So many believers are waiting for increase while neglecting the Spirit who reveals it.

John 14:26 says, "*But the Helper, the Holy Spirit ... will teach you all things, and bring to your remembrance all things that I said to you.*" If abundance feels distant, maybe it's time to ask the Holy Spirit to remind you of what's already yours.

He's not distant. He's personal. He's not waiting until you're perfect. He's ready right now to partner with you. Whether it's how you use your afternoon or how you pursue your life's calling, He has wisdom, clarity, and peace available for you.

So invite Him in, not just on Sundays, but every moment. Let Him be the manager of your minutes, the curator of your calling, and the activator of your abundance. You'll never want to walk alone again.

Busyness Versus Fruitfulness

There's a difference between being busy and being fruitful. The world applauds hustle and multitasking, but the kingdom calls us to intentionality and obedience. Busyness can keep you spinning your wheels while going nowhere spiritually. Fruitfulness, on the other hand, is the evidence of abiding in Christ and aligning with His will.

The enemy loves busyness. Why? Because it feels spiritual. It looks responsible. But it often keeps us from the very thing we were created for: intimacy with God and effectiveness in our calling.

When you walk in sync with God's vision, you eliminate distractions. That means not every open door is your assignment. Fruitfulness means doing what God asks, not everything people expect.

John 15:16 says, "*You did not choose Me, but I chose you and appointed you that you should go and bear fruit, and* that *your fruit should remain ....*" You're not called to burn out for God; you're called to bear lasting fruit. Fruit that remains. That requires pruning, intentionality, and saying no to good things so you can say yes to God things.

I met a woman who shared with me how overwhelmed she felt trying to juggle every ministry opportunity. When she heard the teaching on priorities and fruitfulness, she said, "I realized I was performing for approval. I let go of the things God never asked me to carry, and suddenly, I had peace." And with that peace came fruitfulness. What she let go of made room for more anointing in what she kept.

Fruitfulness is a reflection of abiding. You don't strive to produce; it comes naturally when you are planted in the right soil. Psalm 1:2–3 captures this beautifully: "*But his delight* is *in the law of the Lord, And in His law he meditates day and night. He shall be like a tree Planted by the rivers of water, That brings forth its fruit in its season, Whose leaf also shall not wither; And whatever he does shall prosper.*"

The goal isn't to do everything; it's to do the right things in the right season. God wants you to live in rhythm with His Spirit, not rush against the clock of performance. Productivity doesn't impress God; obedience does.

Ask yourself: am I busy or fruitful? Am I led by peace or driven by pressure? Am I doing what God asked, or what people expect? It's not about how much you do. It's about who you become and what remains when you do it with Him.

Choose fruitfulness. Choose alignment. And watch as your life overflows, not with chaos, but with purpose.

Vision Grows Where Love Is Rooted

So often, people search for vision by looking outward, at opportunities, trends, or needs, but true vision begins inward, rooted in the revelation of God's love. Before you can walk in the vision God has for you, you must know how deeply you are loved by Him. It is in that place of security that boldness rises, identity solidifies, and vision becomes clear.

It's in a revelation of God's love that we can truly surrender to the vision of letting His love flow out into our lives in unique and powerful ways. If your calling isn't built on love, it won't last. You'll either be striving to earn approval or be afraid to step out. But when you know you're loved, you stop performing and start producing.

God wants you to live in rhythm with His Spirit, not rush against the clock of performance. Productivity doesn't impress God; obedience does.

Ephesians 3:17–19 beautifully expresses this foundation: "... *that Christ may dwell in your hearts through faith; that you, being rooted and grounded in love, may be able to comprehend with all the saints what* is *the width and length and depth and height—to know the love of Christ which passes knowledge; that you may be filled with all the fullness of God.*"

The fullness of God, His direction, provision, and abundance, flows from being *rooted* in love. That's where vision begins. It's not a business plan. It's not a five-year goal. It's a heart that says, "God, I trust Your love enough to follow wherever You lead."

There have been times when I was faced with a decision that would stretch me far beyond what I felt qualified for. My first reaction was, "Lord, I don't know if I can do this." But His response was simple: "I didn't ask you to do it without Me. I asked you to trust that I love you." That settled it. I wasn't stepping into the unknown; I was stepping deeper into the arms of the One who had already prepared the way.

God's love is not just a comfort; it's the overflow. When you know you are deeply loved, you stop living from scarcity and start living from supply. You stop asking, "Do I have enough?" and begin declaring, "I have more than enough because I have Him."

First John 4:18 reinforces this truth: "*There is no fear in love; but perfect love casts out fear, because fear involves torment. But he who fears has not been made perfect in love.*"

When fear is removed, boldness can rise, and boldness is what fuels vision. It's not arrogance. It's confidence in the One who loves you and equips you.

One woman once shared with me how she was terrified to pursue a call into missions. She felt underqualified, too broken, and overwhelmed. But after one session where we talked about the love of God, she came back to class and said, "I feel like I can finally breathe. I'm not earning my place; I'm walking in it." That year, she took her first trip and never looked back. She now oversees mission teams around the globe, and it all started with this: knowing she was loved.

The greatest investment of your time is in your relationship with God. That relationship is where love grows and where vision is conceived. It's no coincidence that people who spend time in God's presence tend to walk with clarity and joy. Why? Because love makes you bold. Love makes you whole. Love makes you available for His purposes.

If you feel confused about your calling or stuck in fear, don't look for a louder voice; look for deeper love. The more you receive His love, the more you'll see His plans unfold naturally. Love is the soil where vision grows.

Divine Vision Is Strengthened Through Resistance, Not Weakened by It

When you step into God's plan for your life, you won't float through it without opposition. In fact, stepping into divine vision often activates resistance. The enemy doesn't attack what isn't a threat. But here's the truth: resistance doesn't mean you're off track; it's often confirmation that you're right where you're supposed to be.

When you step into the greatness of God's plan for your life, you will begin to experience the resistance of the enemy. But here's the encouragement: don't fear and don't quit. God never calls you without equipping you, and He never equips you without empowering you to stand when pressure comes.

Isaiah 54:17 declares, "'*No weapon formed against you shall prosper, And every tongue* which *rises against you in judgment You shall condemn. This* is *the heritage of the servants of the* LORD, *and their righteousness* is *from* Me,' Says the *LORD*."

It doesn't say weapons won't form; it says they won't prosper. The promise isn't a life without battle; it's victory in the midst of it.

> *The greatest investment of your time is in your relationship with God. That relationship is where love grows and where vision is conceived.*

I remember when we launched a major new outreach ministry. I had a word from the Lord. I had confirmation. I had peace. But then, right after launching, we were hit with all kinds of challenges: miscommunication, resource delays, criticism. Everything that could go wrong, did. In the past, I might have thought, *Did I miss it?* But the Holy Spirit reminded me: "This isn't failure; it's friction. Keep pressing forward." And we did.

Within months, the fruit of that outreach exploded. The resistance had been a signpost, not a stop sign.

James 1:2–4 reveals the refining purpose of pressure: "*My brethren, count it all joy when you fall into various trials, knowing that the testing of your faith produces patience. But let patience have its perfect work, that you may be perfect and complete, lacking nothing.*"

There is something that forms in us during resistance that can't be formed any other way. The grit of faith. The clarity of conviction. The depth of dependency on God. When your vision hits friction, don't shrink back, lean in.

It doesn't say weapons won't form; it says they won't prosper. The promise isn't a life without battle; it's victory in the midst of it.

This applies to time as well. The enemy will try to destroy your purpose by filling your life with distractions, discouragement, or even over-commitment. But the Holy Spirit is always guiding you back to the main thing. You may face resistance, but you don't have to face it alone. You've been given grace for every step.

One woman I mentored faced enormous spiritual resistance the moment she stepped into her ministry call. People she trusted turned away. Her finances got tight. Her schedule felt overwhelming. But as we walked through the Word together, she began to see the pressure not as punishment, but as preparation. She said, "I've never been more sure I'm doing what God called me to do because the enemy is working overtime to stop it!" And sure enough, the fruit came because she didn't quit.

Abundance is not the absence of trial; it's the presence of provision *in* the trial. It's the unwavering awareness that God is enough, even when things feel tough.

Romans 8:37 reminds us: "*Yet in all these things we are more than conquerors through Him who loved us.*" Not just conquerors, more than conquerors. That's who you are when resistance rises and you choose to stand in God's vision with God's power.

When opposition comes, don't panic. Don't retreat. Don't let fear narrate your story. Let resistance refine you. Let it build your muscles of faith. Let it expose your reliance on Him. Resistance doesn't destroy divine vision; it deepens it.

Staying in Your Lane Is the Strength of Destiny

In a world filled with distractions, detours, and comparison traps, one of the greatest spiritual disciplines is focus. Staying in your lane, faithfully running your race, is not about ignoring others, but about honoring the unique path God has marked out for *you*. You can't walk in the fullness of your vision if you're constantly glancing at someone else's.

Many times, life, others, and even our own laziness can sway us to abandon our visions. Life throws curveballs. People have opinions. Our flesh craves comfort. And if we're not grounded in purpose, it becomes easy to detour from the direction God gave us.

That's why Hebrews 12:1–2 is so vital: "... *let us run with endurance the race that is set before us; looking unto Jesus, the author and finisher of* our *faith* ...."

You are called to your race, not someone else's. The enemy loves to whisper, "You're behind... Look at them... You're not enough." But Jesus, the One who authored your calling, is also the One who will finish it if you don't give up.

There was a time when I was tempted to compare my progress in ministry to others. I saw what looked like faster growth, wider reach, more followers. But the Holy Spirit lovingly corrected me: "I called you to impact, not to impress." That one statement realigned my heart. Impact comes from intimacy. Destiny flows from devotion. Staying in your lane keeps you connected to both.

When you know the vision God has destined for your life, it empowers you to eliminate distractions. That's the beauty of focus; it gives you permission to say no without guilt. You don't have to say yes to every opportunity. If it doesn't line up with your lane, you can let it pass without fear of missing out.

Once a woman said to me, "I feel like I'm always saying yes because I don't want to disappoint people." But after learning about priorities and purpose, she said something profound: "I realized I was disappointing *God* by not doing what He asked." She began to scale back, focus in, and pour her energy into what God had shown her. The peace and fruitfulness that followed were undeniable.

Philippians 3:13–14 captures this heart: "... *but one thing I do, forgetting those things which are behind and reaching forward to those things which are ahead, I press toward the goal for the prize of the upward call of God in Christ Jesus.*"

Staying in your lane means you don't live stuck in the past or paralyzed by regret. You keep moving forward. You forgive. You release. You rise. Your lane is sacred because it's God-designed.

Abundance flows when you live with intentionality. You stop wasting energy on side-paths and dead ends. You begin to see every step as meaningful. Even small steps, when taken in obedience, move you toward divine destiny.

Impact comes from intimacy. Destiny flows from devotion. Staying in your lane keeps you connected to both.

You weren't made to zigzag through life with uncertainty. You were made to move forward with purpose. That's why staying in your lane isn't restriction; it's *power*. It's how you protect the anointing on your life. It's how you multiply your impact without multiplying your stress.

Take inventory today. Are you running your race or reacting to someone else's? Are you moving with heaven's cadence or chasing external approval? Ask the Holy Spirit to clarify your lane and then stay in it, walk in it, thrive in it.

Your lane leads to legacy.

The Posture of Pressing Unlocks the Fullness of Purpose

There is a holy tension in the kingdom, a spiritual stretching, that comes when you're fully committed to the call of God. You're not just waiting around for God to move; you're leaning forward, pressing in, and laying hold of what's already been given to you. This isn't striving in the flesh; it's surrender in motion. The posture of pressing is faith in action.

Apostle Paul said in Philippians 3:12–14, "*Not that I have already attained, or am already perfected; but I press on, that I may lay hold of that for which Christ Jesus has also laid hold of me ... forgetting those things which are behind and reaching forward to those things which are ahead, I press toward the goal ....*"

This "pressing" is not about performing; it's about prioritizing what matters most. It's saying, "I'm not going to stay stuck where I've been. I'm reaching forward into what He's called me to."

Pressing into the things of God means letting go of everything that's trying to press in on you. The distractions. The regrets. The "what ifs" and the "if onlys." God wants you to press with confidence, not looking back, but leaning forward into the direction of the Spirit.

There was a time when we were believing for breakthrough in a specific area of ministry. It felt like everything had stalled, and we began to wonder, *Did we miss it?* But in prayer, I felt the Holy Spirit whisper, "Press." Not in panic, but in persistence. We prayed. We fasted. We re-centered. And then doors began to swing wide open. It wasn't the pressing that opened the doors; it was our hearts positioned in trust and faith. That is the power of the press.

Hebrews 6:12 confirms this truth: "... *imitate those who through faith and patience inherit the promises.*"

It's not just faith; it's faith and patience. That means perseverance. That means not letting delays make you doubt. Pressing is trusting that even when you don't see fruit yet, something is happening beneath the surface.

Pressing in brings the shift from natural to supernatural. You're not waiting on the economy, people, or ideal timing. You're drawing from the supply of heaven, and that takes spiritual tenacity.

I remember a lady shared that she had given up on a God-given dream after too many closed doors. But as she sat in class and heard this message of pressing, something awakened in her. She said, "I realized I had stopped asking. I had stopped believing. But God hadn't stopped calling." That week, she began praying again, and not long after, a door opened that had been shut for years. All it took was one move of obedience, birthed out of renewed faith.

This posture is described in Isaiah 40:31: "*But those who wait on the LORD Shall renew* their *strength; They shall mount up with wings like eagles, They shall run and not be weary, They shall walk and not faint.*"

To wait on the Lord isn't passive; it's active pressing. It's living in such close proximity to His presence that your strength is constantly renewed.

Don't let delays define you. Don't let setbacks stall you. Choose today to press. To reach forward. To expect. To believe again. You don't have to push your way into the will of God, but you do have to pursue it with focus and faith.

The prize isn't something you earn; it's something you lay hold of. Press in. His fullness is waiting.

God Is More Committed to Your Growth than Your Comfort

We often desire the destination of purpose without embracing the process of transformation. But God is not in a hurry. He's not just trying to get you to a platform. He's shaping your heart to carry the weight of His call. He cares more about who you're becoming than where you're going. Why? Because only a transformed life can steward a vision that brings lasting impact.

God is committed to your growth and transformation. It's not about your list of changes that have to occur before God can use you. God uses us *as* we grow, not just after we grow. He meets us in the middle. The enemy says, "You're not ready." But God says, "Just walk with Me. I'll transform you as you go."

Romans 12:2 speaks directly to this process: "*And do not be conformed to this world, but be transformed by the renewing of your mind, that you may prove what* is *that good and acceptable and perfect will of God.*"

Notice that transformation comes before the proving of the will of God. You don't walk in divine vision through natural strength; you walk in it through renewed thinking. That's why growth is essential: it's what aligns your heart with His thoughts.

Time is a gift to steward. Every season is a classroom where God is teaching you how to think like Him. One of the most precious testimonies I've seen in students is when they realize that the delays, struggles, and even frustrations were not wasted. God used it all to deepen their roots and develop their discernment.

I remember a young woman who felt stuck in transition. She wasn't where she used to be, but not yet where she wanted to be. Through tears, she told me, "I feel like I'm in a holding pattern." But I gently shared, "You're not in a holding pattern, you're in a healing pattern. God's preparing you to carry what's coming." A few months later, she stepped into full-time ministry, and the maturity she brought to that role was the direct result of her season of growth.

We often desire the destination of purpose without embracing the process of transformation.

Second Corinthians 3:18 captures the divine process beautifully: "*But we all, with unveiled face, beholding as in a mirror the glory of the Lord, are being transformed into the same image from glory to glory, just as by the Spirit of the Lord.*"

Transformation isn't an event; it's a journey. And the more you behold Jesus, the more you become like Him. Vision without transformation is dangerous, because it will magnify unhealed places. But vision birthed from transformation will release healing, wisdom, and power to others.

The overflow of God isn't just material; it's spiritual. You're not just being equipped with provision; you're being equipped with perspective. God wants you to grow into someone who can carry His abundance with integrity and generosity. That means pruning. That means surrender. That means change.

John 15:2 reminds us, "*Every branch in Me that does not bear fruit He takes away; and every* branch *that bears fruit He prunes, that it may bear more fruit.*"

Transformation isn't an event; it's a journey. And the more you behold Jesus, the more you become like Him.

God doesn't prune because you're failing. He prunes because you're fruitful, and He wants you to be even more fruitful. That pruning often looks like conviction, redirection, or even slowing down. But it's never punishment. It's preparation.

If you're in a stretching season, lean into it. If you feel like nothing's happening, trust that something is growing under the surface. You don't need to rush through transformation. Just remain. Just receive. Just keep saying yes.

God is faithful to complete what He started in you, and growth is the pathway to glory.

Your Connection to God's Plans Produces Divine Fruitfulness

You were never created to live aimlessly or barely survive. You were created to abide, to be fruitful, and to multiply, not in your own strength, but through your connection to the One who knows the end from the beginning. When you surrender your time, vision, and life to God, you align yourself with divine productivity, the kind of fruitfulness that glorifies Him and changes lives.

You were created to be fruitful, so that you can multiply and glorify God. What a grand future when you are connected to the plans and directions of the One who has thoughts of peace and a future for you! That's not just a motivational phrase; it's a kingdom promise.

Jeremiah 29:11 puts it plainly: "F*or I know the thoughts that I think toward you, says the Lord, thoughts of peace and not of evil, to give you a future and a hope*."

Your future isn't a mystery to God. It's a masterpiece waiting to unfold as you yield to His direction. That's why time isn't something you manage apart from Him; it's something you surrender to Him. When your calendar is under His Lordship, your days become purposeful. You stop just checking boxes and start living by divine rhythm.

Relationship is the source and sustainer of all vision. Vision isn't just an assignment; it's a response to intimacy. As you walk with Him, He unfolds His thoughts. He reveals the next step. He fine-tunes the desires of your heart to match His own.

One testimony I often share is about a season in my life where I thought I was in the fullness of what God had called me to do: traveling, teaching, and leading. But one day in prayer, He whispered, "I have more for you." At first, I hesitated. I was comfortable. But when I finally said yes, He launched me into a whole new dimension of influence: new nations, new students, new impact. Why? Because I stayed connected to Him, not just the vision.

John 15:5 says it so clearly: "*I am the vine, you* are *the branches. He who abides in Me, and I in him, bears much fruit; for without Me you can do nothing*."

Fruitfulness isn't about striving; it's about abiding. And in that abiding, you find supernatural effectiveness. Things begin to align. Opportunities come without manipulation. Favor flows without forcing it. That's divine fruitfulness.

We are not called to live normal, average lives, but to live as people who demonstrate the fullness of salvation, showing the world what it looks like to be connected to a good and faithful God.

In fact, Ephesians 3:20 promises, "*Now to Him who is able to do exceedingly abundantly above all that we ask or think, according to the power that works in us.*" Notice the power doesn't just work around us; it works in us. That power is the Spirit guiding us into all truth, including the truth of our purpose, provision, and position.

Your future isn't a mystery to God. It's a masterpiece waiting to unfold as you yield to His direction.

You may feel like your life is too ordinary to produce anything meaningful. But that's the beauty of fruitfulness; it happens when you're connected, not when you're impressive. It happens when you say, "Lord, I surrender my time, my vision, and my very life to You. Use me."

Don't try to produce fruit through effort. Position yourself in relationship. Surrender your daily plans. Watch what grows. God's plans for you are fruitful by design, and when you remain in Him, your life becomes an orchard of everlasting impact.

Reflection

Time. Vision. Abundance. These aren't three separate compartments of life; they are intimately woven together by one core principle: surrender.

You were never called to manage your time by human striving. Time was never meant to be a burden or a pressure. It's a gift that belongs to God, a resource that, when placed in the hands of the Holy Spirit, becomes supernatural. It's not about fitting God into your schedule; it's about letting Him become your schedule. When you give time to the Spirit, He aligns your steps, redeems your minutes, and causes even delays to serve your purpose.

You may feel like your life is too ordinary to produce anything meaningful. But that's the beauty of fruitfulness; it happens when you're connected, not when you're impressive.

Vision doesn't begin with ambition. It begins with surrender. Vision is not something you manufacture; it's something you receive. It's the joy of walking in step with the Father's heart, discovering that your calling is simply the outflow of your intimacy with Him. As you give Him space to speak and lead, vision unfolds. Sometimes quietly, sometimes surprisingly, but always with power and purpose.

And abundance? It's not about accumulation. It's not about wealth or image or productivity. It begins with the Shepherd. "*The LORD is my shepherd; I shall not want*" (Psalm 23:1). When He leads, lack disappears, not because you have everything the world says you need, but because you have Him. Abundance is His nature flowing through your yielded life. It's a river of provision, identity, fruitfulness, and peace that starts the moment you stop trying to control and start following.

This is divine order: time submitted, vision received, and abundance released. When we live from that place of surrender, we move out of chaos and into calling. We stop reacting and begin reigning. And in that space, overflow becomes our new normal, not just for ourselves, but for everyone around us.

My Challenge to You

- Pause and Surrender: Take time to stop and intentionally surrender, not just in words, but in your daily practice.
- Open Your Calendar: Bring your schedule before the Lord and ask, "Where do You want my time?"

- Invite the Holy Spirit: Welcome Him into your margins, your plans, and your priorities.
- Realign Your Commitments: Ask God to reveal what needs to shift, be removed, or be strengthened in your schedule.
- Receive Fresh Vision: Go beyond your past experiences or natural talents, ask God to speak vision into you based on His love and promises. Write it down. Let it take root and grow.
- Evaluate Your Source: Reflect honestly. Have you been depending on yourself, your job, or your own strength for provision? Or have you been trusting the Shepherd to lead?
- Choose Trust Again: Give God room to guide, multiply, and fill your life.
- Remember This Truth: Surrender isn't weakness; it's wisdom. It is the beginning of divine order and the doorway to living in abundant overflow.

Scripture References

Romans 12:2
Ephesians 2:10
Luke 10:41–42
John 15:4–5
Jeremiah 29:11–13
Proverbs 19:21
Psalm 32:8
Hebrews 12:1–2
Philippians 3:12–14
Hebrews 6:12
2 Corinthians 3:18
Ephesians 3:20
John 15:16
John 14:26
Proverbs 29:18
Romans 8:14
3 John 1:2
Psalm 23:1–3
Galatians 6:7–8
Luke 5:15-16
Ecclesiastes 3:1
1 Corinthians 2:10–12
1 Corinthians 10:23
Acts 17: 28
Psalm 16:11
Isaiah 30:15

Matthew 11:28–30
Hebrews 4:9–11
John 10:10
Deuteronomy 28:2
Proverbs 3:5–6
John 15:2
Isaiah 40:31
Romans 8:37
James 1:2–4
Isaiah 54:17
1 John 4:18
Ephesians 3:17–19
Psalm 1:2-3

Chapter Two

Busyness: The Enemy of Purpose

Introduction

We live in a world that applauds busyness. If your calendar is full, if you're running from one thing to the next, if you're exhausted, then somehow you're doing life right. But what if all that busyness is actually robbing you? What if it's not a badge of productivity, but a distraction from true purpose?

I've seen it time and again, in others and in myself. When we fill every space with activity, we lose sensitivity. We stop hearing God clearly. We stop recognizing His leading. We begin to confuse motion with meaning and performance with fruitfulness. But God never asked us to be busy. He asked us to be surrendered.

Busyness isn't a personality trait; it's a spiritual thief. It steals our focus, depletes our joy, and most dangerously, robs our spiritual authority. When we live cluttered lives, it's easy to forget that we've been seated with Christ in heavenly places, called to reign in life through Him, not run ourselves ragged trying to earn what He's already given.

When I began to let the Holy Spirit show me how much of my life was filled with striving rather than trusting, everything shifted. I realized that my excuses were rooted in the false belief that it all depended on me. But when we come to know His strength—really know it—our excuses melt away, and we step into His supernatural grace, which empowers purpose.

When we fill every space with activity, we lose sensitivity.

God is not in a hurry; He's not pushing us to keep up with the world's pace. Instead, He invites us into His rest, a rest that is deeply spiritual, powerful, and completely anchored in trust. Satisfaction, true satisfaction, doesn't come from achievement; it comes from trust. From knowing we're in the center of His will, right where we're supposed to be.

In this chapter, we're going to explore the dangerous deception of busyness. You'll see how your authority, your vision, and your abundance are all connected to how you steward your time and attention. More than anything, I pray you'll be reminded that your purpose isn't found in what you do, but in who you belong to.

Let's dive into what it really means to live on purpose, without the pressure.

Fix Your Focus

I want to expose the subtle, yet destructive, trap of busyness and how it keeps believers from stepping into the fullness of their God-given purpose. While the world glorifies hustle and constant activity, the kingdom of God invites us into divine rhythm—one where rest, surrender, and trust produce lasting fruit.

We'll uncover how busyness is more than just a scheduling issue; it's a spiritual battle that can rob us of vision, authority, and peace. When we are overwhelmed, distracted, or constantly on the go, we lose clarity. We start surviving—rather than thriving—and reacting, rather than responding to the Spirit. Busyness becomes the enemy of purpose by keeping us too preoccupied to hear God's voice or follow His leading with confidence.

But there's freedom. Through surrender, we find true strength, not our own, but His. As we recognize that purpose doesn't come from performance, but from intimacy with God, excuses fall away. The strength to walk in our calling comes not from striving, but from trust. And from that trust flows a deep satisfaction—a soul at rest, knowing that God is directing every step.

This focus will be explored in this chapter through real stories, scripture, and personal moments of transformation. You'll see how letting go of busyness isn't a loss—it's a breakthrough. When we give God our time, we receive something far more valuable: divine order, joyful vision, and a life of abundance that cannot be shaken.

Busyness Is a Thief of Spiritual Authority

One of the most deceptive things about busyness is how spiritual it can feel. We tell ourselves we're doing things "for God," when, in reality, we're often doing them apart from Him. Busyness can become a counterfeit of purpose—looking fruitful on the outside while draining us on the inside. I've seen firsthand how being constantly busy dulled my spiritual sensitivity. I could still quote Scripture, still pray, still show up, but my authority had been compromised because I was operating from pressure, not presence.

I used to wear my full calendar like a badge of honor. I thought saying yes to everything was a sign of obedience and maturity. But all I was doing was saying no to God's priorities for my life. I had to come face-to-face with the truth: I wasn't managing time—I was misplacing my authority.

As I've said before, when the enemy can't stop you with sin, he'll distract you with good things—and busyness is one of his favorite tactics. It gets us to trade intimacy for activity. We need to sit in the stillness, where God's authority is built in the quiet moments of abiding, listening, and obeying. Without those moments, we end up moving in our own strength—and the enemy knows we're no threat to him when we're burned out and spiritually dull.

Jesus modeled the opposite of busyness. He didn't strive; He abided. Even in the face of massive need and constant demand, He withdrew to be with the Father. And because of that, He always knew what to say, where to go, and who to heal. His authority wasn't in His schedule; it was in His surrender.

Authority in the kingdom is birthed from abiding. When we're running ahead of God, trying to make things happen, we forfeit the strength that comes from walking in step with Him. If the devil can keep us moving but not hearing, doing but not discerning, he knows we won't walk in the full authority that's been given to us in Christ.

We are seated with Christ in heavenly places (Eph. 2:6). That position is not earned by effort; it's received by rest. When we slow down and ask the Holy Spirit, "What is Your assignment for today?" we step back into divine authority. Suddenly, what felt heavy becomes light, and what felt chaotic becomes ordered. Because the moment we exchange busyness for presence, we gain clarity, confidence, and authority.

We need to sit in the stillness, where God's authority is built in the quiet moments of abiding, listening, and obeying.

If busyness has stolen your peace and dulled your spiritual sharpness, you can take it back. You can repent—not in shame, but in realignment. Say, "Lord, I've been running on empty. I've been saying yes out of fear or obligation. But I choose to return to the one thing that matters: abiding in You." And from that place, your authority is restored.

Busyness Blinds Us to Vision

When your schedule is full, but your spirit is empty, you're not walking in vision; you're walking in survival. That's what busyness does—it keeps our heads down, reacting to the urgent instead of responding to the eternal. If the enemy can keep us too busy to see, then he can keep us from stepping into the vision God designed uniquely for us.

I remember a time early in ministry when I was juggling so many roles, trying to be excellent in every area. I had the heart to serve, but I was operating out of obligation more than revelation. I was busy, but not fruitful. And in the middle of all that activity, I lost sight of the vision God had spoken over me. I couldn't even remember the last time I had stopped to ask Him, "Lord, what are You showing me for this season?"

Busyness can mask itself as spiritual growth. We attend every event, sign up for every team, and say yes to every need. But busyness *without* clarity leads to exhaustion *without* purpose. And if we're not guarding our time, we risk trading our God-given vision for everyone else's expectations.

Vision requires margin. Without time to hear God's voice, we can't see what He's doing. Proverbs 29:18 (*KJV*) says, "*Where* there is *no vision, the people perish ....*" Another translation says, "*They cast off restraint.*" That's what busyness does: it strips away the boundaries that keep us focused and fruitful. When we lose vision, we start to drift. We let the loudest voices or the most pressing needs define our direction, rather than the quiet leading of the Holy Spirit.

This is where abundance connects so deeply to vision. God never gives vision without provision. When He calls, He equips. When He sends, He supplies. Abundance isn't about always having more; it's about always having enough for the assignment He's given. When we walk in His vision, we don't strive; we receive.

Psalm 23:1–3 reminds us of this abundance: "*The Lord is my shepherd; I shall not want. He makes me to lie down in green pastures; He leads me beside the still waters. He restores my soul; He leads me in the paths of righteousness for His name's sake.*" That's vision wrapped in provision. He leads us. He restores us. He satisfies us, not through a flurry of activity, but through stillness. When we follow the Shepherd, vision becomes clear, and provision flows naturally.

I've watched people come through our training programs with dreams so big, they make your heart ache—incredible visions from the Lord. But the ones who flourish are not the ones with the busiest calendars or the loudest declarations. It's the ones who have learned to slow down, to wait on the Lord, to protect their time with Him. And because of that, they walk with divine momentum, not human effort.

If busyness has clouded your vision, God is not condemning you. He's calling you back. Back to simplicity. Back to His voice. Back to that place where vision was birthed not from striving, but from encounter. You don't need to run harder; you need to see clearer. Remember that clarity comes when we choose presence over pressure.

Striving Erodes Authority: Yielding Strengthens It

There's a hidden cost to busyness that many believers never recognize: it slowly erodes your spiritual authority. We get so busy doing things for

God that we forget to be with God. And the truth is, when we disconnect from intimacy, we disconnect from power.

Authority in the Spirit doesn't come from working harder; it comes from abiding deeper. You cannot manage spiritual outcomes with fleshly effort. No amount of hustle will produce the kind of breakthrough that only comes through yielding. That's why busyness is not just a distraction; it's a danger. It makes us feel productive while leaving us spiritually depleted.

Abundance isn't about always having more; it's about always having enough for the assignment He's given.

Jesus modeled this perfectly. In Luke 5:15–16 it says: "*However, the report went around concerning Him all the more; and great multitudes came together to hear, and to be healed by Him of their infirmities. So He Himself* often *withdrew into the wilderness and prayed.*"

Even at the height of His influence, Jesus didn't let the demands of people override His time with the Father. That was the source of His authority. He didn't work to prove Himself; He submitted to the Father's voice.

We can't afford to neglect that. Our purpose is tied to hearing and obeying the Lord, not reacting to every opportunity. If the enemy can keep you striving, he can keep you ineffective. He'll use your own sense of responsibility to drain your spiritual power.

In John 10:10 it says: "*The thief does not come except to steal, and to kill, and to destroy. I have come that they may have life, and that they may have* it *more abundantly.*" When we live in a cycle of busyness and burnout, we're letting the thief steal the life Jesus died to give us. That's not abundance—it's spiritual survival.

But there's a better way. When we yield our time, our plans, our efforts to God, we receive grace, not just to endure, but to reign.

Romans 5:17 says: "*For if by the one man's offense death reigned through the one, much more those who receive abundance of grace and of the gift of righteousness will reign in life through the One, Jesus Christ.*" That's real authority. That's reigning, not in our own strength, but through abundance of grace.

There was a season when I was doing everything "right." I was showing up, saying yes, filling every role. But I wasn't seeing fruit. I was tired, anxious, and constantly second-guessing my direction. And then the Lord gently spoke, "You're operating in your strength, not Mine." That word hit deep. I realized I had let striving become my substitute for authority.

So I pulled back. I quieted the noise. I let Him recalibrate my heart. And in that stillness, the authority returned. Not because I worked harder, but because I surrendered deeper.

Let me tell you: spiritual authority flows from a heart that's anchored in God's presence, not driven by performance. The more surrendered you are, the more powerful your walk becomes. Because now you're not just doing things for God, you're moving with God.

If you feel like you've been losing ground spiritually, maybe it's not because you're not doing enough. Maybe it's because you haven't paused to let Him lead. Authority isn't earned—it's received. And it's in the quiet places of yielding that we hear His voice, feel His power, and walk in purpose with boldness.

Excuses Crumble When We Know His Strength

One of the most subtle byproducts of busyness is the excuses it creates. We say, "I just don't have time ... I'm too overwhelmed ... I'm not ready yet ...." But underneath those words is often something deeper: a belief that we have to accomplish our calling in our own strength. And as long as we believe that, we'll keep finding reasons to delay.

Excuses give us a false sense of control. If I can justify my lack of movement, then I don't have to face my fear of failing. But God never called us to live by excuses. He called us to live by grace. And grace doesn't wait until we feel ready; it meets us exactly where we are and says, "Let's go together."

Excuses are often just misplaced identity. When we forget who God is in us, we begin to see our limitations as immovable barriers. But when we remember His strength, excuses begin to crumble.

Consider Moses. When God called him to deliver Israel, Moses had plenty of excuses: "Who am I?" "What if they don't believe me?" "I'm not a good speaker." But what was God's answer? "*I will be with you*" (Ex. 3:12, *New International Version*).

God didn't address Moses' qualifications; He pointed to His presence. That's the key to everything. We aren't qualified because we're talented. We're qualified because He goes with us. And once you know that, your excuses lose their power.

In 2 Corinthians 12:9, Paul shares what the Lord spoke to him: "*My grace is sufficient for you, for My strength is made perfect in weakness.*" And Paul's response? "*Therefore most gladly I will rather boast in my infirmities, that the power of Christ may rest upon me.*"

The same is true for you. Your weakness isn't a disqualification—it's an invitation for His power to be made perfect. When you're aware of His strength, you stop protecting your own limitations. You start walking in grace.

It's not about doing more—it's about doing what matters. Busyness thrives on the lie that "if I just had more time, I'd do what God's called me to do." But the truth is, God has already given you everything you need to begin. What we need is not more hours, but more trust.

And trust is a beautiful doorway into abundance. Because, when you stop leaning on your own ability and begin leaning into His strength, you'll find there's more than enough: more wisdom, more provision, more favor, more peace. You were redeemed out of the norm. You were called to be ... what? Sons and daughters of the Most High God. That means excuses don't define you anymore. Grace does. And grace doesn't just cover your past; it empowers your present.

I remember when God called me to step into a new season of leadership. I had every excuse ready: I'm not qualified; I don't have time; I've never done this before. But the Lord spoke so gently, "Carrie, I didn't call you because you're able. I called you because you're available." That truth broke the power of my excuses. It wasn't about my resume; it was about His sufficiency.

Friend, you are not too late, too small, or too weak. You are called. And the One who calls you is faithful. When you know His strength, your excuses lose their grip. Because now you're not moving in pressure—you're moving in partnership.

Trust Brings Satisfaction, Not Striving

Busyness often masquerades as productivity, but underneath it, there's usually striving. It's an anxious hustle to prove something, earn something, or avoid something. We fill our calendars, check all the boxes, and wonder why we still feel so empty. That's because striving isn't a fruit of the Spirit. Trust is.

When I began to understand the difference between striving and trusting, it was like my entire walk with God shifted. I wasn't meant to carry the weight of performance; I was created for relationship. And relationships don't thrive in frantic activity. They flourish in rest, in stillness, in trust.

We don't manage time by trying to fit God into our schedule; we surrender it by letting Him lead. The difference is massive. One leads to control, the other to peace. One fuels striving, the other cultivates satisfaction.

Isaiah 30:15 says, "*In returning and rest you shall be saved; In quietness and confidence shall be your strength.*" That verse doesn't tell us our strength is in working harder. It says our strength is found in stillness, returning to Him, resting in Him, and walking with quiet confidence.

We don't often equate rest with abundance, but they are deeply connected.

Psalm 23:1-2 says, "*The Lord* is *my shepherd; I shall not want. He makes me to lie down in green pastures ....*"

Notice, it says He makes me lie down. Sometimes we're so busy trying to "produce" for God that He has to lovingly interrupt us and say, "Rest. Let Me restore you." That's abundance, not running on fumes, but walking in overflow. You weren't created to grind—you were created to be led.

There was a season in ministry where I felt stretched in every direction. I was doing good things, kingdom things, but I was doing them in my own strength. I started noticing irritability, fatigue, and an internal sense that I was somehow missing God's voice. One morning during prayer, the Holy Spirit whispered, "You're chasing My purpose without My pace."

We don't manage time by trying to fit God into our schedule; we surrender it by letting Him lead.

That moment realigned me. God never intended for purpose to feel like pressure. True vision isn't a race against time; it's a walk of trust. And when we return to that place of trust, satisfaction replaces striving.

Hebrews 4:10 reinforces this truth: "*For he who has entered His rest has himself also ceased from his works as God* did *from His.*" Ceased from his works. That means we no longer perform for approval; we walk in response to love. That's what makes vision joyful instead of heavy. That's what opens the door for abundance to flow without fear.

It is important to find satisfaction in God's voice before we try to satisfy anyone else's expectations. If you're driven by what others think, you'll always be tired. But if you're led by the Spirit, you will walk in peace, even in seasons of great responsibility.

We must remember: abundance doesn't mean having everything you want. It means having exactly what He wants for you, when you need it. And that's deeply satisfying. Trust makes room for that kind of living. Trust teaches us to delight in the Lord and let Him set the pace.

Striving tells you, "You're not enough." Trust tells you, "He is more than enough." And when you truly believe that, you can breathe again. You can serve with joy. You can rest without guilt. You can walk, not run, into the next step of your calling.

Trust Him with your time. Trust Him with your calling. Trust Him with your pace. Because when trust takes the lead, striving loses its grip, and satisfaction fills the space where stress used to live.

Excuses Disappear When We Trust His Sufficiency

One of the greatest lies busyness whispers is, "You can't afford to slow down." And yet, beneath that lie, a more fundamental one resides: "You're not enough." We keep ourselves in constant motion, not just out of obligation, but out of fear—fear of not measuring up, fear of failing, fear of letting someone down. And when we feel inadequate, the easiest way to cope is with excuses.

We must remember: abundance doesn't mean having everything you want. It means having exactly what He wants for you, when you need it.

But here's the good news: every excuse melts in the presence of God's strength. When we know who He is, we stop worrying about who we are not.

I remember times early in ministry when I would hesitate to step into new roles or take on new responsibilities, not because I didn't believe in God, but because I didn't believe in myself. I was aware of all my limits, my past, my personality quirks. I would think, *Surely, someone else is more qualified.* But God kept drawing me back to one truth: It's not about your strength; it's about Mine.

Second Corinthians 12:9 says it plainly: "*And He said to me, 'My grace is sufficient for you, for My strength is made perfect in weakness.' Therefore most gladly I will rather boast in my infirmities, that the power of Christ may rest upon me.*"

That means your weakness isn't a disqualifier; it's a landing strip for His power. When we stop striving in our own strength and start leaning into His, excuses lose their power over us.

Can I tell you, stepping into God's purpose isn't about confidence in yourself; it's about confidence in your God. You don't have to have all the answers to say yes. You just need to be available. And availability is born in rest.

When you slow down and stop trying to manufacture your own success, you'll start to see where God has already made a way. And in those moments, you'll realize you don't need another excuse; you just need His strength.

It is important to recognize the patterns of avoidance that disguise themselves as busyness. Sometimes we keep ourselves busy so we don't have to face the fear of failure. But busyness won't protect you from fear; it will just exhaust you while you try to hide it.

When we stop striving in our own strength and start leaning into His, excuses lose their power over us.

Isaiah 41:10 says, "*Fear not, for I am with you, Be not dismayed, for I am your God. I will strengthen you, Yes, I will help you, I will uphold you with My righteous right hand.*"

That verse doesn't say, "Try harder." It says, "*I will strengthen you.*" That's the voice of a Father who isn't asking you to figure it all out. He's asking you to trust that He already has.

One testimony I often think about is a young woman who came through our ministry training feeling unsure of her ability to lead. She would say things like, "I'm not good at speaking. I don't think I'm ready. I don't want to mess this up." But through the course of her time with us, she began to understand that her adequacy wasn't the point. God's faithfulness was. When she leaned on Him instead of hiding behind excuses, boldness began to rise. And what was once fear turned into fruitfulness.

The same is true for all of us. God never required you to be enough; He just asks you to trust that He is. When you trust His sufficiency, excuses lose their grip. When you lean into His strength, the very thing you thought disqualified you becomes a testimony of His power.

That's how busyness gets dismantled. Not by trying harder but by trusting deeper.

God's Presence Is the Priority That Anchors Everything Else

In a world that demands constant movement, we're often tempted to prioritize productivity over presence. But when we allow God's presence to become our highest priority, everything else aligns. This is not about doing less; it's about doing what matters most first. Purpose flows from presence. When we make time for God, we receive clarity, direction, and the strength to walk in vision and abundance.

The truth is so clear in Luke 10:41–42 when Jesus gently corrects Martha: "*Martha, Martha, you are worried and troubled about many things. But one thing is needed, and Mary has chosen that good part, which will not be taken away from her.*"

Martha was busy, doing good things. But Mary was positioned at Jesus' feet, drawing strength, vision, and identity from His words. In the same way, we may be investing our energy into valuable efforts, but if we've neglected the One who directs our purpose, we'll eventually run dry.

God never required you to be enough; He just asks you to trust that He is.

When I first stepped into full-time ministry, I had to learn this the hard way. There were seasons when I let the schedule take over and ministry became a list of tasks rather than an overflow of intimacy. It wasn't until I returned to that place of prioritizing His presence above all that things began to realign, not only spiritually but practically. My time was more fruitful, my vision clearer, and I had the grace to accomplish what He assigned, without being drained by what He didn't.

This is the intersection where time management, vision, and abundance meet. When you start with presence, priorities become clearer. The joy of walking in your vision becomes sustainable. Abundance flows not just financially or emotionally, but spiritually, because you're no longer operating from depletion, but from overflow.

Psalm 16:11 reminds us: "*You will show me the path of life; In Your presence is fullness of joy; at Your right hand* are *pleasures forevermore.*"

The path of life is not uncovered by pushing harder, but by abiding deeper. Fullness of joy isn't found in arriving at a destination, but in walking with the One who leads. When we give Him the first of our day, the first of our thoughts, the first of our decisions, He shows us how to order the rest.

There's no abundance apart from His presence. You may gain the world, but you'll forfeit the soul-level satisfaction only God can give. When His voice leads your calendar, when His Word anchors your purpose, when His presence guides your pace, you'll step into something far greater than balance—you'll step into divine order.

The real battle isn't for your time; it's for your attention. It's not whether you can do it all; it's whether you're listening for what really matters. When God is the center, everything else falls into place.

Clarity Comes When We Stop the Noise

One of the greatest casualties of busyness is clarity. When our minds are filled with to-do lists, comparisons, and unending expectations, it becomes nearly impossible to hear the still, small voice of God. The chaos around us drowns out the calm within us. Yet it is in that calm, when the noise ceases, that vision is renewed and the next step becomes clear.

In Psalm 46:10, the Lord says: "*Be still, and know that I* am *God; I will be exalted among the nations, I will be exalted in the earth!*"

There is a knowing that only comes in stillness. We often seek answers while rushing through our schedules, but God speaks to the heart that pauses. Stillness is not inactivity; it's intentional focus. It's the refusal to let pressure dictate our pace.

I want to share with you a time when I was wrestling with multiple opportunities—things that were good, exciting even—but I felt stretched too thin. I tried to rationalize and evaluate each one logically, but I still couldn't decide. So I paused. I stopped trying to figure it out and just sat in His presence. And it was there, in that sacred stillness, that the Lord whispered clarity. I knew which door was mine to walk through, and which one, though good, wasn't meant for me. That one moment of stillness saved me from months of misalignment.

When His Word anchors your purpose, when His presence guides your pace, you'll step into something far greater than balance—you'll step into divine order.

This is what we must realize: purpose thrives in clarity, and clarity is found in the presence of peace. When we're overwhelmed, we begin chasing tasks that are not even ours. We confuse motion for momentum and action for obedience. But when we slow down enough to listen, God reveals what's essential and what's just noise.

In Matthew 6:33, Jesus reminds us: "*But seek first the kingdom of God and His righteousness, and all these things shall be added to you.*" We often seek all the other things first: results, recognition, provision, and then hope God will bless it. But His promise is clear: when we seek Him first, everything else flows from that alignment. That's not a poetic idea; it's a divine principle of order.

You might be thinking, *But I don't have time to stop.* Friend, can I gently tell you, you don't have time not to. If you're unclear, if your days feel like a blur, if your vision feels buried under busyness, the solution isn't to push harder; it's to get quiet. Let God lift the fog. Let Him remind you why you started. Let Him refresh your focus.

Abundance isn't found in a packed schedule; it's found in a clear one. When time is surrendered, vision is recovered. And in that focused clarity, you'll walk with purpose, not panic. God's peace will go before you, and His voice will be unmistakable.

Vision Thrives in Surrendered Seasons

Many of us wait for a perfect season before we pursue the vision God has placed in our hearts. We want fewer distractions, more time, a better support system, or more favorable circumstances. But the truth is, vision is not dependent on perfect conditions; it's revealed and refined in surrendered seasons.

Purpose thrives in clarity, and clarity is found in the presence of peace.

Ecclesiastes 3:1 says, "*To everything* there is *a season, a time for every purpose under heaven.*" That word "purpose" is key. Your current season is not an accident; it's been appointed. And within it is a purpose tailor-made for your growth and God's glory. When you hand over the season you're in to the Lord, rather than resist or try to escape it, you begin to see it through His eyes. Suddenly, what felt like a delay becomes divine preparation. What seemed like lack becomes a lesson in His sufficiency.

I walked through a season where the pace of ministry, family, and leadership collided in a way that left me feeling stretched and unclear. I wanted clarity about the next step, but instead of answers, I felt the Lord whisper, "Give me this season." It wasn't about finding an escape route or waiting for things to calm down. It was about yielding the season and trusting that even in the tension, God was doing something deep.

In that time, I began to write a vision, not for what I hoped someday might happen, but for what God was already doing within me. I allowed His clarity to rise above my chaos. And now I know many of the opportunities I walk in today were birthed in seasons I almost tried to skip.

Proverbs 19:21 confirms this beautifully: "*There are many plans in a man's heart, Nevertheless the Lord's counsel—that will stand.*" When we hand over our season, our vision aligns with God's counsel. He clarifies what truly matters and leads us into fruitfulness without striving.

This is also where abundance flows. When we stop trying to manipulate time or control the path, we discover that God's timing is perfect. We stop rushing and start resting. Not in inactivity, but in peace-filled trust. That's when doors open, favor flows, and vision becomes more than a hope; it becomes our reality.

Don't despise your season. Don't discount it because it feels messy or unfinished. God doesn't need you to be in a different place; He just needs you surrendered in this one. Your yielded yes in this season is the soil where your next season will bloom.

Abundance Begins with Renewed Mindsets

Many people misunderstand abundance because they see it only through the lens of material wealth. But God's abundance begins as a transformation in the way we think, shifting us from a "lack" mentality to a "life" mentality. It's not about what you have in your hands; it's about what you hold in your heart and mind.

People can have a poverty mentality even while holding abundance in their hands. You can have everything, and still feel like you're not enough, never chosen, always behind. Abundance isn't about accumulation; it's about revelation. It's a mindset shift that says, "Because I am a child of God, I lack nothing."

Romans 12:2 says: "*Do not be conformed to this world, but be transformed by the renewing of your mind, that you may prove what* is *that good and acceptable and perfect will of God.*"

This transformation isn't just about morality; it's about identity. When your mind is renewed to who God is and what He has given you, abundance begins to manifest in every area: your peace, your confidence, your time, your creativity, your boldness.

I remember seasons in my own life where I kept hitting walls, not because of lack on God's end, but because my thinking still reflected fear, unworthiness, and limits. I had to choose to let God shift my internal narrative. I had to forsake the old ways of thinking and return to the Lord's truth, just as Isaiah 55:7 says: "*Let the wicked forsake his way, And the unrighteous man his thoughts; Let him return to the* Lord, *and He will have mercy on him; And to our God, For He will abundantly pardon.*"

God's invitation into abundance starts with how you think about Him, about yourself, and about your future. You might be saying things like, "That's just not for me," or "I've already missed my chance." But the Lord says, "[My benefits] *are new every morning*" (Lam. 3:23).

I met this woman who believed for so long that her life was over because of a series of failures. But the moment she let God renew her mindset, when she stopped identifying with her past and started agreeing with His Word, things began to shift. Opportunities opened, joy returned, and peace replaced fear. Not because everything outside changed, but because her inside did.

The world will always say, "Do more, get more, prove more." But God says, "*Be still, and know that I* am *God*" (Ps. 46:10). When your mindset is aligned with truth, you stop striving for significance and start living from it.

Abundance is not a destination. It's a way of thinking that flows from the Spirit of God within you.

Divine Order Opens the Door to Supernatural Living

When we allow God to bring order to our time and priorities, we're not just becoming more "organized" people; we're becoming more available vessels. The structure of divine order isn't limiting; it's liberating. It positions us to hear God's voice more clearly, walk out His vision more confidently, and receive His abundance more freely.

So many times, we say we want to see the supernatural, healing, provision, favor, open doors, but we're living in chaos. God doesn't bring miracles into disordered lives just to have them collapse under the weight of misalignment. His abundance flows through order. His vision unfolds through time that's been surrendered to Him.

Time is not meant to be controlled but entrusted. We are not stewards of the clock; we are stewards of the calling. And when we surrender our schedule to the Spirit, He begins to breathe divine appointments into ordinary days. The vision becomes clearer not because we try harder, but because we've made space to listen.

Ephesians 5:15–17 gives us this clear instruction: "*See then that you walk circumspectly, not as fools but as wise, redeeming the time, because the days are evil. Therefore do not be unwise, but understand what the will of the Lord* is."

To walk in vision, you must understand the will of the Lord, and that only happens when time is redeemed. This means your calendar isn't just full of tasks; but aligned with purpose.

There was a time in my life when ministry, family, and travel all collided. I thought I had to hold it all together in my own strength. But I was missing something vital: peace. I had to step back and ask, "Lord, what's eternal in this season? What is truly You?" And as I released what was urgent to focus on what was eternal, the vision for my life became clearer, and surprisingly, abundance followed. Not just financial blessing, but time, rest, clarity, and favor.

God doesn't bring miracles into disordered lives just to have them collapse under the weight of misalignment.

Proverbs 3:5–6 reminds us: "*Trust in the Lord with all your heart, and lean not on your own understanding; In all your ways acknowledge Him, And He shall direct your paths.*"

When your paths are directed by God, vision doesn't feel like pressure; it feels like peace. And that's when abundance flows: not because we hustle for it, but because we've prepared a place for it. Abundance isn't accidental. It comes where there is room. And room is made through surrendered priorities.

Vision without order quickly turns to burnout. You might be chasing ten "God ideas" but missing the God assignment. That's why divine order isn't optional; it's essential.

If you feel like you're running in circles, doing good things but not seeing fruit, take a moment and ask: Is my time surrendered? Is my vision cluttered? Is there space for His abundance to land?

Because when divine order is established, the supernatural is no longer occasional; it becomes your lifestyle.

When You Know Who Leads, You Stop Chasing and Start Dwelling

Another danger of busyness is that it tricks us into thinking we are in control. It lures us into chasing opportunities, people's approval, financial goals, or even ministry achievements, all in the name of "purpose." But when you really know the One who leads you, you stop running and start dwelling.

The Lord isn't interested in you burning out in the name of vision. He's inviting you into a rhythm where rest becomes a weapon and peace becomes your strategy. When you know the Shepherd, you no longer have to chase green pastures; you are led into them.

Psalm 23:1-3 must become more than a memory verse; it needs to become a lifestyle: "*The Lord is my shepherd; I shall not want. He makes me to lie* down *in green pastures; He leads me beside the still waters. He restores my soul ...*"

> *Vision without order quickly turns to burnout.*

He makes me lie down. Sometimes the Spirit will interrupt your pace because He knows your soul needs restoration more than your hands need another task. That's not laziness; it's leadership. That's not failure; it's flourishing.

There was a time when I kept saying yes to things that sounded good, even spiritual things. But slowly, I began to notice that I was no longer operating from overflow. I was pouring out but not being filled. The Lord gently asked me, "Did I lead you here, or did you lead yourself?" That question marked me. I had to realign—not my calendar first, but my heart.

This is why walking in your vision doesn't start with doing; it starts with dwelling.

John 15:5 gives us this powerful reminder straight from Jesus: "*I am the vine, you are the branches. He who abides in Me, and I in him, bears much fruit; for without Me you can do nothing.*"

Abiding is where true fruit comes from. Not striving. Not networking. Not hustling. Just abiding. Vision without abiding becomes vanity. But when you're rooted in Him, fruit comes, abundantly and effortlessly.

Abiding is also where abundance stops being about possessions and becomes about presence. You can have a full house and an empty soul. Or you can have a quiet place with the Lord and feel the wealth of heaven in your bones. That's why we don't measure abundance by what's in our bank account; we measure it by who is leading us.

Proverbs 10:22 says, "*The blessing of the Lord makes one rich, and He adds no sorrow with it.*" That's the difference between a vision you strive for and a vision you dwell in. The first brings exhaustion. The second brings rich blessing with no sorrow attached.

If you're feeling drained, disoriented, or doubtful, ask yourself: Am I still following the Shepherd? Or have I run ahead of Him in my desire to prove, produce, or perform?

The beauty of knowing who leads is that you stop chasing. You find rest in His pace, clarity in His direction, and provision in His timing. That's how vision flows. That's how abundance multiplies. And that's how divine order is restored when we dwell, not just do.

Abiding is also where abundance stops being about possessions and becomes about presence.

Redeeming the Season You're in Opens the Door to Overflow

Sometimes we're so focused on the future, what's next, what's more, what's better, that we miss the power of the now. We pray for God to use us "someday," not realizing He's already positioned us in a season He wants to bless today. The concept of redeeming time isn't about squeezing more productivity out of your day; it's about recognizing the divine purpose of your current season and surrendering it to God.

I used to view certain seasons of my life as wasted time. I was waiting for the "real" part of my calling to begin. But God challenged me: "Will you let Me use this season for preparation, or will you complain your way through it?" That moment changed my perspective forever. I realized that vision is not on pause just because you're not where you think you should be. If you're surrendered, you're already in motion.

Paul writes this in Ephesians 5:15–17, "*See then that you walk circumspectly, not as fools but as wise, redeeming the time, because the days are evil. Therefore do not be unwise, but understand what the will of the Lord* is."

Redeeming time is not just about keeping a tight schedule; it's about aligning your heart with the will of the Lord in this moment. I already shared with you that the enemy wants to distract you with busyness or discourage you with delay. But when you understand that your time is not wasted but invested in eternity, you begin to walk in wisdom, purpose, and peace.

I remember when I spoke with a woman who thought her past failures disqualified her from living in abundance. But as she surrendered her present season to the Lord, despite her regrets, He began to restore her hope, confidence, and joy. That's what it looks like to redeem the time: not undoing the past but unlocking God's grace in the present.

This is also where abundance becomes personal. You don't step into overflow by longing for the "next." You step into overflow by trusting the Shepherd in the "now." Psalm 23:3 says: "*He restores my soul; He leads me in the paths of righteousness for His name's sake.*"

Vision is not on pause just because you're not where you think you should be. If you're surrendered, you're already in motion.

That's restoration in real time. Not when your circumstances change. But when your posture before Him changes.

Sometimes the enemy can't steal your calling, so he tries to steal your sense of timing. He'll whisper, "You're too late," "You missed it," or "It's not your season." But that's not what the Word says. Joel 2:25 declares, "*So I will restore to you the years that the swarming locust has eaten ....*"

God knows how to restore lost years and redeem broken moments. But that restoration begins when we stop despising where we are and start partnering with what God is doing now.

When you let Him redeem your time, He will multiply your influence. When you stop fighting the season and start flowing with His Spirit, vision comes alive. And when you let go of regret or delay, abundance isn't just a promise; it becomes your testimony.

This is divine order: time no longer serves your fear; it serves your faith. Vision is no longer delayed; it's discovered. And abundance isn't a wish; it's your witness.

The Lie of "Not Enough Time" Steals Your Faith for More

Another one of the enemy's most effective lies is: "You don't have enough time." He'll whisper it when God calls you to rest. He'll shout it when you begin to dream. He'll use it as a weapon of distraction, fear, and defeat. But what I've learned and what I've taught over and over again is that the issue is not how much time we have. The issue is whether we've given our time to God.

Sometimes we wear busyness like a badge of honor. We think it proves our value. But busyness isn't the same as fruitfulness. Busyness often reflects disordered priorities. When we fill our days with what feels urgent rather than what is eternally important, we end up tired, frustrated, and spiritually dry. And worse, we start blaming time, when what we really need is trust.

The truth is, we always have enough time to do what God has called us to do. Always. God didn't forget how to be the Author of your day. He's not surprised by your schedule or the season you're in. Ecclesiastes 3:1 assures us: "*To everything* there is *a season, A time for every purpose under heaven.*" That means time is not your enemy. It's your ally when it's given to God.

When you stop fighting the season and start flowing with His Spirit, vision comes alive.

The "not enough time" mentality once held me back from stepping into what God had put on my heart. I believed I had to earn the time, create the margin, and then, maybe, I could begin. But the Holy Spirit challenged me: "If I gave you the vision, don't you think I've also given you the time?" That question cut through the excuses. I realized I wasn't waiting for time; I was waiting for permission. And that permission had already been granted by grace.

Isaiah 55:12 says: "*For you shall go out with joy, And be led out with peace ....*" When you're following God's lead, your time flows in peace, not pressure. You're no longer driven by comparison or fear of missing out. You're led by the Spirit into what matters most.

The abundance message supports this truth beautifully. God's definition of overflow is never dependent on time, status, or opportunity. It's rooted in His character.

Psalm 86:15 says: "*But You, O Lord, are a God full of compassion, and gracious, Longsuffering and abundant in mercy and truth.*" That's abundance: God's willingness to work with us where we are, patiently and generously, as we follow Him. He is not in a hurry, but He's always on time.

I remember counseling a woman who believed she had missed her window to walk in purpose. "I had my chance," she said, "but I blew it. That was years ago." I told her, "Your clock may have ticked forward, but God never stopped speaking." Within weeks, she began to see new doors open because she decided to believe the voice of grace over the voice of guilt.

God's not measuring your vision by a stopwatch. He's measuring your willingness to trust. And when you do, time begins to multiply. Clarity increases. Peace flows. Joy rises. Why? Because you're no longer racing the clock. You're resting in the Shepherd.

Let's destroy the lie of "not enough time." You are not too late. You are not too busy. You are not disqualified. You are right on time to do what matters most, because God is still speaking, still redeeming, and still inviting you to step into more.

Vision Isn't a Destination; It's a Daily Walk with the Shepherd

So many people approach vision like it's a far-off destination, something you run toward in the future after you get your life in order, find more time, and feel "spiritually ready." But that mindset delay's purpose and disconnects us from the abundant life available right now. Vision isn't out there somewhere. Vision is here because Jesus is here.

Our relationship with God is the vision. He is the vision. He doesn't just hand us a five-year plan and say, "Good luck." He walks with us step by step. That means the joy of your vision isn't in the arrival; it's in the intimacy of the journey.

Early in ministry, I was so eager to do everything "right." I had all the lists and plans, and I wanted to check every box. But one day the Holy Spirit whispered to my heart, "I didn't call you to build something apart from Me. I called you to walk with Me." That changed everything. The pressure to perform lifted. I stopped striving to finish and started learning to follow. That's where real purpose begins.

The Shepherd leads us beside still waters. He doesn't drive us like cattle. When God leads, it restores. When we run ahead, it drains. That's how you know if you're walking in His vision—you'll feel peace even in the unknown.

Vision is not separate from time management. In fact, good time management is simply agreeing with God about what really matters. When you prioritize His voice, everything else begins to fall into place. It's not that life gets easier. It's that clarity comes. And in clarity, you find strength.

> *The joy of your vision isn't in the arrival; it's in the intimacy of the journey.*

God doesn't give us vision and leave us to figure out the how. He supplies grace upon grace, that's powerful. In John 1:16, it says: "*And of His fullness we have all received, and grace for grace.*" Vision that is walked out with God will always be accompanied by His grace. That means when the path looks too hard, or the calling feels too big, your job isn't to shrink the vision; it's to draw nearer to God. Because the vision is Him.

And here's what's amazing: as you walk with Him, you start to live in abundance without even realizing it. Your heart gets filled. Your relationships deepen. Your time becomes fruitful. And suddenly, you're not just surviving days you're fulfilling destiny All because you chose to walk.

One of my favorite testimonies came from a woman who said, "Carrie, I thought I missed my calling because I never found that 'big vision' everyone talks about. But then I realized, walking with God every day, that's the vision." That still brings tears to my eyes. That's the truth. The most powerful vision you can live out is one that is surrendered daily to the Lord.

Let's stop waiting for something bigger and start walking with Someone greater. His vision for your life unfolds not on the mountaintop, but in the daily steps of obedience and trust. Vision isn't a destination. It's a relationship. And that relationship leads you into green pastures, still waters, and a life more abundant than you ever imagined.

Order Precedes Overflow—God Builds Before He Fills

One of the most powerful truths I've learned in walking with the Lord is this: God brings order before He brings overflow. Many times, we cry out for abundance: more time, more clarity, more provision, but God, in His wisdom, begins by putting things in order so you're not just busy, but have direction. That's not punishment; order is preparation. He wants to bless you in a way that won't crush you. So He builds before He fills.

Often, we want increase without adjustment. We want multiplication without management. But even Jesus, before He performed the miracle of feeding the five thousand, told the disciples to have the people sit down in groups. There had to be structure before the supernatural.

Luke 9:14–17 tells us: "*For there were about five thousand men. Then He said to His disciples, 'Make them sit down in groups of fifty.' And they did so, and made them all sit down. Then He took the five loaves and the two fish, and looking up to heaven, He blessed and broke them ... So they all ate and were filled, and twelve baskets of the leftover fragments were taken up by them.*"

His vision for your life unfolds not on the mountaintop, but in the daily steps of obedience and trust.

Jesus didn't need organization for Himself. He needed it for them. The same is true for us. We ask God for abundance, but if we're too busy to sit down with Him, how can we receive it? If we don't make space, we won't make room for overflow.

This connects deeply with walking in vision. Sometimes we get frustrated because the vision seems delayed, or nothing is "happening." But what I've learned is that in those quiet, hidden seasons, God is working deeply in me. He's building a foundation, restoring my soul, ordering my thoughts, clarifying my values. That is vision work. That's how purpose is built to last.

One woman I mentored had this powerful encounter. She said, "Carrie, I thought I had a vision for my life, but it was based on pressure, not peace. Once I let the Lord reorganize my days and realign my focus, He started speaking fresh vision again." That's what order does: it opens the door for God to speak.

God is abundant in mercy and truth (Ps. 86:15). But that abundance isn't chaotic. It flows in unity with His nature. His mercy doesn't ignore disorder; it transforms it. His truth doesn't shame; it aligns. So, when we invite God into our time, our vision, and our expectations, He doesn't just bless us; He rebuilds us.

He wants to bless you in a way that won't crush you. So He builds before He fills.

That's what happened in my own life. There was a season when I was begging God for breakthrough in ministry. I felt like I had all these great ideas, but no traction. But the Lord gently showed me how out of alignment my own schedule and heart were. I had let busyness steal my spiritual authority. So, I gave Him my time. I let Him reorder my days. And once that order came, His grace flowed in ways I couldn't have imagined.

This is not about being perfect. It's about being willing. Willing to let God examine our calendars, our conversations, our checklists, and our dreams. And say, "Lord, if there's anything out of alignment, I trust You to bring it into order."

When God is first, everything else finds its place. That's the divine order that opens the floodgates of abundant living. Because He's not a God of striving. He's a God of structure and supply.

If you feel stuck or stretched or like you're missing something, ask this simple question: "Lord, what needs to be brought into order so You can fill it?" You'll be amazed at how quickly the overflow comes once the foundation is surrendered.

Identity-Fueled Vision Reclaims Wasted Time

A lie the enemy tries to sell us, especially when we've been busy but unfruitful, is that we've lost too much time to ever walk in purpose. But the truth is, when we surrender to God's timing, He redeems the time. He gives back what busyness tried to steal. And it all starts with identity.

You'll never fully walk in your vision until you know who you are. Vision without identity becomes performance. But when you know you're a beloved child of God, called, equipped, and filled with His Spirit, you stop chasing approval and start walking in confidence. And when your identity is rooted in Him, He begins to show you how even your wasted seasons weren't wasted to Him.

Ephesians 5:15–16 says, "*See then that you walk circumspectly, not as fools but as wise, redeeming the time, because the days are evil.*" That phrase "redeeming the time" is powerful. It means that what felt wasted can be reclaimed, restored, and made fruitful again.

When we give Him our "yes", our surrendered time and hearts, He won't just start where we left off. He rearranges everything and gives us back more than we thought we'd lost. Relationships are restored. Dreams come alive again. Energy and focus return. And vision becomes joy again, not pressure.

That's what happens when we let Him remind us of who we are. We begin to make decisions from a place of grace, not guilt. We start saying yes to what matters, and no to what distracts. That's where true time management begins: not with a planner, but with the planner of your life.

We often think our calling is "out there," something we have to strive to achieve. But the truth is, it's already in us. It's in the Word planted in our hearts. It's in the identity we've received in Christ. When we believe that, we don't waste time searching. We start living. And that's when joy rushes back in.

> *You'll never fully walk in your vision until you know who you are. Vision without identity becomes performance.*

Abundance, too, is deeply connected to this revelation. It's not just more stuff or more success. It's the fullness of walking with the Father in every area, spirit, soul, and body. As

Psalm 23:3 reminds us, "*He restores my soul.*" Sometimes the restoration of time begins with the restoration of the soul. When your soul is whole, your time bears fruit. Your vision clears. Your heart becomes peaceful again.

If you've felt like you've lost time, don't agree with that lie. Your Father holds time in His hands, and He is well able to redeem it. Start today by coming back to who He says you are. Let that identity become the foundation for your time, your vision, and your abundance. Because nothing is wasted in His hands.

Reflection

If I could leave you with one thing from this chapter, it would be this: You were never created for a life of busyness. You were created for a life of purpose. The world may celebrate the hustle, the constant striving, and the calendar packed to the brim. But heaven celebrates something else entirely: intimacy with the Father, clarity of purpose, and fruit that remains.

Busyness may look productive on the outside, but if it's not anchored in God's priorities, it robs you of spiritual authority. It steals your joy, dulls your discernment, and distracts you from the very thing God is trying to do in and through your life. But the good news is, you don't have to live that way anymore.

We've seen throughout this chapter that when we yield our time, God doesn't just give us better schedules; He gives us better vision. He brings satisfaction where there was striving. He turns noise into peace and chaos into clarity. And in that place of divine alignment, abundance starts to flow, not just in finances, but in wholeness, joy, fruitfulness, and impact.

You were never created for a life of busyness. You were created for a life of purpose.

I've lived on both sides of this. I know what it feels like to be so busy doing "good things" that I miss the God things. I also know the incredible freedom that comes when you slow down, get honest, and say, "God, I trust You to lead my time, my vision, and my life." That's where restoration begins. That's where strength replaces excuses and authority replaces anxiety.

You don't have to earn your way into purpose. You don't have to prove yourself to walk in vision. You don't have to strive to deserve abundance. All of it, every single part, flows from your relationship with Him.

So, as you reflect on what you've read, remember, you were never meant to manage life on your own. You were meant to walk in divine order, and from that place, live in abundant overflow—redeemed time, reclaimed vision, restored life.

My Challenge to You

- Stop and Realign: Take a step back and look at your calendar, routines, and daily rhythms through the lens of the Spirit. Ask yourself: Am I being led by divine purpose, or just pulled along by pressure, performance, and people's expectations?
- Invite God into Your Time: Sit with Him and ask, "Lord, what have I said yes to that You never asked me to carry?" Allow Him to highlight where busyness has crept in.
- Release the Unnecessary: Be bold enough to let go of what's good if it's not God. Trust that what you release in obedience, He will redeem with fruitfulness.
- Reclaim Joy in Vision: Choose to walk in your vision, not from stress or striving, but from rest, knowing that you're led by the Shepherd who restores your soul.

- Let Go of Excuses: Embrace His strength instead of your own. Remember, He's not asking for perfection, just permission to lead.
- Trust His Redemption: Believe that your time is not too far gone, your priorities can be rebuilt, and your heart can be restored.
- Make Room for Abundance: When you surrender the weight of busyness, you create space for clarity, margin, peace, and purpose.

Scripture References

Ephesians 2:6
Proverbs 29:18
Psalm 23:1–3
Luke 5:15–16
John 10:10
Romans 5:17
Exodus 3:12
2 Corinthians 12:9
Isaiah 30:15
Hebrews 4:10
Isaiah 41:10
Luke 10:41–42
Psalm 16:11
Psalm 46:10
Matthew 6:33
Ecclesiastes 3:1
Proverbs 19:21
Romans 12:2
Isaiah 55:17
Lamentations 3:23
Ephesians 5:15–17
Proverbs 3:5–6
John 15:5
Proverbs 10:22
Joel 2:25
Isaiah 55:12
Psalm 86:15
John 1:16
Luke 9:14–17

Chapter Three

A Life God Leads

Introduction

In the last chapters, we began this journey by looking at time as something to be surrendered, not managed. We saw how busyness can rob us of joy and purpose, and how letting go of control opens the door to divine order and true overflow. Surrendering our time and vision was never about losing; it was about making space for God to fill.

Now, in this chapter, we take that truth a step further. What does it look like to actually live a life God leads? This isn't about a perfect schedule or a flawless plan; it's about recognizing that your days are not your own, and that's the best news you'll ever hear. God never designed you to lead yourself. He designed you to walk with Him, led by His Spirit, carried by His love, and guided by His vision pulsing within you.

Here, we'll discover that surrender is not weakness but the very doorway to peace, clarity, and abundant overflow. When you realize that Christ already lives in you, you stop striving to become something you already are and start living out of what He has already given. This chapter is an invitation to shift from performance to abiding, from pressure to peace, and from confusion to the clarity of a Spirit-led life.

Fix Your Focus

1. Surrendered Time Becomes Spirit-Led Time

Discover that effective time management isn't about fitting God into our schedule. It's about handing our schedule to God. Much of our day already belongs to Him, and when we surrender control, we begin to operate in divine rhythm. Our days gain purpose, not because we manage them perfectly, but because we invite the Holy Spirit into the details.

2. Vision Begins with Relationship, Not Performance

Vision isn't birthed out of pressure or self-discovery; it's born in the presence of God. True vision begins the moment we ask, "Lord, how do You want to express Your love through me?" When we stop trying to figure out our calling and start receiving God's love, His vision flows naturally from that relationship. Joy comes not from knowing all the steps, but from knowing the One who leads us.

3. Abundance Is Already Yours in Christ

Abundance isn't a reward for your performance; it's the inheritance of those who belong to Christ. You're not working for it; you already possess it. When you stop striving and start receiving, you become both a reservoir and a distributor of God's goodness. Focus on the truth that we've been translated out of the kingdom of lack into the kingdom of overflow. The journey begins with letting God lead.

A Life of Vision Begins with Relationship

So many times, we approach vision like it's a destination. We treat it like it's this future assignment we have to chase down or figure out on our own. But vision doesn't start with a plan; it starts with a Person. It starts in relationship with the Holy Spirit.

While I was sitting on the back porch in Africa, reflecting on everything God was doing, I was overwhelmed with the beauty of what it means to simply be with Him. We'd just finished a whirlwind of ministry, eleven flights in fifteen days, powerful meetings with men and women of the area, and leaders all across Africa, and now we were resting as a family. In that still moment, God said something I had never heard before: "Carrie, vision is how I want to express My love through you."

That one sentence wrecked me. It simplified everything. It reminded me that vision is not something I manufacture or strive to discover. It's the overflow of my intimacy with God. It's the natural fruit of knowing Him and letting Him lead. If I stay connected, He'll do the revealing.

Jesus said in John 15:5, "*I am the vine, you* are *the branches. He who abides in Me, and I in him, bears much fruit; for without Me you can do nothing.*" That's where true vision comes from, abiding in Him. You don't have to go on a hunt for your destiny. Just spend time with the One who designed it.

When we walk with the Spirit, He shows us who we're called to love, who we're called to serve, and how we're called to give. Sometimes that love looks like parenting your children. Sometimes it's launching a business, pastoring a church, or reaching a specific group of people you never thought you'd connect with. That's how it happened for me in Russia. I had no experience with drugs or prostitution, but God gave me compassion for the addicts and the trafficked. His love became my vision.

And that's how it starts. Not with your qualifications. Not with your education or credentials. But with God saying, "Let Me love through you." That's the kind of life He leads. It's a life full of purpose, but one that flows from His presence.

You may be tempted to ask, like Moses did, "Who am I?" But vision doesn't come from who you are; it comes from who He is. And when you know Him, when you see yourself through His love, everything changes. Exodus 3:11–12 says, "*But Moses said to God, 'Who* am *I that I should go to Pharaoh ...?' So* [God] *said, 'I will certainly be with you.'*" That's the promise of a life God leads: He will be with you.

So today, don't rush to define your future. Don't try to force vision. Rest in Him. Spend time in the Word. Let the Holy Spirit whisper His love. That's where your journey begins—in His presence.

Daily Surrender Makes Room for Supernatural Living

I have found that one of the most powerful shifts that happens when you start letting God lead your life is that you realize you don't own your day anymore. And that's not a burden; it's a beautiful invitation.

When you connect with the Holy Spirit, your calendar changes. Your sense of urgency changes. Your value system changes. You're not just living to cross off tasks; you're walking in step with the Spirit. Suddenly, you realize that your time is not your own and that much of your day belongs to Him.

If God is Lord of your life, He must also be Lord of your time. That doesn't mean we don't make plans or have responsibilities; it means we give Him the right to interrupt them. And it means we start our day asking, "Lord, what do You want to do with my time?"

This surrender is not rooted in striving; it's rooted in love. That's what makes it sustainable. When we know how deeply we're loved, surrender doesn't feel like loss, it feels like alignment. Galatians 2:20 says, "*I have been crucified with Christ; it is no longer I who live, but Christ lives in me; and the* life *which I now live in the flesh I live by faith in the Son of God, who loved me and gave Himself for me.*" That is powerful. Christ in you changes how you live moment by moment.

During our trip to Africa, I had so many plans. But God had His own appointments. Some of the most powerful times of ministry didn't happen on a stage; they happened while we were traveling, in conversations, in quiet moments. I had to continually check in with the Holy Spirit, laying down my agenda to make room for His.

That's how vision comes alive, through obedience in the small things. Abundance doesn't come by overstuffing your schedule. It comes by letting the Lord guide each step. Psalm 37:23 says, "*The steps of a* good *man are ordered by the* Lord, *and He delights in his way.*" Did you catch that? He delights in your way. God wants to partner with you in your daily life, not just your big dreams.

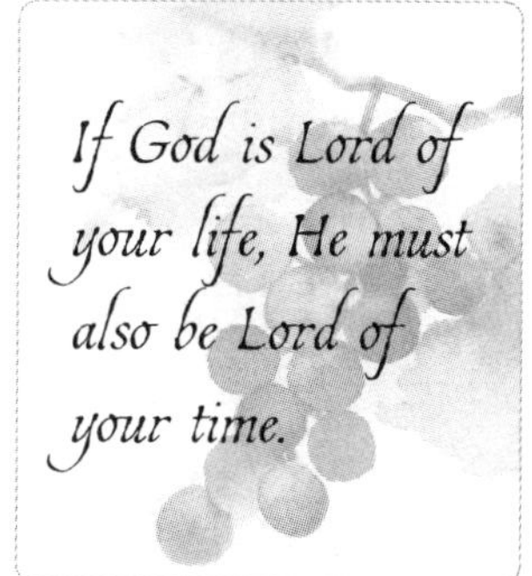

Too often, we think surrender is only for massive life decisions like where to go to school, who to marry, and what job to take. But real surrender is daily. It happens when you invite God into the quiet, ordinary moments and say, "Lord, these next thirty minutes are Yours. Speak. Lead. Interrupt me if You need to."

I used to fill every gap in my day with activity, but I began to notice that God couldn't get a word in. He wasn't competing with my busyness; He was waiting for my stillness.

Surrendering your time is where you'll find the rhythm of grace. It's where you'll realize that supernatural living is not for "special moments";

it's for every moment. And that's when the abundance of God's presence, wisdom, and provision starts flowing—not just to you, but through you.

Let today be a reset. Pause, breathe, and invite Him in. Ask the Holy Spirit, "What parts of my day have I been holding onto?" Then open your hands. There's no better time manager than the One who holds eternity in His hands.

Knowing God's Voice Clarifies Your Path

When we talk about a life that God leads, it has to begin with this truth: You can hear God. Not just occasionally. Not just in crisis. But every day. The ability to walk in divine order and overflow starts by recognizing the voice of the One who's leading you.

That life which God leads is a life tuned to His voice—not in just isolated moments, but in the quiet rhythm of your day, He's speaking, guiding, correcting, and encouraging. When you begin to discern His voice in the midst of all the noise, you gain clarity about what truly matters.

Most people are not struggling with a lack of time; they're struggling with a lack of direction. The deeper issue isn't how to fit everything in—it's knowing what actually belongs in your life to begin with. And that's something only the Holy Spirit can reveal.

Jesus said in John 10:27, "*My sheep hear My voice, and I know them, and they follow Me.*" That's not a vague promise. That's a description of relationship. He knows you. He speaks to you. And you can follow because you recognize His voice.

But let me be honest—there were seasons where I was doing all the right things: ministry, leadership, raising my kids, building programs. But my peace was leaking. I wasn't running from God; I was just running ahead of Him. And I had to ask, "Whose voice am I listening to today? God's? Or the expectations of people?"

When you begin your day by asking, "Holy Spirit, what's on Your heart today?" it reframes your to-do list. You stop living reactively. You stop chasing opportunities that aren't your assignment. And you start moving with purpose.

I remember a time when I had said yes to too many good things. Ministry, events, people, needs, and things that looked right on the surface. But inside, I could feel the strain. It wasn't sin that I was entangled in. It was busyness. Busyness can masquerade as purpose. But only the Holy Spirit can show you what truly belongs.

The Word confirms this over and over. Proverbs 3:5–6 says, "*Trust in the Lord with all your heart, and lean not on your own understanding; in all your ways acknowledge Him, and He shall direct your paths.*" Paths, plural. He doesn't just direct your "big life plan." He directs the moments. The conversations. The transitions. Every path you take can be led by His voice.

> *When you begin to discern His voice in the midst of all the noise, you gain clarity about what truly matters.*

But here's the key: You have to value His voice enough to make space for it. The discipline of margin is what makes room for intimacy. That's how we shift from being led by circumstances to being led by the Spirit.

The truth is, abundance doesn't just show up when we get everything perfect.

It shows up when we follow the Shepherd. Psalm 23:1–3 reminds us, "*The* L*ORD* *is my shepherd; I shall not want. He makes me to lie down in green pastures; He leads me beside the still waters. He restores my soul; He leads me in the paths of righteousness for His name's sake.*"

Vision gets clearer when you rest in who He is. Your purpose comes into focus not because you finally figured it all out, but because you trust the One who already knows the way.

As you grow in hearing God's voice, vision becomes more than a distant dream—it becomes a daily walk. You begin to steward time differently. You stop investing energy into things He never assigned. And suddenly, life becomes a divine collaboration where heaven touches earth through your simple obedience. And that's the kind of path God loves to lead.

Love-Fueled Vision Breaks the Limits

When vision is born from love, it becomes unstoppable. Love, real divine love, removes fear, silences excuses, and demolishes limitations. You don't need a perfect resume to walk in purpose. You need a revelation of God's heart.

You already possess Christ. That changes everything. When you know that Christ lives in you, you stop asking, "Can I?" and start asking, "Lord, how do You want to love others through me today?" That's where divine vision is born—not from talent, not from credentials—but from love.

This is where time management intersects powerfully with purpose. When you follow God's heart, you stop wasting time on unassigned burdens. Love becomes the filter for your schedule. What's rooted in love will bear fruit. What's not will drain you.

And that love leads you to the truth that God is not stingy with vision. He's not withholding plans from you, waiting for you to earn it. No, He's eager to reveal His heart—because He's already given you His Spirit. As Romans 5:5 says, "*The love of God has been poured out in our hearts by the Holy Spirit who was given to us.*" You don't need to dig deep to find purpose. You need to recognize what's already been deposited.

When God told Moses, "*I Am who I Am*" (Ex. 3:14), He wasn't trying to be mysterious. He was revealing, "You're not the source—I Am. And I'm with you." That's all Moses needed. That's all you need. Because when you understand that love is the source of your vision, you stop putting yourself on trial. You stop hesitating. You stop waiting for the perfect moment. You say, "God, if You're leading me, I'll go." And as you go, the overflow comes.

God's Timing Protects What He's Building

When we commit to letting God lead our lives, it's easy to get impatient. We sense the vision, we feel the passion, and we want to run forward. But God's timing isn't just about delay; it's about protection. We often take on things out of season—rushing into assignments God never told us to start yet. What ends up happening is we mismanage the weight, or we try to carry something in our own strength that we weren't ready to steward. That's why surrendering to the Holy Spirit's timing is essential.

> *When vision is born from love, it becomes unstoppable. Love, real divine love, removes fear, silences excuses, and demolishes limitations.*

God doesn't give you vision to torment you with unfulfilled dreams. He reveals things so you can walk with Him in trust, day by day, into the fullness of what He's building. But the foundation has to be Him, His Word, His presence, His character. You don't build your life's purpose on passion alone. You build it by walking in step with the Spirit.

One of the most freeing moments I've experienced was when the Lord reminded me, "Carrie, I'm not in a rush—and neither should you be." That stopped me in my tracks. I was trying to do too much, too fast. But He showed me that some of the things I was rushing into weren't wrong—they were just premature. And premature obedience can sometimes carry the same pain as disobedience. There's protection in the timing of God.

This protection applies to abundance as well. See, abundance isn't just about having more; it's about receiving what is yours when you're ready to walk in it. God desires to multiply grace and peace to us. "*May grace and peace be multiplied to you in the knowledge of God and of Jesus our Lord*" (2 Pet. 1:2, *English Standard Version*). But that multiplication flows best when we've learned to abide and rest in His lead. You don't demand harvest before seedtime has been honored. There is a divine order. God builds your character, deepens your dependence, and prepares your heart before the breakthrough arrives.

You don't build your life's purpose on passion alone. You build it by walking in step with the Spirit.

Look at Moses. When God called him, Moses wanted to know, "What if they won't listen?" (Ex. 4:1). He had so many objections. But God didn't answer with timing charts or task lists. He answered with His presence. He revealed who He was: "I AM." That's how God leads, with Himself. And when you have Him, you don't need to force your way into your future.

The truth is, when you slow down to be led, you speed up your effectiveness. Waiting on God isn't passive; it's powerful. It produces endurance, clarity, and peace. And when the season turns and God says, "Go," you'll have more than vision, you'll have divine momentum.

The Holy Spirit Reclaims the Day

So much of our time feels consumed by what we have to do, work, responsibilities, schedules, and obligations. But when the Holy Spirit leads, you begin to discover that much of your day actually belongs to Him. That was a turning point for me. I used to think I had to segment time for God into a neat, little devotional block. But God doesn't want visitation rights—He wants habitation. The Holy Spirit is ready to lead you *in* your responsibilities, not just *around* them.

What we often see as interruptions, God sees as invitations. And that shift comes when we surrender control. Often, we're tempted to treat time like a commodity we must guard. But when you start seeing time as something to steward *with* God instead of *for* Him, your days take on new meaning.

One day, I was heading into a full schedule, and I felt a nudge from the Lord: "Let Me direct today." I had no idea what that meant in the moment, but I paused and said, "Okay, Lord. I surrender the schedule." That day was radically different. Divine conversations happened. Things I thought were urgent got postponed, and things I had no idea were coming suddenly became the priority. The joy that filled my heart wasn't because the to-do list got done; it was because I knew I was being led.

The truth is, when you slow down to be led, you speed up your effectiveness.

Vision isn't about plotting the next big step; it's about living relationally with God in the small steps. So many people are waiting for a lightning bolt of destiny, but often, God is whispering through the seemingly mundane: "Can I lead you in this errand? Can I guide you in this meeting? Will you let Me interrupt your plan with My love?"

That's where abundance comes in, too, not just financial or material, but an overflow of wisdom, clarity, and peace when you give the Holy Spirit authority in your time. You might not get everything done your way, but you'll end the day with a sense of fullness because He used it His way.

Letting God lead doesn't make your schedule chaotic; it makes it consecrated. You begin to trust that what's not finished was never the priority, and what was accomplished carried eternal value.

And that's the beauty of a life God leads: He redeems the minutes, realigns your focus, and reclaims your day as His own. Every meeting, every moment becomes sacred ground when you're walking with the Spirit.

Stop Negotiating with God's Call

There's a tendency we all share, especially when God calls us to something big, something beyond our abilities. We start negotiating. We play the "what if" game, just like Moses did. God gives us an assignment, and immediately we respond with, "Well, what if they don't believe me? What if it doesn't work? What if the money doesn't come in?" That inner dialogue might sound responsible or realistic, but really it's fear in disguise. It's our flesh trying to maintain control instead of surrendering to the Spirit.

I've been there. I've had the Lord ask me to step out, and my mind immediately went to all the ways it might not work. "But Lord, what if the timing's off?" or "What if this interrupts everything else I'm juggling?" I was still trying to manage my life as if were mine to lead. But if you and I are truly going to live a life God leads, we have to stop negotiating with Him and start trusting His voice.

So many of us think we can only say yes to God once our schedule allows it, once the bills are paid, or once we feel more prepared. But God isn't waiting for our calendar to open up. He's inviting us to yield to His plan so that He can redeem our time. The moment we agree with His direction, we find that He's already gone ahead of us—with provision, strength, and strategy.

This is where vision and surrender collide. God doesn't give you vision and then say, "Good luck figuring out how to make it happen." He gives you vision and then says, "I will be with you. My strength will carry you. My grace is sufficient." But we won't experience that sufficiency if we keep putting His call through our approval process.

Think about what happens when we finally let go of the "what ifs." That's when vision starts to flow again. That's when peace returns. That's when joy becomes our default, because we've stepped out of control and into trust. God never called us to fear-based planning. He called us to faith-filled obedience.

And yes, there are things we will have to say no to, good things, comfortable things, even logical things. But every time we surrender our plan for His, what we find is far better than what we were afraid of losing. We have to stop putting our excuses on the table like a deck of cards we're trying to play against God. That's not faith. That's hesitation.

It's time to throw out the "what ifs" and start saying, "Lord, if You've called me, I will go. You know the future. You are already there. So, I step in, not with fear, but with faith."

Vision Isn't About Qualification; It's About Possession

One of the greatest misconceptions that keeps believers from stepping into vision is this idea: "I'm not qualified." We look at our background, education, past mistakes, or even just the stage of life we're in and say, "There's no way God could use me for something big." But that thinking completely ignores one crucial truth: you already possess Christ.

When I look back at some of the people God used in the Bible—like Moses, Gideon, and Peter—they all had something in common: a long list

God never called us to fear-based planning. He called us to faith-filled obedience.

of reasons why they shouldn't have been chosen. But God didn't choose them based on what they brought to the table. He chose them because He saw what He had already placed inside of them. That's why the call to walk in vision isn't about natural qualifications; it's about spiritual possession. You have the living God inside of you. That changes everything.

We waste time questioning whether we're ready when, in reality, God has already prepared us with every spiritual blessing in Christ. But too often we spend so much time looking outward instead of inward. We think vision is about finding the perfect opportunity, the right timing, or a platform that makes us feel important. But vision begins with recognizing the fullness of what we've already been given.

That's where abundance enters the conversation. We don't operate from lack. We operate from overflow. You already possess Christ—the wisdom, the power, the Spirit of God. We have the mind of Christ. So, what more are we waiting for?

God is not asking you to impress Him with your résumé. He's asking you to believe Him, to believe that His love qualifies you, His Word equips you, and His Spirit empowers you. When you know who lives in you, those opportunities that once felt too big suddenly become a natural next step.

That doesn't mean you won't feel the pressure or the temptation to compare yourself to others. But when your confidence is rooted in Christ—not in yourself—it frees you to say yes to God, even when everything in the natural says "You're not ready." I've walked into rooms and stood behind pulpits thinking, "Lord, are You sure You picked the right girl?" But the moment I yielded, I saw the anointing flow. That's because I wasn't standing there in my strength; I was standing in the strength of the One I already possess.

If you've been holding back because you don't feel prepared, let this be the moment you stop waiting for perfect conditions. Vision doesn't need your perfection. It just needs you to know you're the possession of Christ and that you live surrendered to His plan.

Let's stop disqualifying ourselves from what God has already qualified us for. You don't have to get ready—you are already ready. Now, walk like it.

Provision Is Found in Obedience

There is a big lie the enemy uses to paralyze believers, and it is this: "If I follow God, I'll lack something." Whether it's finances, safety, community, or success, the fear of not having enough can keep us from stepping into the very life God is leading us toward. But here's what I've learned after years of ministry and saying yes to God: provision is always found on the path of obedience.

When our family was in Africa on a ministry trip, we'd poured ourselves out in teaching, encouraging, and loving on the students. After it was all said and done, we were surprised with a gift: a three-day safari retreat. We didn't ask for it. We didn't plan for it. We weren't striving to make it happen. It was simply God saying, "Thank you for trusting Me." That little pocket of rest and beauty was a reminder that God's goodness follows obedience.

The call to walk in vision isn't about natural qualifications; it's about spiritual possession.

When you say yes to the life God leads, you're not stepping into a desert—you're stepping into a place where His rivers of provision already flow. That's what abundance really looks like. It's not the world's version of hustle, stress, or accumulation. It's God's invitation to live in the flow of His provision—right on time, in the right place, and with peace.

I've learned that the more I prioritize His presence in my time—saying no to distractions and yes to the Spirit's nudges—the more I realize God has already gone before me. He knows the people I'll meet, the answers I'll need, and the strength I'll require. He's not trying to catch up with my plans—He's leading me in His.

So often, we want to map everything out—to understand how it all connects—before we take the first step. But God doesn't work like that. He calls us to trust. To go. It's in the going that the provision shows up. God isn't withholding until we earn it—the blessing is simply tied to the place of obedience.

Think of Elijah at the brook. God told him, "Go to the brook, and I will command the ravens to feed you there." If Elijah had gone anywhere else, he would have missed the very provision God had already arranged. The ravens weren't going to chase him. The miracle was tied to the obedience.

When you live a life that God leads, you stop being afraid of lack. You stop stressing over how it's going to work out. Instead, you begin to expect that your obedience will unlock blessing, not because you earned it, but because God is that good.

So don't let fear of not having enough keep you from stepping out. The abundance is already there. The table has already been prepared. Your part is simple: listen, follow, and trust that provision flows on the path of obedience.

A God-Led Life Is Marked by Supernatural Rest

When you're truly led by the Lord, when your time, vision, and resources are submitted to Him, one of the most surprising results is rest. Not exhaustion, not striving, not burnout. Supernatural rest. That rest doesn't come from everything being easy. It comes from trusting the One who leads.

There's a beautiful picture of this in Hebrews 4. It speaks of a "rest" that remains for the people of God. Not just physical rest, but a deep spiritual confidence—a ceasing from our own labors and an entering into the finished work of Christ.

Hebrews 4:10 says, "*For he who has entered His rest has himself also ceased from his works as God* did *from His.*" That's the place where God wants you to live from, His rest, not your pressure. That was the shift that happened in me when I surrendered my time management to the Lord. For so long, I tried to juggle the responsibilities of ministry, family, teaching, mentoring, travel, and deadlines—until I realized that peace isn't found in a perfect schedule; it's found in a Person.

When you live a life that God leads, you stop being afraid of lack.

When I connected with the Holy Spirit and let Him order my day, I found He didn't just make me more productive, He made me more peaceful. He showed me that much of what I thought was urgent, wasn't. He taught me that some things could wait, and others could simply fall away. And in that surrender, I stopped feeling guilty for resting. I stopped apologizing for saying no. I started letting God lead my time, not my task list.

Jesus modeled this so powerfully. In Mark 6, the disciples return to Jesus after ministry and miracles. They're excited, worn out, and ready to share. But Jesus didn't rush into the next assignment. He didn't say, "Great job, now go out again." Instead, He invited them to rest.

Mark 6:31 says, "*And He said to them, 'Come aside by yourselves to a deserted place and rest a while.' For there were many coming and going, and they did not even have time to eat.*"

Jesus knew the rhythm of grace: rest and release. That's the cadence of a life God leads. It's not all gas pedal, all the time. It's grace and guidance. Movement and margin. And that's where real abundance shows up, not just in what you produce, but in what you enjoy.

When we obey God's leading, we don't have to fear that rest will make us fall behind. In fact, rest becomes our strategy. God doesn't bless our stress; He blesses our surrender. And that surrender includes resting when He says to rest.

This is still growing in my life. As I learn to give Him my schedule, I also learn to receive His refreshment. Even in seasons that are full, I now expect there to be a supernatural rest because I'm not carrying the weight; He is.

Matthew 11:28–30 is one of my favorite invitations from Jesus: "*Come to Me, all* you *who labor and are heavy laden, and I will give you rest. Take My yoke upon you and learn from Me, for I am gentle and lowly in heart, and you will find rest for your souls. For My yoke* is *easy and My burden is light.*" That's the life you and I are called to—a life where the burden is light, not because life is easy, but because we're not carrying it alone.

Fear Tries to Forecast What God Has Already Finished

There's a sneaky tactic the enemy uses when we begin to take steps of obedience: he tries to make us afraid of the future. It's not just fear of failure; it's fear of the unknown, fear of rejection, fear of losing control. But when your life is led by God, you learn to recognize fear as a counterfeit guide.

Remember the story of Moses at the burning bush in Exodus 3, when he received a call bigger than anything he could imagine. God told him to go to Pharaoh and lead His people out of Egypt. Remember what he did? Moses did what many of us do: he began negotiating with God. "Who am

I?" "What if they don't believe me?" "What if they won't listen?" Moses was already picturing rejection, resistance, and failure.

Exodus 4:1 says, "*Then Moses answered and said, 'But suppose they will not believe me or listen to my voice; suppose they say, 'The Lord has not appeared to you.*'"

Do you see it? Suppose ... suppose ... suppose. Fear always speaks in future tense. It paints false pictures and demands we make present decisions based on imagined disasters. That's how the enemy traps so many believers; they don't move forward, not because they heard a no from God, but because they listened to a "maybe not" from fear.

I've done this before, too. I thought I was being wise and logical when I was actually just being anxious. I wasn't counting the cost by faith; I was calculating failure through fear. The Lord had called me to something, and instead of agreeing with what He said, I started offering excuses: What if the finances don't come in? What if people don't understand? What if it's too hard?

But let me tell you—God doesn't call you into uncertainty. He calls you into trust. Where He leads you, His provision is already waiting.

When you're surrendered to God, your time becomes a seed of obedience. Every yes to God comes with heaven's backing. So instead of spending our days worrying over hypotheticals, we can spend them worshiping with confidence.

Fear always speaks in future tense. It paints false pictures and demands we make present decisions based on imagined disasters.

Second Timothy 1:7 reminds us, "*For God has not given us a spirit of fear, but of power and of love and of a sound mind.*"

That means every fearful "What if..." scenario didn't come from God. If it didn't come from Him, we have the authority to reject it. Fear tries to limit you before you ever begin. When you know what God has spoken—when you're in relationship with His Word and His Spirit—you stop letting fear forecast your future.

You begin to declare, "God has called me. He's provided for me. He's going before me. And I refuse to let the enemy's what-if rob me of my what-is."

I once said this, and it still sticks with me: The enemy wants you paralyzed by imagination, but God wants you mobilized by revelation. What has God already said? That's your anchor. That's your guide. That's your strategy for silencing fear.

Isaiah 41:10 says, "*Fear not, for I am with you; Be not dismayed, for I* am *your God. I will strengthen you, Yes, I will help you, I will uphold you with My righteous right hand.*"

A life led by God doesn't mean we never hear fear—it means we stop obeying it. We stop making room for it. We stop letting it sound wiser than God's Word. And when we do that, when we surrender to truth instead of trembling over lies, that's when vision flourishes. That's when time multiplies. That's when abundance is released.

True Surrender Is Rooted in God's Love

If you've ever wrestled with the idea of surrender, you're not alone. We often equate surrender with giving up—laying down dreams, sacrificing comfort, or letting go of control. But here's what the Lord has shown me: Surrender is not about losing; it's about receiving. It's about making room for the life God wants to lead you into.

So many of us make vision harder than it needs to be. We ask, "What's my calling? What's my talent? Where should I go?" And while those are sincere questions, we often skip the foundational one: Do I know His love?

When you don't start from love, surrender feels like sacrifice. But when love is your root, surrender becomes joy.

A life led by God doesn't mean we never hear fear—it means we stop obeying it. We stop making room for it.

First John 4:18 says, "*There is no fear in love; but perfect love casts out fear, because fear involves torment. But he who fears has not been made perfect in love.*"

Only in the revelation of God's love does fear loses its grip, and true surrender begin. You stop clinging to your own timing, your own plans, and your own definition of what feels "safe." You start trusting that His love is better, fuller, and stronger than anything you can build yourself.

During one of my early years serving at Charis, I found myself in a season of busyness. I was doing good things, teaching, ministering, traveling. But something felt off. I was trying to keep everything together—to be everything to everyone. And I remember the Holy Spirit gently whispering, "You're trying to lead a life I'm supposed to lead for you."

I had to come face-to-face with the fact that I'd let busyness become a form of control. I thought that if I could manage it all, then nothing would fall apart. But that mindset left me tired, anxious, and disconnected. So I surrendered, not because I had to, but because I finally trusted His love enough to let go.

That's when I discovered that God is not trying to take from you; He's trying to overflow through you. But He can't fill hands that are still clinging. Surrender is the posture that positions us to receive everything He's already placed inside us in Christ. Surrender doesn't diminish you; it fills you. It reorders your schedule to reflect heaven's priorities.

You can plan your day from the flesh, or you can prioritize your time from the Spirit. The former leads to burnout. The latter leads to fruitfulness. And the difference is found in surrender. Not once, but daily.

When you surrender to God's love, when you let Him love you, lead you, and live through you, then your life becomes the message. Your vision flows from a place of wholeness. And the choices you make, how you spend your time, how you treat people, how you invest your resources, they all begin to look like Jesus.

Stop seeing surrender as loss. Start seeing it as alignment. You're aligning with the One who knows the end from the beginning. And He loves you enough to lead you step by step.

Psalm 32:8 promises, "*I will instruct you and teach you in the way you should go; I will guide you with My eye.*"

That's not the voice of a dictator; that's the voice of a loving Father. And when you surrender to Him, you're not giving up; you're growing up. You're walking into the life He leads, and let me tell you, it's abundant.

His Grace Multiplies as You Trust Him

Another one of the greatest lies the enemy whispers is that we must earn what God freely gives. Whether it's vision, provision, or peace, we feel like we've got to work hard enough, be good enough, or prove ourselves worthy before God will move on our behalf. But can I tell you something the Lord has taught me? Grace doesn't multiply through performance; it multiplies through trust.

We're not just called to be reservoirs of God's blessing, but distributors. You're meant to carry more than enough, not just for yourself, but for others. But here's the thing: that kind of overflow doesn't come from working harder. It comes from learning to rest in the finished work of Jesus and receiving what's already yours in Him.

Let's look at 2 Peter 1:2 again; "*Grace and peace be multiplied to you in the knowledge of God and of Jesus our Lord.*"

I love that. Grace and peace aren't added; they're multiplied. And not by effort, but by knowing God. When you know Him, really know Him as your source, your Shepherd, your daily strength, then grace and peace increase. And suddenly, you're walking through life with focus, confidence, and a calmness not because everything's easy, but because you know you're not alone.

> *When you surrender to God's love, when you let Him love you, lead you, and live through you, then your life becomes the message.*

Busyness can become a thief of grace. We get so caught up trying to juggle all the pieces that we crowd God out of our priorities. But when we allow Him to be Lord of our calendar, when we pause to invite Him into the planning, He brings supernatural ease to what used to feel overwhelming. That's the kind of life you were designed for.

Second Corinthians 9:8 promises: "*And God is able to make all grace abound toward you, that you, always having all sufficiency in all things, may have an abundance for every good work.*"

You don't have to panic when new opportunities come. You don't have to feel overwhelmed when God asks you to take a bold step. Grace abounds toward you—not trickles, not drips—but abounds. And it's always enough.

I urge you to stop making vision complicated. It's not about your qualifications. It's about your connection. When you walk with God, vision becomes the overflow of intimacy. His love pours in, and vision flows out. And grace multiplies because you're not walking alone. You're walking in rhythm with the Spirit.

We're not just called to be reservoirs of God's blessing, but distributors.

When we learn to stop, listen, and trust, when we quiet the noise and truly acknowledge Him, He leads us into wide-open spaces where grace isn't scarce but is multiplied.

Proverbs 3:5–6 reminds us: "*Trust in the Lord with all your heart, And lean not on your own understanding; In all your ways acknowledge Him, And He shall direct your paths.*"

If your path today feels cluttered or uncertain, pause and acknowledge Him. Let Him lead as grace rearranges your pace.

The Voice of God Simplifies Obedience

When you surrender your day to God, He simplifies your steps. He doesn't overwhelm you with the full picture. He simply speaks to your heart in a way you can understand. See, walking in God's vision isn't about knowing all the details ahead of time. It's about staying connected to the voice of the Holy Spirit so you can move when He says move, speak when He says speak, and rest when He says rest.

So many times, we get stuck waiting for a grand unveiling of purpose, thinking we need to see the entire map before we take a single step. But God doesn't work that way. He gives us vision in relationship, not just direction. And when you're in relationship with Him, hearing His voice, trusting His Word, abiding in His presence, that's when obedience becomes a joy instead of a burden.

I remember another time when I was preparing to step into a new area of ministry that I didn't feel qualified for. All the logistics seemed too complicated, and I started wrestling with fear—what if I fail? What if I missed something? But the Holy Spirit reminded me of the simplicity of obedience. He said, "Carrie, just say yes to the next step. That's all I'm asking for." And when I did, things started falling into place one by one.

This is the beauty of divine order. When God leads your life, He doesn't throw you into chaos. He brings peace and clarity to your path, even if you don't have all the answers yet. He leads you with His voice, and His voice is always filled with love.

Jesus said it this way: "*My sheep hear My voice, and I know them, and they follow Me*" (John 10:27).

He knows you. And He wants you to know Him, not just His will, but His heart. When you tune your ear to hear the Shepherd, following Him becomes less about figuring everything out and more about trusting Him with everything you have.

When you surrender your day to God, He simplifies your steps.

So instead of overthinking the plan, let God lead your life. Ask the Lord today: What are You speaking to me right now? Then say yes to that. You'll be amazed how much joy, clarity, and supernatural provision unfolds from surrendering your day to the Holy Spirit with a single yes in the right direction.

Reflection

So often, we try to lead our lives with our own wisdom, our own strategies, and our own timelines. But what I've discovered, and what I hope you've seen through this chapter, is that a truly abundant life isn't one we lead. It's one we surrender.

God didn't design us to run ourselves ragged trying to earn His blessing or figure out our future. He designed us to walk with Him. When we stop treating vision like a checklist and instead make it a relationship, something powerful happens. Our time begins to align with His priorities. Our purpose becomes clearer because we're not chasing achievement, we're listening to love. And in that surrender, peace shows up. Joy multiplies. Abundance flows.

Throughout this journey, we've looked at how excuses lose their grip when we know His strength. We've seen how provision meets us in motion, not before we obey, but in our obedience. We've watched how fear tries to project false futures, but the Holy Spirit guides us back into the present reality of God's promises. And perhaps most importantly, we've realized that vision isn't about performance. It's about partnership with a God who delights in revealing Himself through us.

I want you to know that wherever you are in your journey, whether you feel stuck, unsure, overwhelmed, or maybe even overlooked, God is not done with you. His Spirit lives inside of you. His grace is enough for you. And His vision for your life is not some lofty mystery; it's a daily invitation to walk in love, to live by faith, and to flourish under the leadership of the One who knows you best.

Let your days belong to Him. Let your vision be born from His love. Let your abundance be the fruit of surrender. This is not a life you have to strive for; this is the life God leads.

My Challenge to You

- Pause Before You Plan: Resist the urge to immediately fill your calendar or chase the next task.
- Invite the Holy Spirit: Each day, ask Him to lead your time, your heart, and your steps.

- Ask a Simple Question: Pray, "What part of my life do You want to lead today?" Then wait and listen.
- Allow Him to Rearrange Priorities: Be open to letting go of what is merely "good" so you can embrace what is truly God.
- Watch for His Prompting: Pay attention as He highlights people, places, or moments where His love wants to flow through you.
- Respond with Surrender: Make your first decision each morning a choice to yield. Let your first response to pressure be trust.
- Walk in His Peace: Remember that His leadership never leads to lack; it brings clarity, overflow, and rest.
- Let Your Vision Be Shaped by Him: Don't focus on what you can do; focus on how He wants to express His love through your life.

Scripture References

John 15:5
Exodus 3:11–12
Galatians 2:20
Psalm 37:23
John 10:27
Proverbs 3:5–6
Psalm 23:1–3
Romans 5:5
Exodus 3:14
2 Peter 1:2
Hebrews 4:10
Mark 6:31
Matthew 11:28–30
2 Timothy 1:7
Isaiah 41:10
1 John 4:18
Psalm 32:8
2 Corinthians 9:8
John 10:27

Chapter Four

Serving Without Striving

Introduction

Have you ever found yourself serving God, yet feeling tired, drained, or even resentful? I know I have. Sometimes we step into service with sincere hearts, but somewhere along the way, we begin to strive. We pile on responsibilities, respond to every need, and assume that "more equals faithful." But service without intimacy leads to burnout. That's not what God designed for us. He didn't call us to run faster. He called us to abide.

One of the most freeing revelations I've received is this: I am not the source. I don't have to be. You and I were never meant to pour out without staying connected to the One who fills us. Jesus said in John 15:5, "*I am the vine, you are the branches. He who abides in Me, and I in him, bears much fruit; for without Me you can do nothing.*" You don't have to produce anything apart from Him. In fact, trying to serve without abiding only leaves us feeling inadequate.

But here's the truth that sets us free: Your inadequacy is not a disqualification; it's an opportunity. In God's hands, what feels like lack becomes overflow. What looks like weakness becomes glory. And what once depleted you becomes the very place where His grace abounds. That's the heart of this chapter. We're going to discover how to serve from rest, how to embrace the sufficiency of Christ, and how to step out in obedience without burning out.

You'll see that real abundance doesn't come from effort; it comes from connection. God's vision for your life isn't about striving; it's about obedience. It's not about being good enough; it's about realizing you already have everything in Him. You don't serve to be approved; you serve because you are empowered.

Let's explore together how you can stop trying to do it all and start abiding in the One who already did it all. Let's trade busyness for intimacy, pressure for peace, and weariness for joy.

Fix Your Focus

In this chapter, I want to talk to you about what it means to truly serve from a place of rest, not religion. We've all been tempted to do things "for God" instead of living "with God." But misplaced service will drain you. It might look spiritual on the outside, but inside, you feel dry and worn thin. That's not how God designed us to live.

He invites us to abide, not achieve. When we stay connected to Him, grace flows, purpose becomes clear, and strength rises. Striving fades when we remember that the fruit He desires comes through intimacy, not effort.

I've learned that feelings of inadequacy aren't a disqualification. They're actually a doorway. That's where God shows up strong. He turns our weakness into His testimony. It has never been about what we can do; it's always been about what He can do through us.

And don't forget, your life was never meant to just "get by." You were created to live in overflow, touching the lives within your sphere of influence. But that kind of impact doesn't come through hustle. It comes through abiding.

In this chapter, we'll unpack how abiding guards us from burnout, how vision flows from intimacy, and how our position in Christ leads us into real abundance, right where we are.

Fruitfulness Doesn't Come from Effort; It Comes from Abiding

There is a trap I see believers fall into, myself included, which is the temptation to measure our value by what we do for God. We get caught up in our assignments, our ministries, our schedules, and before we know it, our identity becomes tangled up in how much we've produced. But that's not the life Jesus designed for us. He never asked us to strive to be fruitful; He invited us to abide.

In John 15:4–5, He makes it so clear: "*Abide in Me, and I in you. As the branch cannot bear fruit of itself, unless it abides in the vine, neither can you, unless you abide in Me ... He who abides in Me, and I in him, bears much fruit; for without Me you can do nothing.*"

He doesn't say, "Work harder, and you'll be fruitful." He says, "Stay connected, and fruit will come." The word "abide" has become an anchor for me. It means to dwell, to remain, to live in. So many times, when I start feeling dry or tired, the Holy Spirit brings me back to these verses. He reminds me that fruitfulness flows from intimacy, not performance.

I've seen this in my own life over and over again. There were seasons where I was doing all the "right things": ministering, traveling, teaching, raising kids, supporting my husband, but I felt worn thin. Not because the things I was doing were wrong, but because I was doing them in my own strength. I had to stop and ask, "Lord, am I abiding? Or am I just performing?"

And when I paused and turned my heart back to Him, it was like the sap of the Vine came rushing in again. Grace returned. Joy returned. Vision became clear. I wasn't called to be the vine. I was always meant to be the branch.

You and I were designed to receive, not just to do. We were never meant to be the source of our own strength. When we start abiding, the fruit comes naturally because it's His life flowing through us. Healing flows. Wisdom flows. Provision flows. Peace flows. You don't have to generate it; you just have to remain in Him.

This is what I mean by serving without striving. You can't manufacture fruit, but you can multiply it by staying planted in the right place, in Him.

Your Inadequacy Is the Perfect Place for God's Glory

I can't tell you how many times I've looked at the things God was asking me to do and thought, "Lord, are You sure You picked the right person?" The truth is, we all have moments where we feel inadequate, underqualified, too weak, too broken, too busy. But do you know what I've discovered over and over again? My inadequacy is not a liability in the kingdom. It's actually the very place where God shows up in His glory.

See, God is not looking for the most polished or the most perfect. He's looking for those who are willing. I've had to learn to stop disqualifying myself based on my own limitations. Just because I don't have it all figured out doesn't mean God can't work through me. In fact, it usually means I'm in the exact position where His power can shine brightest.

Colossians 2:9–10 has been a cornerstone truth for me: "*For in Him dwells all the fullness of the Godhead bodily; and you are complete in Him, who is the head of all principality and power.*"

Let that sink in. You are complete in Him. Not almost complete. Not trying to earn it. Not halfway there. You've been filled with the fullness of God. That means everything you need to accomplish what He's called you to do is already inside of you because Christ is in you.

I've seen this firsthand so many times. Whether I was standing in front of a class of students, ministering to women in desperate situations, or raising my children with no manual and a lot of prayer, there were moments I felt totally unqualified. But every single time, the Holy Spirit reminded me, "Carrie, you're not doing this alone."

And maybe you need that reminder today, too. It's not about trying to prove something. It's about receiving what He's already placed inside of you. That's what transforms inadequacy into glory. Because when you stop striving to be "enough" and start abiding in the One who is more than enough, you'll begin to see fruit that has nothing to do with your talent and everything to do with His presence.

That's the abundant life Jesus promised, not a life free of responsibility but full of His sufficiency. When you stop resisting your weakness and start embracing His strength, you'll see the miraculous flow right through the ordinary.

Abundance Is Found in the Abiding Life

One of the truths I've come to cling to over the years is this: the most fruitful life isn't born out of effort; it's born out of abiding. I've seen so many believers, myself included, fall into the trap of striving. We serve and serve, hoping that our performance will somehow unlock more of God.

But the truth is, He's already given us everything we need. He's just waiting for us to connect.

As I stated before, John 15:4 has been a lifeline to me. Whenever I start to feel dry, scattered, or overwhelmed, the Holy Spirit leads me right back to these verses. Jesus said: "*Abide in Me, and I in you. As the branch cannot bear fruit of itself, unless it abides in the vine, neither can you, unless you abide in Me.*"

That's the abundant life Jesus promised, not a life free of responsibility but full of His sufficiency.

You know what that tells me? If I'm running on empty, it's not because God has withheld anything from me. It's because I've disconnected somewhere. And the beautiful thing is, He's always inviting me back in. There's no condemnation in that, just a sweet reminder: "Come back to the source."

See, fruit doesn't grow by force. It grows because it's attached to the vine. That's how it works in the natural, and that's exactly how it works in the spirit. When we try to manufacture fruit in our own strength—joy, peace, purpose, and love—we end up exhausted. But when we abide in Jesus, that fruit flows supernaturally.

I've had to ask myself, even in ministry and in motherhood: *Am I abiding or am I striving? Am I trying to bear fruit to prove something, or am I resting in the Vine and letting Him produce it through me?*

When Jesus said, "*Without Me you can do nothing*" (John 15:5), He wasn't trying to discourage us. He was lovingly inviting us into the secret of real effectiveness. He's the source. I'm the branch. And when I stay connected, when I remain in that place of intimacy with Him, I bear much fruit.

And let me just say this: abiding isn't passive. It's not sitting around doing nothing, hoping God fixes our mess. It's intentional connection. It's choosing to open the Word, choosing to listen, choosing to agree with what He says. And in that space, abundance begins to multiply.

You don't have to strive to get more of God. You already have Him. Abiding is how you receive what you've already been given. And that changes everything.

You're Not Called to Serve Empty

A key lesson I've had to learn is that God never asked me to serve empty. And yet, there have been times I've found myself running on fumes, pouring out, ministering, meeting needs, while quietly, inwardly, I was feeling dry. And that's not the abundant life Jesus died to give me.

Sometimes, in ministry or even in daily life, we fall into the trap of performance, doing what we think God expects, instead of flowing from what He's already provided. We serve because we're supposed to, not because we're filled. But that kind of service depletes rather than overflows.

If we serve without being fully connected to the Vine, what's the result? Burnout. Resentment. Confusion. But the moment we come back to abiding, when we let the Word fill us again, when we sit with Jesus and let Him minister to our hearts, everything changes. Suddenly, our service isn't forced; it is fueled.

You don't have to strive to get more of God. You already have Him. Abiding is how you receive what you've already been given.

The key to fruitfulness is tapping into the source. We were built to receive. You and I are the branches, not the vine. That means it's not our job to create the life; it's our job to carry it.

"If you abide in Me, and My words abide in you, you will ask what you desire, and it shall be done for you" (John 15:7).

That's not just about getting your prayers answered. It's about alignment. When you abide, your desires align with His, and your service flows from His strength, not your own.

So if you're feeling worn out today, if you're serving, but you feel like you're drowning, stop and ask yourself, *Am I connected?* Because God didn't call you to rely on your own strength. He called you to serve from overflow. And that kind of service changes everything.

The Provision Was Already There

Sometimes we're waiting for provision, like it's still on its way. Maybe if we just fast a little more, pray a little harder, or work ourselves into greater faith, then it will show up. But the truth is, the abundance is already there.

Many believers are walking around like they're still waiting for God to deliver what He already put inside of them. They look at their circumstances, at their mistakes, and they filter the Word of God through the lens of failure. And that kind of lens will always shrink the promise down to your own performance. But here's the reality: God gave you His fullness, not in part, not as a future reward, but right now. We get to have that fullness and live in the abundance He wants for us because of salvation, which is "*Christ in* [us] *the hope of glory*" (Col. 1:27).

I want you to look at another reality that is ours when we stay connected to Him: "*For in Him dwells all the fullness of the Godhead bodily; and you are complete in Him*" (Col. 2:9–10).

You are complete. That word changed everything for me. It means we don't have to beg God for more when He's already placed it inside us. And if we are feeling dry or depleted, it's not because the supply is missing; it's because we've stopped drawing from the well.

You know, so many times, the enemy gets us to focus on our lack: not enough time, not enough resources, not enough strength. But God's Word tells a different story. Second Corinthians 9:8 says we have everything we need for every good work. It says His riches are in glory, not in human effort or self-made success.

Abundance isn't what we earn. It's what we abide in. And when we start to serve from that revelation, knowing that we're already filled, already equipped, already anointed, then our giving becomes joyful. Then our time becomes ordered. Then our service becomes fruitful.

You don't need more of God to be abundant. You need more awareness of what you've already been given. The well is full. The supply is ready. Draw from it and let every part of your life, your service, and your calling reflect the truth that the provision was already there.

True Abundance Is Measured by Fruitfulness, Not Effort

A liberating truth God has shown me is that fruitfulness is not the result of effort; it's the result of abiding. It's not the long list of tasks, ministry goals, or spiritual checkboxes that define our success in the kingdom. It's the presence of His life flowing through ours. That's what multiplies. That's what lasts.

In John 15:4, Jesus made it clear: "*Abide in Me, and I in you. As the branch cannot bear fruit of itself, unless it abides in the vine, neither can you, unless you abide in Me.*"

This verse has been an anchor for me, especially in seasons where I've felt pulled in a thousand directions. Sometimes I would catch myself starting the day in the Word, but then racing ahead, trying to carry everything on my own strength. And while it looked productive on the outside, inside, I was starting to run dry.

That's when the Lord would gently bring me back to this truth: "You're a branch. You were never meant to be the vine."

Fruitfulness in your marriage, your ministry, your career, and your calling isn't born from pushing harder; it's born from staying connected. When we abide in Him, His joy becomes our strength. His peace becomes our compass. His love becomes the very fuel for everything we touch.

I've seen this in my own life over and over again. When I stop measuring success by how much I've accomplished and start asking whether I've stayed connected, everything shifts. The pressure lifts. The striving breaks. Suddenly, I'm not focused on doing more; I'm focused on being in Him. And that's where the real overflow begins.

In Ephesians 2:10, it says, "*For we are His workmanship, created in Christ Jesus for good works, which God prepared beforehand that we should walk in them.*"

That word "walk" isn't rushed or panicked; it's steady. It's a walk of relationship, not performance. God didn't design you to burn out in misplaced service. He designed you to flourish in pre-appointed fruitfulness.

So let's stop asking, "Am I doing enough?" and start asking, "Am I abiding enough?"

Because when you stay in Him, the fruit will come.

Speak Life into the Places You Serve

Sometimes we speak lack over our lives without even realizing it. We say things like, "I don't know how this is going to work," or "I don't think I can do this anymore," or even, "Nothing ever changes." But I've learned something powerful: when I partner my words with the truth of God's Word, everything begins to shift. Not because I'm trying to manipulate outcomes, but because I'm aligning my heart with what heaven is already saying.

God showed me this when I started declaring truth over the places where I was weary. Instead of saying, "I'm too tired for this," I'd declare, "I have all sufficiency in all things." Instead of saying, "This ministry is too much," I'd say, "Lord, thank You that I abound in every good work." The difference wasn't just in my words—it was in what I began to believe.

Second Corinthians 9:8 (*NIV*) says, "*And God is able to bless you abundantly, so that in all things at all times, having all that you need, you will abound in every good work.*" That means every place God has called us to, whether it's our homes, a team, a conference, or a quiet one-on-one conversation, He's already provided what we need to abound.

We don't have to brace ourselves for burnout. We can enter each space with an attitude of authority, not because we're strong but because He is. The Spirit of God lives in us, and He's not passive. He's present. He's leading. That's why we can start taking spiritual ownership of the areas where we are serving, not out of pressure, but out of purpose.

The world wants to drain us with noise and negativity, convincing us that we're barely making it. But when we abide in Christ, we start to speak from a different position. We're no longer trying to survive the day; we're declaring life over it.

I remember telling the Lord, "I want to be the kind of woman who speaks abundance over every space I walk into." And He said, "Then fill your mouth with My Word." That was a shift for me. I stopped just quoting verses to fix situations, and I started living those verses out loud in my everyday rhythms.

When you declare God's truth over your time, your schedule, your family, and your calling, you're not pretending things are perfect; you're activating what's already yours in Christ. It's not striving; it's aligning.

Now, the question becomes: What are you speaking over your life? What are you releasing over your service? Because you'll see fruit in the direction of your confession. Don't speak dry ground when you've been given living water. Speak life. Speak abundance. Speak vision. That's not just optimism; that's abiding.

Your Sphere Is Meant to Overflow

We've looked at surrendering our time. I think it is important that we start talking about surrendering our mindset. We often underestimate the influence God has entrusted to us. Sometimes we look at our lives, our jobs, families, churches, relationships, and think, *What difference can I really make?* But I want to remind you today that you have a God-given sphere, and that sphere isn't random. It's where your overflow is meant to pour.

In one of my times with the Lord, He showed me that my sphere—my place of responsibility, leadership, motherhood, marriage, and ministry—was not a burden to manage. It was a place to pour out the abundance He was pouring into me. And not just in big, flashy ways. I'm talking about the everyday kind of overflow that comes from intimacy with Him. The kind that saturates a meeting with peace, or shifts the tone in a tense conversation, or brings clarity when others feel confused.

You have a sphere. And in that sphere, God wants to liberally supply everything you need, not so you can barely make it, but so you can abound. In the last section, I shared 2 Corinthians 9:8 with you, and it stated that "*you will abound in every good work.*"

Your sphere is your "good work": your family, your classroom, your small group, your business. And the abundance He supplies isn't just finances; it's wisdom, strength, patience, joy, strategy, and peace. But here's the key: He can only overflow through you if you let Him fill you first.

The Lord spoke this to me once: "You're trying to carry your sphere instead of letting Me carry you into it." That changed the way I saw ministry and leadership. I stopped asking, "What do I have to get done?" I stopped entering rooms with a burden and started entering with a sense of divine appointment.

When we abide in Him, He brings fruit into our sphere. We don't manufacture the fruit; we just stay connected to the Vine. We get to rest in the truth of John 15:5, "*I am the vine, you are the branches. He who abides in Me, and I in him, bears much fruit ....*"

You'll see fruit in the direction of your confession.

That "much fruit" shows up in our sphere, in conversations, projects, assignments, and decisions. It shows up in the peace that disarms tension, in the joy that changes atmospheres, and in the wisdom that silences confusion. And let me tell you, it's not about personality or skill. It's about being connected to the source of all life.

When we start seeing our sphere through God's eyes, everything changes. We stop serving from depletion and start serving from overflow. We stop striving to maintain and start abiding to multiply. We start to believe that we are equipped for every good work, right here, right now.

Don't Resist the Blessing

There was a time in my life when, honestly, I wasn't sure if I was allowed to be fully blessed. I didn't think I was resisting God, but the way I talked, the way I saw myself, and the way I handled situations made it clear that I wasn't fully receiving what He had already provided. I kept thinking things like, "I don't know if this couple's marriage can be saved," or "I'm not sure I'll ever figure out how to lead this team," all while asking God to bless those very areas.

That's when the Lord interrupted me and said, "Stop asking for blessing and then speaking curses over your life." And He was right. I was canceling His provision with my own words. I had the theology, but not the trust. I knew God was good, but I kept talking like I had to fix everything on my own.

So I had to shift, completely. I had to stop measuring His promises by my performance and start receiving them because of His love.

Sometimes we come into the presence of God, asking Him to do something, bless us, help us, and guide us, but we're doing it from a place of striving, not surrender. And God wants to bless us abundantly. He's already made provision for everything we need. The only thing that blocks it is us, our doubt, our self-talk, our small vision of His goodness.

Abundance is not something we're waiting to qualify for; it's something we've already inherited in Christ. We read in Ephesians 1 that we've been blessed with every spiritual blessing in heavenly places, but too often, we resist those blessings without realizing it.

Here's what I've learned: You've got to let yourself be blessed. That doesn't mean just being open to it in theory; it means changing your posture. Instead of praying, "Lord, help me survive today," I now say, "Lord, I receive wisdom for this day, I receive joy for this moment, I receive favor for this assignment."

These are very different mindsets. One is rooted in lack and striving. The other is rooted in abundance and abiding.

I remember the Lord challenging me: "What if you stopped treating your needs like emergencies and started treating them like opportunities for Me to be God in your life?" With this new insight, I began to see my needs, whether financial, emotional, or spiritual, as places of partnership, not panic.

You must do the same. When things feel overwhelming, choose to speak differently:

"Lord, I receive Your grace for my marriage."
"Lord, I receive Your peace for my mind."
"Lord, I receive Your favor in this meeting."

We're not begging Him to move. We're aligning with what He's already doing. Serving without striving starts here: with a heart that says, "Lord, if You've given it, I receive it." And you know what? When we serve from that posture, people notice. They don't just see our efforts; they see our peace. They encounter our joy. And they begin to hunger for the God who blesses like that.

Living as a Son, Not an Orphan

So many times in ministry, work, or even just in our day-to-day responsibilities, we step into moments with this pressure, this sense that we have to perform, produce, and prove something. We act like it's all on us, as if we've got to hustle for the blessing or keep striving to maintain it. But the truth is, that's the mindset of an orphan, not a son.

God never asked us to serve Him from lack. He called us to serve from identity. I've caught myself, even after years of walking with God, slipping into a place of trying to earn results or make something happen.

But in those moments, the Holy Spirit reminds me: "You're not an outsider looking in, you are seated with Me. You're a daughter."

When we live like sons and daughters, striving comes to an end. Our posture shifts. We're no longer running around trying to figure everything out. Instead, we start to trust. We lean in. We listen. We follow.

"You've already been given everything you need in Christ Jesus." That one truth dismantles so much pressure. If we've already been equipped, then why are we living like we still have to prove something? Why are we measuring our fruitfulness by activity instead of by intimacy?

One day, I found myself discouraged, like I wasn't doing enough, producing enough, leading well enough. And God stopped me mid-thought and said, "You're living like a servant who doesn't know the house belongs to her. Come sit with Me." That moment shifted me from striving into rest, and from rest into real effectiveness.

John 15:15 says, "*No longer do I call you servants ... but I have called you friends.*" That's not just a warm sentiment; it's a radical realignment. Friends don't strive; friends abide. Sons don't hustle for their inheritance; they receive it because it's theirs by birthright.

When we live like sons and daughters, striving comes to an end.

And here's the thing: when we stop striving, the fruit doesn't decrease. It multiplies. Not because we pushed harder, but because we got in sync with the source.

When we carry this mindset into every area of life, home, work, and ministry, we stop burning out and start burning brightly. That's the kind of serving that overflows. That's the kind of identity that walks into a room and shifts the atmosphere, not because of effort, but because of God's presence.

Let His Vision Fuel Your Effort

When I used to think about vision, I assumed it came with pressure, plans, deadlines, and expectations to perform. But as I've walked with the Lord, He's shown me that vision, when it's truly from Him, doesn't drive you; it draws you. It doesn't come from exhaustion; it flows from connection.

Sometimes we get caught up chasing what we think God wants, instead of walking with Him daily to discover what He's already prepared. And when that happens, we begin to carry the vision as if it depends on us. But that's not how kingdom vision works.

The Lord reminded me of something powerful in Romans 12:2: "*Do not be conformed to this world, but be transformed by the renewing of your mind, that you may prove what is that good and acceptable and perfect will of God.*"

This isn't about trying to "figure out" God's will like a puzzle. It's about being transformed in how we think, letting go of hustle, performance, and striving, and leaning into the truth that God's will is already good, already acceptable, already perfect. It's not earned. It's revealed as we walk with Him.

This changed everything for me. I stopped trying to produce fruit as proof of obedience and started pursuing intimacy. I stopped chasing the vision and started walking with the Vision-Giver. And do you know what happened? The fruit multiplied, not because I worked harder, but because I stopped resisting grace with my own self-effort.

In John 15:7, Jesus said, "*If you abide in Me, and My words abide in you, you will ask what you desire, and it shall be done for you.*"

That verse doesn't just speak of answered prayer; it speaks of alignment. When we abide, His Word reshapes our desires. His Spirit energizes our steps. And that's how you step into a life that is both purposeful and peaceful.

So if you're feeling overwhelmed in the call God's given you, here's my encouragement: Let Him redefine vision for you. It's not about how much you can carry; it's about how closely you stay connected. When He's the source of your calling, serving becomes a joy, not a burden.

The Power of Saying Yes to the Right Things

One of the most powerful lessons I've learned is this: Just because I can do something, doesn't mean I should. We live in a world that applauds hustle. If you're not busy, if you're not maxed out, people assume you're lazy or lacking ambition. But God doesn't measure our fruitfulness by how full our calendars are. He measures it by how full our hearts are with Him.

There was a time in ministry when I kept saying yes to every opportunity. It looked like I was being fruitful. Travel invitations, speaking engagements, counseling sessions, mentoring, event planning, I was doing it all. But slowly, I began to feel dry inside. I was showing up, but I wasn't overflowing. One day, the Holy Spirit gently corrected me: "Your yes is powerful, but it's not eternal. Only *My* yes produces eternal fruit."

When He's the source of your calling, serving becomes a joy, not a burden.

That hit me so hard. I realized I had been trying to meet every need instead of asking, "Lord, is this my assignment?" Saying yes out of pressure or guilt is a fast way to get spiritually dehydrated. But when you say yes in obedience to God's leading, you're not drained, you're sustained. Grace flows when your yes is connected to His voice.

Jesus modeled this for us. In John 5:19, He said, "*Most assuredly, I say to you, the Son can do nothing of Himself, but what He sees the Father do; for whatever He does, the Son also does in like manner.*"

Jesus didn't run on the approval of the crowd. He didn't rush from town to town trying to be everyone's healer, comforter, or provider. He stayed in sync with the Father's direction. That's why His yes always produced eternal impact.

Ephesians 5:15–17 encourages us, "*See then that you walk circumspectly, not as fools but as wise, redeeming the time, because the days are evil. Therefore do not be unwise, but understand what the will of the Lord* is."

Redeeming the time doesn't mean cramming your schedule with religious activity. It means aligning your yes with heaven's assignment.

I've come to understand that clarity on what to say yes to requires confidence in what to say no to. And that confidence comes from abiding. It comes from recognizing that I am not the source; He is. And when He calls me to something, He equips me with the grace to do it without striving.

If you're in a season where you feel pulled in too many directions, I encourage you to stop and ask: "Lord, what is Your yes for me right now?" That question has brought me more peace and fruitfulness than a thousand strategic plans.

You are not called to serve every need. You are called to serve God's purpose in your generation. And that starts with a surrendered yes. One that flows from abiding, not striving.

Faith Flourishes in a Heart That Knows It's Loved

Sometimes we fall into the trap of thinking that faith is a formula. We think: *If I just confess enough, believe hard enough, or pray long enough, then I'll see results.* But what the Lord has taught me is this: Faith doesn't flourish in pressure; it flourishes in love.

We don't serve God from a place of trying to earn answers. We serve Him from the place of already being answered through Jesus. So many times, we approach our service like it's a test to pass: Am I doing enough? Did I say it right? Did I mess it up? That's striving. That's performance. And that's not the Gospel.

Clarity on what to say yes to requires confidence in what to say no to.

I remember when God really opened my eyes to this through Ephesians 1:17–18. Paul said, "*That the God of our Lord Jesus Christ, the Father of glory, may give to you the spirit of wisdom and revelation in the knowledge of Him, the eyes of your understanding being enlightened ....*"

That was it. I needed my eyes opened to see that I wasn't serving for approval. I was serving from fullness, from the richness of being loved. That's when faith becomes natural. When you know you're already accepted, faith becomes a response to love, not a tool to manipulate outcomes.

Romans 12:2 also says, "*Do not be conformed to this world, but be transformed by the renewing of your mind ....*"

When I began renewing my mind to God's love instead of religious obligation, everything changed. I didn't pray to impress anymore. I didn't serve to prove anything. I began walking in a rhythm of trust, where faith was no longer a weight; it was a response to relationship.

So if you're struggling to believe today, not just for provision, healing, or wisdom, but to believe that you're enough, I want to remind you: You don't have to work to be loved. You already are. And when that settles deep in your heart, you'll be amazed at how faith rises up, not because you're striving, but because you're finally abiding.

Reflection

When we talk about serving without striving, we're not saying we stop giving, building, leading, or investing in others. We're saying we stop doing it from a place of depletion. We stop doing it to prove something or to earn something that's already ours in Christ.

Throughout this chapter, we've looked at what it means to serve from identity, not insecurity, to step into our God-given assignments from rest, not rush. And the more I walk with the Lord, the more I realize everything fruitful in my life has come from abiding, not effort.

There have been seasons where I gave too much, said yes to everything, and ended up drained, not because I was called, but because I was driven. But God in His mercy always brought me back to the vine. He reminded me that I'm not the source, I'm the branch. And as long as I abide in Him, the fruit will come. The strength will come. The wisdom will come.

We're not meant to serve on empty. We're meant to serve out of the overflow. And that overflow doesn't come from hustle, it comes from being with Him. That's the sweet place where inadequacy turns into glory. That's where our "not enough" becomes more than enough in His hands.

So wherever you are today, I want to encourage you: Stop striving. Start abiding. Don't forget His benefits. Don't try to impress Him. Just stay close.

Let His voice set your pace. Let His love be your motivation. And let your life be a demonstration, not of your strength, but of His supply.

My Challenge to You

- Reflect: Take time to evaluate how and why you are serving. Are you pouring out from a place of overflow, or just obligation?
- Connect with Holy Spirit: Invite Him to reveal areas where you've been saying yes out of fear, pressure, or performance instead of love.
- Lay It Down: Surrender every assignment you've picked up that God never asked you to carry. Release the weight of striving.
- Recenter Your Days: Begin each morning not with a to-do list, but with surrender. Let God set your pace and your priorities.
- Remember Your Source: Let Him remind you that He alone is your Strength, your Shepherd, and your Supply.
- Serve from Rest: Choose alignment over exhaustion. Follow the example of Jesus, who served from peace and connection with the Father.
- Breathe in Grace: Relax into the truth that you are not behind, not disqualified, but deeply loved. Watch what God will do through you, without burnout, without striving, and without fear.

Scripture References

Colossians 1:27
Colossians 2:9–10
Ephesians 2:10
John 15:4–5
2 Corinthians 9:8
John 15:7
Romans 12:2
Ephesians 5:15–17
Ephesians 1:17–18
John 15:15
John 5:19

Chapter Five

Invest in the One Who Matters Most

Introduction

I used to think time management was all about scheduling, fitting in everything I could so that nothing got dropped. But I've come to realize it's not about managing minutes; it's about following the Master. Every day is an opportunity to invest, not just our energy and talents, but our time into what truly matters. And what matters most isn't our calling, our to-do list, or even our productivity. What matters most is Him.

God didn't call me to juggle a hundred things for Him. He called me to know Him. And from that place of knowing, everything else flows. Time in His presence isn't a luxury; it's the most strategic, fruitful investment I can make. That's where vision becomes clear, where distractions lose their grip, and where abundance begins—not from effort, but from abiding.

This chapter is for every person who's felt the tug of distractions pulling them in a hundred directions, for every believer who's wondered if they're doing "enough," and for every heart that's hungry for more than survival. We're going to walk through what it really means to invest in the One who matters most and how that single decision can transform your entire life.

Let's talk about what it really means to invest in the One who matters most. Because when we give Him our time, attention, and trust, we receive so much more than we ever imagined.

Fix Your Focus

There's so much noise out there telling us what success looks like, even in ministry: productivity, hustle, achievement. But I've learned the most powerful, life-altering investment I can ever make is in my time with God. When I do that, everything else starts to line up.

This chapter is about shifting the way we think about our time, our calling, and our worth. We're going to talk about what it means to fight distractions with His presence, to see through His eyes instead of through the world's expectations, and to expect abundance, not from what we do, but from who we're abiding in.

You'll see that this kind of investment isn't burdensome; it's freeing. It's not about adding more to your plate; it's about releasing the pressure to perform and embracing the overflow that comes from intimacy with the Father. When your time is His, your life becomes full, full of peace, clarity, purpose, and power.

Let the Holy Spirit show you where true abundance begins.

The Enemy Targets What Matters Most: Your Time with God

A cunning strategy of the enemy is simply to keep us too busy to be with God. He doesn't need to make us rebellious or sinful, just distracted. And I've seen it again and again, not only in the lives of others but in my own life as well. It's subtle. It looks like productivity, service, and even ministry. But underneath, if we're honest, it's a slow drift away from presence, away from abiding.

This is a super spiritual topic. Because how you manage your time will either protect or jeopardize your intimacy with the Lord. And that's exactly why the enemy is after it. He wants to steal your focus, your peace, your fruitfulness, not by scaring you, but by distracting you.

Distractions may look like opportunities, like giving God our yes. But when we're constantly pulled away from stillness, pulled away from hearing His voice, we eventually find ourselves doing all the right things—from an empty place. I've lived that. I've served with zeal and yet found myself feeling depleted, all because I wasn't guarding my time in God's presence.

Matthew 6:33 says, "*But seek first the kingdom of God and His righteousness, and all these things shall be added to you.*"

This is the divine order. When we invest in the One who matters most, everything else gets added. We don't have to chase opportunities, recognition, or outcomes. We chase Him. And in the pursuit of His presence, we find clarity, rest, and supernatural multiplication.

> *A cunning strategy of the enemy is simply to keep us too busy to be with God.*

This is where time management becomes sacred. It's not about better calendars or smarter routines, even though they help. It's about surrender. God doesn't need your efficiency; He wants your heart. And when He has your heart, He can order your steps.

That's why I've learned to begin every season, every week, even every day by surrendering it afresh. "Lord, You lead. I follow." That's not just poetic language; that's a powerful strategy against the chaos of culture and the lies of religion.

Proverbs 3:6 says, "*In all your ways acknowledge Him, and He shall direct your paths.*"

God is not trying to make your life harder; He's trying to lead you into abundance. And that begins with putting Him first. Time with God isn't an obligation. It's your greatest investment.

So, let me ask you: what's been stealing your time with Him? What's masquerading as "good" but pulling you away from the best?

This is your permission to pause. To return. To draw near again, not out of guilt, but with the joyful expectation that abundance flows from abiding.

Your Relationship with God Is the Foundation of Your Calling

We live in a world that pushes productivity as proof of purpose. "Do more, be more, achieve more." And honestly, even in ministry or in our walk with God, it's easy to slip into that mindset. But here's the truth: your greatest calling is not what you do; it's who you're with.

The best place to invest is not in your calling, but in your relationship with God. That turned a light on for me years ago. I had made the mistake of thinking my calling was the thing I did for God. I loved ministry.

I poured my heart into helping people. But somewhere along the way, I started making the mission more important than the relationship.

God gently corrected me. He said, "Carrie, ministry is your relationship with Me." And that revelation changed everything. It redefined how I saw time management, how I saw vision, and how I defined abundance. Because when relationship becomes the foundation, everything else flows in right order.

1 Corinthians 1:9 says, "*God is faithful, by whom you were called into the fellowship of His Son, Jesus Christ our Lord.*"

You've been called into fellowship. That's your first calling. If you don't know how to fellowship with Him, how to be still, how to receive, how to delight in His presence, then all your effort, even your spiritual effort, can quickly turn into striving.

The best place to invest is not in your calling, but in your relationship with God.

The enemy doesn't have to take your calling away to stop your vision; he just has to get you so busy that you stop hearing God clearly. Distraction becomes his tool. But when you prioritize time with the Father, clarity returns. Vision gets refined. Your "why" becomes stronger than any distraction.

There's such joy in that! Because now, instead of chasing a dream in your own strength, you're walking in divine rhythm, fueled by love, not pressure.

John 17:3 says, "*This is eternal life, that they may know You, the only true God, and Jesus Christ whom You have sent.*"

That's what it's always been about, knowing Him. Not just doing for Him. Your calling is holy not because of how much you do, but because of His grace and purpose within it.

Second Timothy 1:9 says, "[God] *saved us and called us to a holy calling, not because of our works but because of His own purpose and grace, which He gave us in Christ Jesus before the ages began.*"

I had to learn to stop measuring myself by output. I had to stop defining my effectiveness by people's reactions. Instead, I started to ask: "Have I met with the Lord today? Have I heard from Him? Have I followed His voice?"

When I live from that place, I'm no longer pulled in a million directions. I can say no without guilt and yes with confidence. Because I know I'm not trying to prove something—I'm walking in relationship with the One who already approved of me.

Your calling begins and ends in fellowship. That's the investment that multiplies. That's the center of your true identity.

Distraction Is the Thief of Destiny

As I mentioned before, one of the enemy's most effective tactics isn't always to tempt you with obvious sin; it's to distract you. If he can't get you to fall, he'll get you busy. And busy doesn't always mean productive. Sometimes, it just means detoured.

We get so consumed with doing things for God that we miss time with Him. We start chasing what we think is the goal, but we're missing the very source of direction. I've often said, "There's no way you can walk in the joy of vision if you're not fighting for your time with the Lord." And I mean that. You've got to fight for it because the world won't hand it to you.

"*In all your ways acknowledge Him, And He shall direct your paths*" (Prov. 3:6).

We get distracted by "good things" all the time—ministry, family, success, opportunities—and we convince ourselves we're being faithful. But here's the truth: faithfulness isn't about activity; it's about intimacy. When you acknowledge Him first, your paths become clear. Not because you're striving to figure it all out, but because you're surrendered.

The Holy Spirit said to me, "Don't make what you do for Me more important than what I've put in you." That hit me hard. Because I had fallen into that trap. I thought I was being fruitful, but I was actually being drained. Why? Because my attention was fragmented. I had taken my eyes off the One who matters most.

Proverbs 4:25 (*ESV*) says, "*Let your eyes look directly forward, and your gaze be straight before you.*"

I want to encourage you: look straight ahead. Stop letting other people's needs or opinions dictate how you spend your time. Yes, we're called to serve. But even Jesus, who was the perfect Servant, regularly withdrew to be alone with the Father.

Distraction may come disguised as obligation. It may look like an open door. But if it pulls you away from the presence of God, it's not a door; it's a detour.

And here's the thing: when you're distracted, you'll start confusing motion for momentum. You'll think, *I'm doing a lot*, but you won't feel any closer to purpose. That's because destiny doesn't grow in chaos. Destiny grows in stillness, in intimacy, and in fellowship.

"*Be still, and know that I* am *God*" (Ps. 46:10).

When you make space to be still, when you clear the noise, you begin to hear again. And when you hear again, vision comes alive. You're no longer pulled in a thousand directions. You're anchored.

And let me tell you something beautiful I've learned: what God speaks in secret will sustain you in public. But if you don't take time to hear it in secret, you'll crumble when pressure comes.

Friend, don't let distraction steal what God designed you to carry. Don't let the noise of the world drown out the whisper of His Spirit. Stay focused. Stay rooted. Invest in the One who sees all things, knows all things, and loves you with an everlasting love.

He's not just the Giver of your calling: He is your calling.

Vision Rooted in Fellowship

So often, people chase purpose based on what looks impressive or what others affirm. But that's not how true vision works. It doesn't come from pressure or performance; it flows out of fellowship. When I was seeking direction, I didn't sit down and brainstorm a five-year plan. I got in the presence of God. And from that place of intimacy, He began to show me the way He sees people: broken, loved, redeemed, and full of purpose.

If it pulls you away from the presence of God, it's not a door; it's a detour.

I didn't have to strain to create vision. I just had to listen.

In 1 Corinthians 1:9, it says, "*God is faithful, by whom you were called into the fellowship of His Son, Jesus Christ our Lord.*" That's our true calling: fellowship. When we abide in Him, His heart becomes our lens. We stop seeing distractions and disappointments through the eyes of fear and start seeing divine opportunities through the eyes of faith.

This is where clarity comes from, not from the world's definitions of success, but from a heart posture of listening to the Father. When you stay connected to Him, you'll see the people and places you're called to, not with striving, but with compassion. You'll sense His heartbeat behind your next step.

There were moments when the Lord would lay something on my heart that didn't make sense on paper. I'd see the need, but more importantly, I'd feel His love for those involved. That love led the vision. And that vision had fruit because it wasn't born from stress; it was born from stillness.

When we fight distractions by choosing presence, we don't just receive vision; we receive His vision. And that's the kind of clarity that can't be shaken.

The Power of Saying "When"

A very liberating truth I've learned in my walk with the Lord is that only He gets to say "when." Not people, not pressure, not obligation. Just Him. When we don't understand this, we let the world around us pile things on our plates, saying yes to everything and everyone until we're spiritually and physically exhausted.

You've probably heard the phrase, "Say when," like when someone's pouring you a cup of tea or ladling mashed potatoes onto your plate. The truth is, people will keep pouring as long as you let them. They don't know your limits. They're not responsible for your peace. And they're not the Holy Spirit.

But when you walk in intimacy with God, He will gently whisper, That's enough. He'll say, "Don't take on that extra night of the week," or "Your family needs you home right now," or "Say no to that opportunity; it's not yours to carry." And it's not rejection; it's protection. His voice helps us guard the good deposit He's placed within us.

Second Timothy 1:14 (*ESV*) says, "*By the Holy Spirit who dwells within us, guard the good deposit entrusted to you.*" You have been given treasure, revelation, vision, relationships, and anointing. But without the guidance of the Holy Spirit, you'll burn out trying to protect it all yourself. And burnout isn't a badge of honor; it's a sign that we've stepped outside of grace and into striving.

So many times, we wait for someone else to tell us when we've had enough. But true maturity is learning to hear it from Him first. He's the only one qualified to say "when."

The Holy Spirit Knows Your "When"

Sometimes the hardest part of managing our time isn't saying yes; it's knowing when to say "when." We say yes to every opportunity, every need, and every person, until we're overflowing, but not with life—with exhaustion.

The Holy Spirit spoke something so gently and personally to me: "No one else can say 'when' for your life. Only I can." People will always need something. The world is constantly shouting for your attention. But only God knows what's best for your current season. He knows when you've poured enough.

People will keep taking your time, your energy, your peace, without considering your family, your margin, or your health. Not because they're evil, but because they're not responsible for guarding your calling. That's your walk with God. That's why we need the Spirit to whisper "enough" when it's time to rest or redirect.

Ecclesiastes 3:1 reminds us: "*To everything* there is *a season, A time for every purpose under heaven.*" But if we don't pause and ask the Spirit what time it is, we'll miss the purpose of the moment we're in.

I've had moments where I felt pulled to do more. But my peace came with a "no" and was just as powerful as a "yes." Because it meant I was in sync with heaven's timing.

You don't have to figure it all out. You're not responsible for carrying everyone. You are responsible for asking the One who dwells within you, "What do You want me to do with this hour?" And when He answers, trust Him, even when it doesn't match what others expect.

This kind of Spirit-led rhythm doesn't just protect your time; it multiplies your impact. Because when you're where God wants you to be, doing what He's asked you to do, grace flows like a river and peace becomes your pace.

Relationship First, Overflow Second

Our relationship with the Lord isn't just the foundation; it is the calling. Everything else, the ministry, the productivity, the vision, it all flows from that intimacy. Remember, 1 Corinthians 1:9 says, "*God is faithful, by whom you were called into the fellowship of His Son, Jesus Christ our Lord.*" Fellowship is the true call. You and Jesus. Heart to heart. Spirit to spirit.

When I finally grasped that, I realized something powerful: investing time in God's presence isn't separate from your purpose; it is your purpose. From that place of abiding, the overflow begins. Clarity comes. Wisdom flows. Creativity is born. Strength is renewed. You don't have to try to muster it all up. When your source is right, everything else aligns.

Spirit-led rhythm doesn't just protect your time; it multiplies your impact.

There were days I'd spend time in the Word and worship, and it felt like nothing "productive" was happening. But then I'd step into a meeting, and suddenly, revelation would come. Insight would flow. I'd have an answer I didn't prepare for, or a word that broke chains in someone's life. And I'd think, *Where did that come from?* and the Lord would whisper, *From that secret place where you spent time with Me.*

We can either live by output or by overflow. One leads to burnout, the other leads to blessing. If you're asking where to start, start here: make your relationship with Him your highest investment. Everything else will follow.

Guard the Treasure Within

When we talk about time, we're not just managing a schedule; we're stewarding something sacred. Your time is connected to your calling, and your calling carries weight because it holds eternal impact. But here's the truth: you cannot protect the call of God on your life in your own strength. You weren't meant to.

That's why 2 Timothy 1:14 (*ESV*) has become such a personal anchor for me: "*By the Holy Spirit who dwells within us, guard the good deposit entrusted to you.*" You've been given something beautiful—revelation, peace, wisdom, grace, purpose—and it's a deposit that needs guarding, not from a place of fear, but from a place of value.

The enemy wants your time because he's after your overflow. He's after the people your life will touch. He knows that when you are full of the Spirit, operating in God's rhythm, walking in grace, you become dangerous to darkness.

But here's the good news: we don't have to be our own security system. The Holy Spirit dwells in us to lead us and guard us. I've experienced this so many times. Just when I was about to say yes to something that seemed good, the Holy Spirit would prompt me to wait, or even say no. At first, it felt strange. Why would I pass up a good opportunity? But later, I'd see clearly that what I was really waiting for was a *God* opportunity.

This isn't about living a closed-off, protective life. It's about walking in step with the Spirit so you can wisely discern where your time, attention, and anointing are best invested. When He says, "not yet," it's not rejection; it's redirection.

You don't have to feel guilty for protecting what God is building in your life. That's not selfishness; it's stewardship. The vision He's planted in you, the intimacy He's cultivating with you, that is precious. Don't cast your pearls before distractions, demands, or the pressure to please everyone.

Let the Holy Spirit show you what to say yes to. Let Him guard what's been entrusted to you. Let Him help you walk in clarity and power, so that every moment becomes a seed planted into eternity.

You are not wasting time when you pause to listen to the Spirit. You are investing it.

Abiding Positions You for Supernatural Multiplication

There is a reason the enemy fights our time with God more than anything else. He knows that when we abide in Him, when our lives are planted deeply in His presence, there is a supernatural multiplication that begins to flow. Abiding isn't about earning; it's about remaining. It's not about striving to produce; it's about being positioned to receive.

I've experienced this in my own life. Seasons where everything around me felt overwhelming with so many demands, people needing things, decisions to be made, and problems to solve. I could feel the temptation to rush, to plan in my own understanding, to jump into work mode. But the Lord would remind me, "Abide first. Sit with Me. Let Me be the One who multiplies what you cannot."

The world teaches us to hustle for results. God teaches us to abide in Him for fruit. John 15:5 says, "*I am the vine, you* are *the branches. He who abides in Me, and I in him, bears much fruit; for without Me you can do nothing.*" True fruitfulness comes when we stop trying to manufacture outcomes and instead remain rooted in the presence of the One who causes increase.

You don't have to feel guilty for protecting what God is building in your life.

This remains true whether at home, at work, in ministry, or even in our marriages. We could have packed our schedule with back-to-back meetings, nonstop travel, and filled every waking hour with tasks. But when we slowed down and invested our first hours with the Lord, something shifted. What used to take hours of effort began to happen with ease. Doors opened without striving. Favor rested on what we set our hands to. Time seemed to stretch. Things that once drained us began to energize us. Why? Because the source changed. It wasn't coming from us anymore. It was coming from Christ in us.

We were never meant to produce spiritual fruit in our own strength. That's why Jesus said, "Apart from Me you can do nothing." He meant it. It's not a motivational phrase; it's a blueprint. The only way we will live a life of lasting impact and divine productivity is by staying connected to the Vine.

When we abide in Him, we are saying, "God, I trust You to bring the increase. I trust You to multiply my time, my resources, my efforts. I'm not placing my faith in what I can do. I'm placing it in who You are." And that changes everything.

The enemy wants us scattered, busy, reactive. But abiding trains our spirit to be still, to listen, to follow. And in that place, God does what only He can do. He breathes on our lives and multiplies them.

This is the supernatural investment plan of heaven. Time with God never returns void. Every moment we spend in His presence is an eternal seed that bears fruit in due season. And when that fruit comes, it isn't small. It's pressed down, shaken together, and running over.

His Presence Is the Priority, Not the Platform

So often, we think that what God really needs from us is productivity, platforms, performances, public ministry, and measurable outcomes. But I've learned that what God truly desires is presence. Not just His presence with us, but our presence with Him. Ministry, success, and calling mean nothing if they are not born out of intimacy with the Father.

I had to learn something very important early on in my walk with God, and that is, we cannot invest more into the work of the Lord than we do in our relationship with Him. It will leave us drained and lead us down the path to burnout. When we start to feel exhausted—mentally, emotionally, and spiritually—we need to stop and ask God, "Did You ask me to do all this?" If the answer is no, then we need to make an adjustment and align our priorities to match His.

Let's look at Luke 10:41-42 from Mary's perspective, because she understood something Martha missed. "*And Jesus answered and said to her, 'Martha, Martha, you are worried and troubled about many things. But one thing is needed, and Mary has chosen that good part, which will not be taken away from her.'*" Mary had come to realize that Jesus didn't need more service; He wanted more time. He wanted someone who would sit, listen, and abide.

What's powerful is that Mary's investment of presence gave her revelation. She heard things others didn't. She anointed Jesus before His death when no one else grasped what was coming. That's the fruit of intimacy: insight that leads to impact. But it started with a choice to sit.

God has taught me that platforms can come and go. Opportunities can increase or decrease. Applause fades. But His presence remains. And if we make that our home, everything else flows with grace. If we neglect it, everything else becomes a burden.

Psalm 27:4 says, "*One* thing *I have desired of the* L*ORD*, *That will I seek: That I may dwell in the house of the* L*ORD* *All the days of my life, To behold the beauty of the* L*ORD*, *And to inquire in His temple.*" David, king, warrior, and leader, had one priority: to dwell in God's presence. That's why he had peace in the wilderness and wisdom on the throne. He wasn't chasing titles. He was chasing God.

We cannot invest more into the work of the Lord than we do in our relationship with Him.

When you invest your time in God's presence, you're not being passive; you're positioning yourself for power. You're tuning your heart to His voice so that your "doing" flows from "being." And that's where real, lasting fruit is born.

You don't have to chase a platform. You don't have to prove your calling. You simply need to pursue the One who called you. His presence is the reward. And from that place, your life becomes a testimony, not of your greatness, but of His glory.

Guard What God Has Entrusted to You

One thing the Lord has had to teach me again and again is how to protect what He's placed inside me. Not in fear or hiding, but through wisdom. When you truly recognize the value of what God has deposited in your heart—His truth, His vision, His anointing—you don't casually spend your life; you steward it. You guard it by drawing close to the Holy Spirit and letting Him lead your yes and your no.

Paul wrote to Timothy in 2 Timothy 1:14 (*ESV*), "*By the Holy Spirit who dwells within us, guard the good deposit entrusted to you.*" That verse can become an anchor for us. We can't protect the call of God in our own strength. We can't safeguard the dreams He's put in us just by being more disciplined or setting up stronger boundaries. We need the Holy Spirit's leadership in every decision because the things God has entrusted to us are sacred.

I've had seasons where I gave out so much—my time, my energy, my creativity—that I started to lose clarity. It wasn't because the work was wrong. It was because I wasn't staying anchored in the Spirit. I was trying to guard the deposit with my flesh instead of depending on the One who gave it. And when you try to guard your calling without the Holy Spirit, it becomes a heavy weight instead of a holy trust.

There are going to be a lot of good things that come your way: opportunities, requests, and even ministry. But not every good thing is a God thing. Some invitations are distractions dressed as purpose. And if we don't discern with the Spirit, we'll spend our time on things that don't bear eternal fruit. Only the Holy Spirit knows the cost of each commitment. Only He can see the ripple effect of our yes or no.

We see this echoed again in 1 Thessalonians 2:12 (*ESV*): "*We exhorted each one of you and encouraged you and charged you to walk in a manner worthy of God, who calls you into his own kingdom and glory.*" When you're called into His kingdom and glory, it means you carry something precious. Your voice is not just an influence; it is an assignment.

The more I invest in my relationship with the Lord, the more I recognize what needs protecting. His peace in my heart: that's worth guarding. His clarity in my schedule: that's worth defending. And I don't do it alone; I do it by the Spirit who dwells in me.

So let me encourage you: If you feel like you're losing the joy, or the clarity, or the focus God once gave you, it's not too late. Go back to the

Holy Spirit. Ask Him to help you guard the good deposit. Let Him show you what needs to stay and what needs to go. Let Him remind you of who you are and what you carry. Because when you guard what God has given you, you make room for even more to grow.

Protect the Good Deposit Within You

There's a powerful truth in 2 Timothy 1:14 (*ESV*) that's easy to miss if we're not careful: "*By the Holy Spirit who dwells within us, guard the good deposit entrusted to you.*" That deposit is everything God has poured into your life: His truth, His promises, His assignments, and your testimony. That deposit is worth protecting.

We can't guard the good deposit by working harder. We can't protect it by building walls of fear or self-dependence. We can only protect it by yielding to the Spirit who dwells within us. He shows us where to put our focus. He nudges us when something's draining us. He convicts us when we've said yes out of guilt instead of grace. He reminds us of who we are and what we carry.

When we live from that place of protected investment, we're no longer running on empty. We're living from overflow. That's why this isn't just about time management; it's about soul stewardship. Because everything God has put in us—His anointing, His truth, His love—is meant to be preserved, protected, and multiplied. But it starts with partnering with the Holy Spirit to protect it well.

We don't have to fear losing what God has given us. But we do need to intentionally protect our time with Him, our revelation from Him, and the peace that comes in knowing Him. When we do that, we're not just investing in our relationship with God; we're investing in every life that will be changed because of it.

Investing in God Isn't a Sacrifice; It's Your Greatest Privilege

Sometimes people look at time with God as something they have to do, like it's a chore or another religious checkbox to check off before the "real" work begins. But here's what I've learned: time with God isn't something we sacrifice for Him; it's something He graciously gives to us as our highest privilege.

I used to think that carving out time for the Lord was me doing something noble. "Look, God, I'm putting You first. I'm setting aside time for You." But He gently corrected me and said, "Carrie, you're not making a sacrifice; you're stepping into the supply." I began to realize that my quiet time wasn't just about me honoring Him; it was where I received everything I would need for the day.

The Lord never asked us to come to Him empty and leave depleted. No, He's always drawing us in so He can fill us up. And the more we prioritize Him, the more we realize this isn't about duty; it's about overflow. Everything we pour into our relationship with God—our time, attention, worship, stillness—He multiplies it back into our lives in ways we could never orchestrate on our own.

This is what Psalm 36:8–9 (*ESV*) says: "*They feast on the abundance of your house, and you give them drink from your river of delights. For with you is the fountain of life; in your light do we see light.*"

That's what it's like to dwell with Him. It's not a dry, religious act; it's a feast. And He's the fountain of life. If we try to serve people, lead ministries, or build vision without feasting first at His table, we're handing out crumbs. But when we drink from His river, we have living water to give others.

The enemy wants us to think we're losing something by choosing Jesus over the world's schedule or the culture's pressure to hustle. But let me tell you, you're not losing anything. You're gaining everything.

Paul told Timothy in 1 Timothy 6:6 (*ESV*): "*But godliness with contentment is great gain.*"

Notice it doesn't say "great loss." It says great gain. That's what investment in the One who matters most looks like. When you choose Him first, when you say, "This is Your day, Lord. Lead me. Speak to me. Multiply my time as You will," He responds with abundance because you've opened your heart to let Him be your source.

The more we prioritize Him, the more we realize this isn't about duty; it's about overflow.

So let me encourage you: stop viewing time with God as a cost. See it for what it truly is: a divine invitation to abundance, vision, peace, strength, and joy. You're not sacrificing your agenda. You're gaining His.

Reflection

When I look back over my life and ministry, I can see that every season of true fruitfulness and joy has flowed out of my time with the Lord. Not from striving, not from running harder or filling every moment with "important" things, but from investing in the One who matters most. The enemy loves to distract us with busyness, with the urgent, with the noise of this world, because he knows that if he can steal our time with God, he can weaken our vision and drain our strength. But when we make intimacy with God our highest priority, everything else aligns. Our calling, our relationships, our ability to discern His voice, all of it grows out of the overflow of being with Him.

The truth is, we will never regret the time we spend with God. We will never look back and wish we had sent one more email or attended one more meeting instead of seeking His face. But we will look back and see that every moment invested in His presence brought multiplication, clarity, and peace that no amount of hustle could ever produce. Abiding with Him isn't just an act of devotion; it's the key to a life of abundance and vision.

When we give our time to God first, we're saying, "Lord, I trust You to lead me. I trust You to guard my energy, my priorities, and my purpose." That's not a loss; it's a divine exchange. We give Him our time, and He gives us His wisdom, His strength, and His supernatural ability to accomplish more with less. Our yes to Him often requires saying no to other things, but those "noes" are what protect the "yeses" that truly matter.

This chapter is not just a reminder to manage time better; it's an invitation to live surrendered, to let your calendar reflect your priorities, and to abide so deeply in Him that His life flows through every decision, every conversation, and every dream. Invest in Him, and you will never run dry.

Abiding with Him isn't just an act of devotion; it's the key to a life of abundance and vision.

My Challenge to You

- Take Time to Reflect: Look at your schedule, not just to see where you spend your time, but to ask why. Are your priorities showing that knowing God is your greatest calling, or have distractions crept in?
- Set Aside Intentional Time: Choose a daily moment to meet with the Lord. Even just fifteen minutes of uninterrupted time, with no phone or noise, can shift your heart.

- Receive Before You Pour Out: Ask the Holy Spirit, "Where have I been giving without first receiving from You?" Listen for His answer and let Him refill you.
- Root Identity in Him: Remind yourself that your worth isn't in your accomplishments. Your identity is secure because you are chosen by God.
- Trust the Flow: Believe that as you abide in Him, clarity, peace, and fruitfulness will naturally follow. You don't need to chase significance because you already have it in Christ.
- Invest in What Matters Most: Adjust your schedule so you can be sure to invest in your relationship with Him. Your calendar may not grow busier, but your heart will grow fuller, your vision clearer, andå your life more aligned with heaven's purpose.

Scripture References

Ecclesiastes 3:1
2 Timothy 1:14
Luke 10:41–42
Psalm 27:4
Psalm 36:8–9
1 Timothy 6:6
Proverbs 3:6
John 15:5
Psalm 46:10
Matthew 6:33
Proverbs 4:25
1 Corinthians 1:9
John 17:3
1 Thessalonians 2:12
2 Timothy 1:9

Chapter Six

The Divine Calendar

Introduction

God isn't trying to cram your life full of noise and hustle. He's not adding burdens to your shoulders. He's inviting you into divine timing. He's offering a rhythm that leads to peace and fruitfulness. The Holy Spirit is our Helper, our Counselor, and He knows the full picture. When we align with His timing, we find ourselves doing the right things at the right time, with the right heart. And there's a grace on it.

Maybe you've been busy but not fulfilled. Maybe you're craving a deeper peace or clarity about your purpose. I get it, I've been there. But I want to walk with you through this chapter and show you how God has already authored a divine calendar for your life. When we surrender to His timing, we don't live behind or ahead; we live full. We live free.

So let's go on this journey together. Let's find His timing, His voice, and His abundance in the moments we surrender. Let's step off the treadmill of performance and walk boldly into the schedule heaven has written for us.

Fix Your Focus

As I've walked with the Lord, one of the biggest revelations He's taught me is this: His timing is always better than mine. I used to think that managing my time well meant filling every slot with something productive. But the Holy Spirit showed me that divine timing isn't about productivity; it's about intimacy and obedience.

One of the first things I had to learn was how to hand over my calendar. That wasn't easy. I liked to plan and check boxes. But I realized that surrendering my time to God didn't mean doing less; it meant doing what actually mattered. The more I gave Him access to my schedule, the more fruit I saw in my life.

I also discovered that real purpose flows from being with Him, not from proving something to Him. If we're honest, many of us feel like we have to perform for God, especially when we're passionate about our ministries, businesses, or making an impact. But I've learned that the greatest impact comes from the secret place. It's in abiding that purpose is birthed.

And through it all, the Holy Spirit has been our compass. He reminds us when to pause, when to say yes, and when to say no. He knows what's ahead. And when we listen to Him, there's peace, even in a full schedule. There's confidence, even when things don't go according to plan. He brings fullness in every season.

In this chapter, we will discuss what it means to live in God's divine calendar, not striving to keep up, but surrendering to His pace. We'll explore how distraction loses its grip when we're anchored in His presence. We'll look at how seeing as God sees lifts us above the stress of comparison and pressure. And we'll dig deep into the truth that abundance doesn't come from doing more; it comes from abiding in the One who is more than enough.

So, get ready. God has a divine rhythm for your life, and it's time to walk in sync with Him.

Your Calendar Is Not Your Master

I used to treat my calendar like it was a scoreboard; every slot filled meant I was winning. Ministry, family, discipleship, outreach, mentoring, teaching—if there was a space on the calendar, I believed I had to fill it for God to be pleased. But I've learned that a full calendar isn't the same as a full life.

I remember looking at my schedule one day and thinking, Lord, I can't do this. And I heard the Holy Spirit whisper, "I never asked you to." So much of what I had committed to was good, but not necessarily God-breathed for that season.

Many of us live like we're trying to prove something with our time. We cram our calendars with appointments, meetings, responsibilities, and even ministry, thinking we're being faithful. But faithfulness is not measured by how much you do; it's measured by your obedience to what God asks of you.

The truth is, your calendar will be shaped by culture, crisis, or the King. If you don't invite the Holy Spirit into your schedule, your time will be hijacked by distractions and demands that pull you out of alignment with your calling.

God showed me that managing my time well isn't about time management; it's about time surrender. I had to stop asking, "What do I have time for?" and start asking, "Lord, what do You want me to prioritize?" That one shift will bring peace. It removes guilt. And it will teach you to live led, rather than driven.

This is the heart behind divine order. When we give God access to our calendar, He gives us access to His divine timing. That's where fruitfulness comes from, not from hustle, but from harmony with Him.

Psalm 90:12 (KJV) says, "*So teach us to number our days, that we may apply* our *hearts unto wisdom.*" God isn't asking you to fill your schedule; He's inviting you to steward your life in partnership with Him. When you do, you'll stop being reactive and start being Spirit-led.

If you feel overwhelmed or behind, maybe it's time to take your calendar off the throne and give it back to God. He's not interested in you doing more. He's interested in you walking with Him, day by day, assignment by assignment.

Purpose Flows from Intimacy, Not Performance

You cannot measure your effectiveness for the kingdom by how much you get done. I've tried that. I've had days when I checked every box, met every deadline, and pushed myself to keep going, but my heart was worn out and far from God. And then I've had days when I spent time with the Lord, heard His voice, and did only what He led me to do, and those days were the most fruitful, peaceful, and filled with eternal impact.

God never intended for us to find our worth in our productivity. That's what the world and religion teach. But the Lord teaches something so different. He teaches that your purpose flows from intimacy, not performance. It's in the quiet place with Him that He reveals what truly matters and what doesn't.

Start your day in intimacy, and walk out your day in assignment. Don't start with your assignment and try to squeeze in intimacy. That may sound like a small shift, but it shifts everything. When we prioritize our relationship with Him first, He organizes our day, shows us what really needs our attention, and gives us the grace to walk in it without striving.

We all want to bear fruit. We want to be effective, purposeful, and have meaningful lives. But Jesus is clear, fruit doesn't come from effort alone. It comes from abiding. It comes from being connected. It comes from knowing Him, not just working for Him.

When we abide, the Holy Spirit speaks into our day. He reveals the divine assignments that might look small to the world, like sitting with your child, pausing to pray for someone, or making a phone call you've been nudged to make, but in God's eyes, those things are eternally significant.

Start your day in intimacy, and walk out your day in assignment. Don't start with your assignment and try to squeeze in intimacy.

There's such freedom in this truth. You don't have to strive to prove yourself. You don't have to hustle to validate your calling. You're already chosen. And when you spend time with the One who chose you, He'll guide you into a divine purpose that is bigger, more beautiful, and more fruitful than anything you could accomplish on your own.

Hand Your Calendar over to God

One of the greatest revelations I've had in my walk with God is that I don't have to manage time; I have to surrender it.

Like I said, I used to think that being organized meant fitting everything into my planner: appointments, meetings, deadlines, family events, and ministry goals. But that's not time management in the kingdom. That's control. And control will wear you out because it's driven by fear—fear of not accomplishing enough, not being good enough, and of missing out.

But when you hand your calendar over to God, you exchange fear for peace and control for trust. You're no longer reacting to the tyranny of the urgent; you're responding to the gentle leading of the Holy Spirit.

If you'll learn how to live by the Spirit of God, then the steps of the righteous are ordered by the Lord, not micromanaged by your fear of "missing it."

God is a much better time manager than we are. He sees the end from the beginning. He knows what's coming tomorrow. He knows whom you'll meet today. He knows where the divine appointments are. And if you'll invite Him into your schedule, you'll find that not only do you have time, but you have purposeful time.

Proverbs 3:5–6 says, "*Trust in the Lord with all your heart, And lean not on your own understanding; In all your ways acknowledge Him, And He shall direct your paths.*"

Acknowledging Him in all your ways includes your calendar. Let Him highlight what needs to stay and what needs to go. Let Him reveal the hidden things: relationships that need tending, rest you've been avoiding, tasks that are more about people-pleasing than purpose.

When we let God set the pace, we discover something beautiful: His calendar always includes margin. He leads with grace. He builds in rest. He multiplies our efforts. And somehow, when we surrender our time to Him, we find we have more time than we thought because He is in it.

Your Calendar Isn't Yours; It's His

I want to dive a little deeper into the truth about our calendars. Our time, every minute of it, actually belongs to the Lord. And when we try to manage it all ourselves, even with the best intentions, we miss the divine opportunities He has planned for us.

We can be so good at filling our days with "good" things. But the question we need to ask ourselves is this: are these God-things, or just good things? Because when we say yes to everything, we're often saying no to the very thing the Holy Spirit is trying to orchestrate in our lives.

There's a scripture that's anchored my heart regarding this: Psalm 31:15 says, "*My times are in Your hand.*" Not just my eternity. Not just the major life decisions. My times, my daily rhythms, my quiet moments, my availability to hear His whisper. If we truly believe our time is in His hands, then we have to surrender the illusion of control and let Him lead.

The Holy Spirit asked me one day, "Carrie, who built your calendar?" And when I looked at it, I had to admit, I had. I had filled it, approved it, stacked it, and now I was asking Him to bless it. But He hadn't authored it.

When we place our calendar back in God's hands, everything shifts. There's clarity. There's peace. There's margin. It doesn't mean we don't work hard; it just means our effort is directed, not drained. Purpose flows from intimacy, not performance.

That's why I started taking my calendar and physically laying it before the Lord. I'd open my planner or phone and say, "Okay, Holy Spirit, what's You and what's me? What do You want me to let go of? Where are the open spaces where You want to move?" And it was amazing. He would highlight things that didn't carry eternal weight, and He would breathe on things I thought were small but turned out to be kingdom moments.

The divine calendar isn't about doing less; it's about being led. It's about living with intentionality birthed from intimacy. When you seek Him first, all the other things—appointments, goals, dreams, needs—are added in proper order. He's not trying to make your life smaller. He's trying to make your life fuller.

Don't just pencil in time with God. Make Him the architect of your whole day. Let the Holy Spirit be your time manager. I promise you, when you do, you'll walk in more fruit, more peace, and more divine appointments than you ever could have scheduled for yourself.

Purpose Flows from Presence, Not Productivity

We often confuse productivity with purpose. But in God's kingdom, purpose doesn't come from a checklist. It comes from closeness.

I used to be a performer. Not intentionally, but like so many of us, I found value in getting things done. I felt secure when I saw progress and meaningful when I could show results. Maybe this is you, but the thing is, God doesn't want your performance. He wants your presence.

When you live from intimacy with God, you're not striving to find your purpose; you're receiving it daily in His presence. Jesus modeled this so clearly. He didn't wake up every morning and grab a to-do list. He went off to be alone with the Father. And out of that place, He healed, taught, corrected, comforted, and raised the dead. He lived from intimacy, not obligation.

Jesus makes it clear what our to-do list should look like. He says in John 5:19, "*Most assuredly, I say to you, the Son can do nothing of Himself, but what He sees the Father do; for whatever He does, the Son also does in like manner.*" Since that is how Jesus lived, it makes sense that we should do the same. Through intimacy with God, we discern what should be on our lists.

The divine calendar isn't about doing less; it's about being led. It's about living with intentionality birthed from intimacy.

Purpose isn't found in the spotlight, the platform, or the planner. Purpose flows from knowing the heart of the One who created you—not serving from habit, but from intimacy.

Psalm 16:11 (NIV) says: "*You make known to me the path of life; you will fill me with joy in your presence, with eternal pleasures at your right hand.*"

That's where clarity comes from. In His presence, the confusion lifts. In His presence, the pressure to impress disappears. In His presence, we're reminded that we were created for relationship, not results.

So if you're feeling unclear about your calling, don't run harder, rest deeper. Let God breathe fresh vision into your heart. That's the only calendar worth following.

The Holy Spirit Knows Your Divine Timing

There is a rhythm to the Spirit of God, an internal pace that doesn't match the world's pressure or our own panic. The Holy Spirit is the One who aligns us with the divine calendar of heaven, and He knows exactly when to say yes, when to say no, and when to wait.

There is a trap we fall into when trying to rush what God is still preparing. We want doors to open now, answers to come now, fruit to appear now. However, if we move according to our own timeline, we often end up exhausted, misaligned, and disappointed. Why? Because we weren't led, we were driven.

Galatians 5:25 says: "*If we live in the Spirit, let us also walk in the Spirit.*"

Walking with the Spirit means letting Him set the pace. It means being okay with not having all the answers yet. It means trusting that even in silence, God is orchestrating something beautiful.

I remember a time when I was eager to start a new project, one I knew God had placed in my heart. Everything in me wanted to begin, to gather the team, to move forward. But each time I brought it to the Lord, I felt Him say, "Wait." He wasn't saying, "no," just "not yet." That was hard for me. But I knew better than to run ahead of the Spirit. So I waited, and when the right time came, the provision and grace were already there waiting for me. The launch was smoother, the impact greater, and I had peace because I had obeyed His timing.

Romans 8:14 says: "*For as many as are led by the Spirit of God, these are sons of God.*"

To walk in your divine purpose, you must first walk with the divine Guide. The Holy Spirit doesn't just give direction; He is direction. He's not trying to fit your busy schedule; He's inviting you to rebuild your schedule around Him.

In Luke 24, after Jesus rose from the dead, He told His disciples to wait in Jerusalem until they were endued with power from on high (Luke 24:49). They weren't told to run out and preach right away. They were told to wait because timing matters. And when the Holy Spirit came, they were launched with power, boldness, and purpose.

Walking with the Spirit means letting Him set the pace. It means being okay with not having all the answers yet.

Let me tell you, when you trust the Holy Spirit's calendar, things fall into place with supernatural precision. The meetings, the open doors, the divine connections, they all show up right on time. Not your time. His.

So let Him lead. Let Him pause you when you're tempted to push ahead. Let Him say "not yet" when you want to say "yes." He sees the full picture, and He's never late.

Peace Comes When We Yield to God's Timing

If we're honest, many of the stressors in our lives don't come from what we're doing, but when we're doing it. We race against the clock, we say yes to too much, and we internalize pressure that God never asked us to carry. The result? Chaos, anxiety, burnout. But peace isn't the absence of activity. It's the presence of alignment.

Isaiah 26:3 declares: "*You will keep* him *in perfect peace*, Whose *mind* is *stayed* on You, *Because He trusts in You.*"

When we fix our thoughts on God instead of our calendar, something shifts. Peace comes, not from everything going our way, but from everything going His way. When our heart is stayed on Him, we stop striving to control outcomes and start resting in His outcomes. Colossians 3:15 instructs: "*And let the peace of God rule in your hearts, to which also you were called in one body; and be thankful.*"

That word "rule" means to act as an umpire. The peace of God is supposed to be the referee of your decisions. If God's peace is absent, God's voice might be missing too. So instead of charging ahead with fear-driven urgency, we pause. We let peace guide us. We let peace say "go," or "wait," or "stop."

But peace isn't the absence of activity. It's the presence of alignment.

God's timing is not just more effective, it's more peaceful. He's not in a hurry. He's not wringing His hands, wondering if things will get done. He sees the end from the beginning and asks us to walk with Him, not ahead of Him.

Philippians 4:6–7 reminds us: "*Be anxious for nothing, but in everything by prayer and supplication, with thanksgiving, let your requests be made known to God; and the peace of God, which surpasses all understanding, will guard your hearts and minds through Christ Jesus."*

You can have peace in the middle of a full calendar if your heart is yielded to Him. That's the difference between striving and serving. That's the power of trusting the divine calendar.

Learn to Listen Before Your Calendar Leads to Burnout

One of the most transformative lessons I ever learned about the cost of burnout didn't come in a classroom. It came while I was driving in Russia. At that time, I was living on the mission field, trying to do "all the things": teach, minister, meet needs, save people. But I wasn't doing them in the strength of the Lord. I was striving in my own strength, trying to be everything for everyone.

God had been showing me that I needed to slow down. And I would say, "Okay, yeah, yeah. I just need to finish this." But there was always another week, another round of commitments I had already made for the next month. I had said yes to too much.

One morning, as I was driving to Bible school in Russia, I literally woke up inside my car and realized I had fallen asleep at the wheel. I had drifted underneath a massive dump truck. The truck was so high off the ground that its big hitch came straight through my windshield and shattered it. As I looked at that steel hitch inches from me, I thought, "Okay, that's not good." Praise God, I wasn't going fast. It was standstill traffic. But I had fallen asleep.

I wish I could say that moment taught me to slow down, but I was still a young missionary in Russia, going on all cylinders. My days started at 6:00 a.m., and I would spend four hours teaching at Bible school, then move into team meetings, mentorship, correction, and training throughout the afternoons. In the evenings, two or three nights a week, and sometimes on weekends, I went to the drug rehab center to teach for two or three hours. After that came a forty-five-minute drive back into town—or a metro ride followed by a half-hour walk to my house. Most nights, I wasn't home until midnight.

That was just Monday through Friday. Saturdays were filled with mentorship, volunteering, and student outreach. On Sundays, I helped pastor a church with a couple, then I would attend the drug rehab center's church in the afternoons. After teaching, we'd stay for fellowship, mentoring, and praying with the young leaders who asked, "How do we do ministry?" I would encourage them late into the evening.

Everyone around me was warning me: "You need to slow down. You need to rest. You're going to burn out before you even get a decade into ministry, Carrie. You're not going to last." I said, "Okay, I'll slow down." But the truth was—I didn't know how to say no.

One evening, I knew I should take the night off. But instead, I said yes again. I went to the rehab center because I told myself they were expecting me. I carried a burden no one else had placed on me.

That morning, I had already preached at church, then joined the other pastors for a strategic planning meeting over lunch. Afterward, as I was pulling out of the restaurant parking lot, rushing to the next thing, I wasn't paying attention. I pulled out too quickly and slammed into the door of another car.

This was still in Russia. Yes, by that time I spoke Russian, but not "insurance Russian." So I just started praying in tongues. My heart sank when I saw the car—it was a Mercedes, the kind the mafia drove. And sure enough, when the men stepped out, I knew immediately who I was dealing with. I prayed, "Oh Lord, help me." And then I continued to pray in tongues.

The driver came up to me. I apologized and asked, "What do we need to do?" He looked at me and said in Russian, "Passport."

"What?" I asked.

He said, "Give me your passport and the keys to your car, and everything will be okay."

Something rose up inside me—Holy Spirit boldness. Despite my foolishness, the courage of God came over me. I looked at him and said, "Do you think because I'm a woman and I'm American that I'm stupid?" He stared at me, then grinned and said, "I like you."

That was a good start!

He insisted we go to a Mercedes dealership. I only agreed because he had his wife and his babushka (grandmother) with him in the car. At the dealership, they inspected his car and said the damage would cost $3,000. I told him, "I don't have $3,000. I'm a missionary. I live by faith for every single need." I asked if we could meet the next day. I knew I needed to get some counsel.

In Russia, it's common to exchange passports in a car accident to guarantee that you'll show up to settle things. Of course, he didn't give me his passport, but I gave him mine after the Holy Spirit whispered, "It's okay. I've got this."

That night, I went to the drug rehab center. We had church, worship, and prayer, but my heart was crying out: "Lord, what do I do? I believe You can provide the money." I kept handing it to the Lord because He is my peace. I asked the young pastor and the worship leader to pray for me. When I explained the situation, they immediately said, "You cannot meet him alone. Carrie, no. You have to bring people with you."

I told them I'd have my translator, Volodia. They shook their heads. "Not enough. We have a couple of guys who are former mafia. They'll go with you."

The next day, those two young men came to my house. They had gone through the rehab program themselves and were now serving as volunteers. They looked stern and tough. I told them, "Guys, listen, God's got this. We are going to talk, and it's going to be pleasant. Don't threaten him. That's not who you are anymore. You're new creations now."

So the four of us met the mafia man at a public supermarket. He brought three men of his own. He looked at us, looked at his three guys, then said, "Good for you."

We sat down to talk. My two friends spoke up, "You know this repair won't cost that much. You could get it done for less. We could even fix it for you."

The mafia man waved them off. "No one touches my car."

But then something incredible happened—my friends started sharing their testimony. "We used to be like you. We used to be mafia." They began recounting the things they had done, and then they said, "But we got saved. She's been teaching us this new life." They testified of the transformation Jesus had brought.

God softened his heart. We agreed on $800 instead of $3,000. It was all my rent money, but I said, "Okay. Here you go." I gave him $600 and said that I would bring him the other $200 the next day.

As we were talking, I noticed his men were in communication with three more, roaming around with radios. Later, my friends told me, "Carrie, he had six men with him." They asked me, "Are you afraid?"

I said, "Guys, I'm not afraid. God's with us. You guys just testified. Seeds were planted today. Even in my foolishness, when I was too tired to say no, God still used it for good. And besides, there are more with us than with him. God is with us."

They looked at each other, laughed, and said, "Actually, there are more with us."

To which I said, "Yeah, I know, guys, God is always with you."

Just then, a van pulled up. The door opened, and fifteen more young men from the rehab center were there, ready to stand with me. "Do you need us?" they asked.

I smiled and said, "No, thank you. God's got this."

That day, I learned a lesson I will never forget: if I don't listen to the Spirit and watch for the warning signs, my calendar will run me straight into burnout.

Burnout Doesn't Come All at Once

Burnout doesn't come all at once. It sneaks up on us, but there are clear warning signs that you need to know and recognize. I began to recognize a pattern, and I want to share it with you. I call them the nine symptoms of burnout:

1. You begin to resent the things you once enjoyed. That passion becomes a burden. Ministry becomes a job. Time with God becomes something on a to-do list instead of a lifeline.
2. You say yes out of obligation, not inspiration. The Holy Spirit isn't leading anymore; guilt is. You serve because you should, not because you're called.
3. You struggle to hear the voice of God. It becomes cloudy. Not because He's silent, but because your soul is noisy.
4. You find yourself jealous of others who have "less responsibility." Their lives look easier, and you secretly resent them for it.

5. You lack joy. You can still go through the motions, but something vital is missing. Joy is no longer your strength because joy has gone missing.
6. You are easily offended. Everything feels personal. Criticism feels like an attack. Correction feels like rejection.
7. You feel exhausted even after rest. Sleep doesn't restore you. A day off doesn't refresh you. You're depleted at a deeper level.
8. You isolate yourself. You stop reaching out. You avoid vulnerability. You don't want to talk because you're afraid the emotions might break through.
9. You begin to question your calling. The thing you were so sure about now feels questionable. You start wondering if you even heard God in the first place.

You start to lose the joy you once had in the very things God called you to do. Your quiet time becomes dry. You feel like you're constantly reacting to everything. You get short-tempered with people you love. You stop listening to the Holy Spirit and start powering through in your own strength. You lose your creativity. You become overwhelmed by even small tasks. You neglect your body, sleep, rest, and nutrition. And worst of all, you become numb to His presence.

Burnout doesn't come all at once. It sneaks up on us, but there are clear warning signs that you need to know and recognize.

But burnout doesn't just happen; it comes from deception. These lies want to trip us up, and so it is important to know what the four deceptions are that lead to burnout:

1. We believe: *If I don't do it, it won't get done.* That sounds responsible, but it's actually pride disguised as dedication. God never asked you to carry the whole kingdom.

2. We think: *I can rest later.* But when "later" keeps getting pushed back, we're living in survival, not stewardship.
3. We say: "I'm fine," even when we're clearly not. That denial keeps us from receiving the help God is trying to send.
4. We believe: *God needs me to do this.* But God doesn't need burnt-out servants. He wants sons and daughters who serve from a place of intimacy, not obligation.

Looking back, I see the Holy Spirit warning me all along. He wanted me to live in rest. Even in my mistakes, He covered me, protected me, and used the moment to plant seeds of the Gospel, but I'd rather learn the easy way, and so should you.

You don't have to drive into a dump truck or face the Russian mafia to realize that you're doing too much. You just have to listen. God is already speaking. Slow down before something forces you to. That's not just good advice; it's divine order.

The Holy Spirit Brings the Peace You're Looking For

When you begin to give your time, attention, and heart to the Lord, the Holy Spirit begins to lead, not in chaos, but in peace. Peace is how God leads. Peace is His fingerprint.

It's easy to confuse productivity with purpose. We've been trained to think that the more we do, the more we matter. But in the kingdom, fruitfulness flows from abiding, not striving. It's the Holy Spirit who knows what your day should look like, who you need to call, what meeting needs to shift, when you need to rest, and when you need to step out boldly. The more we follow His leading, the more we see how He orchestrates what we never could have planned ourselves.

I remember one day having six different things scheduled: back-to-back appointments, ministry prep, team meetings, and more. But as I paused that morning in prayer, I felt a clear prompting: "Only three of these are yours." I laughed, but I obeyed. I rescheduled the others, not even fully understanding why. And wouldn't you know it, by the end of the day, three separate divine appointments had opened up. People who needed to talk, who were hurting, showed up at just the right time. If I had bulldozed through my to-do list, I would've missed what He had prepared.

When you begin to give your time, attention, and heart to the Lord, the Holy Spirit begins to lead, not in chaos, but in peace.

Peace doesn't mean your life will always be slow or easy. But when it's God's rhythm, there's grace for it. There's joy in it. That's how I know I'm following the divine calendar, because I'm not frazzled. I'm fruitful.

Scripture tells us in Isaiah 26:3, "*You will keep him in perfect peace,* Whose *mind* is *stayed* on You, *Because he trusts in You.*" Staying our minds on Him means trusting Him with our days, decisions, and duties, and that kind of trust is what opens the door to supernatural peace.

The Holy Spirit isn't the author of confusion. If your schedule feels like a whirlwind, step back and ask Him: "What did You plan for me today?" He's not trying to squeeze more out of you. He's trying to fill you up so you can overflow into others.

Don't let a loud world drown out the voice of peace. Tune your ears to the Spirit. Trust that where He leads, He provides. And remember, peace isn't the absence of motion; it's the presence of God in the middle of it all.

Faith Says "Yes" Before the Path Is Clear

A big distraction from divine timing is waiting until everything feels ready. We keep hoping for the perfect time, the perfect invitation, the perfect resource, or the perfect set of credentials. But here's the truth: faith doesn't wait for perfect conditions; faith says yes before the path is clear. And when you're walking in relationship with the Holy Spirit, His leading is often quiet, subtle, and always anchored in love and peace, not performance or panic.

Often, people are delaying obedience, not because they're rebellious, but because they're perfectionists. But God isn't looking for perfection. I've had so many moments where God called me forward, and honestly, I didn't feel ready. I didn't feel like I had enough experience or that my resources matched the task ahead. But the Spirit of God inside of me was ready. And because He's in me, I could say yes, even when I didn't know exactly how it would all unfold.

Let me tell you, you're never going to have it all figured out in the natural. If you're comparing your life, your timing, or your calling with what someone else is doing, you'll always feel behind. But when your calendar is in God's hands, you're not behind. You're right on time for your assignment. Faith steps forward because it knows the One who walks with us. The more we abide in Him, the more courage grows, not because we see the whole staircase, but because we trust the One who's building it beneath our feet.

Faith doesn't wait for perfect conditions; faith says yes before the path is clear.

I want to encourage you with this: you already have what you need because you already have who you need.

Colossians 2:9–10 (*NIV*) reminds us, "*For in Christ all the fullness of the Deity lives in bodily form, and in Christ you have been brought to fullness.*" You're not trying to get ready; you've already been made ready by the One who lives in you.

Abundance doesn't wait for the stars to align. It flows from the fullness of the Spirit of God inside of you. And that means your yes to God carries eternal weight, even if it's whispered through trembling lips. I've found that when I say yes to Him first, the timing, the clarity, and the provision come rushing in like a flood. But they follow faith; they don't precede it.

So don't hold back. Don't disqualify yourself with all the "I don't have" and "I'm not enough" lies. The Holy Spirit's calendar for your life isn't built around what the world calls adequate. It's built around God's presence in you. And when you respond to His voice with childlike trust, the impossible becomes possible.

A Peaceful Heart Walks in Divine Timing

I've learned over the years that when I'm walking in sync with the Holy Spirit, my life doesn't feel like a rush; it feels like peace. Divine timing isn't something you calculate, plan, or force. It's something you walk in, because you've let the Prince of Peace set the rhythm of your life.

The more our hearts are anchored in trust, the more peace becomes our default setting. And peace is not just a feeling; it's a fruit of the Spirit. You don't have to manufacture it. You just have to stay connected to the One who is peace.

When you release your deadlines, demands, and distractions into God's hands, you begin to operate on His calendar. You don't panic when things seem delayed. You don't measure your worth by your productivity. Instead, you let your soul rest in the assurance that He's not in a hurry, and He's never late.

It's in that place of stillness that clarity comes. Your decisions are no longer driven by fear of missing out or trying to impress others. You stop running and start listening. And the Holy Spirit becomes your counselor, not just in crisis moments, but in your everyday schedule.

I used to think that if I slowed down, I'd fall behind. But I've discovered the opposite: when I slow down to hear God, He accelerates His grace in ways I could never manufacture. That's the rhythm of a life led by Him: full of peace, full of purpose, and full of power.

> *When you release your deadlines, demands, and distractions into God's hands, you begin to operate on His calendar.*

So today, if you're feeling hurried or overwhelmed, I encourage you to do what I've learned to do: breathe deep, turn your heart toward heaven, and ask the Holy Spirit to realign your pace. You don't have to strive to stay on schedule. Just abide, trust, and walk in peace. That's the beauty of living by God's divine calendar.

Reflection

Let me encourage you to walk by His rhythm and not the clock. So much of our stress and burnout comes from trying to live by man-made calendars instead of God's rhythm. We chase deadlines. We overcommit. We strive to perform, thinking that if we just work harder or faster, we'll finally feel peace or purpose. But the truth is that peace isn't found in control. Peace is found in surrender.

This chapter isn't about time management tips or productivity hacks. It's about trust. Do you trust God enough to let Him lead your day? Do you believe that His plan is better than yours, even if it doesn't look efficient on paper? Do you value intimacy more than image?

When we learn to abide in Him, we stop striving and start receiving. The pressure lifts. The joy returns. And instead of being driven by the clock, we are led by the Spirit. That's the invitation of the divine calendar, not to do more, but to do only what He asks, when He asks.

So take a deep breath, my friend. You're not behind. You're not failing. You're not forgotten. God sees you. He holds your days in His hands. And as you align your heart with His, He will lead you, one step, one moment, one divine appointment at a time.

My Challenge to You

- Evaluate Your Calendar: Look at what fills your days. Ask honestly: Did God place this here, or did I? Identify the difference between His assignments and man's expectations.
- Invite the Holy Spirit into Planning: Pray before you schedule. Ask Him to show you what's essential and what's just noise.
- Allow Pruning: Surrender activities that aren't bearing fruit. Don't be afraid to cancel or adjust commitments when peace has lifted.
- Choose His Rhythm over Hustle: Take intentional time in His presence before you commit to tasks. Let Him reorder your priorities around His voice, rather than pressure.
- Expect Divine Appointments: Trust that as you walk in alignment, you'll encounter opportunities that carry joy, rest, fruitfulness, and supernatural timing.
- Release the Weight of Striving: Remember, you don't have to carry every opportunity. You were never meant to live by hustle, but by His holy rhythm. Trust Him daily to order your steps.

As you do these things, you'll find divine appointments tucked into everyday moments, ones that lead to joy, rest, fruitfulness, and supernatural timing.

Scripture References

John 5:19
Psalm 31:15
Psalm 16:11
Romans 8:14
Luke 24:49
Isaiah 26:3
Colossians 3:15
Colossians 2:9–10
Proverbs 3:5–6
Galatians 5:25
Philippians 4:6–7
Psalm 90:12

Chapter Seven

The Power of No

Introduction

Have you ever found yourself so wrapped up in the expectations of others that you start losing sight of what God originally asked you to do? I know what that's like. It's easy to feel pulled in a hundred different directions, overwhelmed by responsibility, under pressure to perform, and subtly led by the voices of other people's urgency. But that's not the divine order God created us for. He didn't call us to a life of chaos or confusion. He called us to clarity—His clarity.

You and I were not designed to live enslaved to a whirlwind of "shoulds," anxiously scrambling to please people while quietly burning out inside. God designed you to walk in peace, in purpose, and with joy. And it's only when we give Him the calendar, the expectations, the burdens, and yes, even the fear of letting others down, that we begin to live from a place of true overflow. Because when you're in the right place, at the right time, as the right you, there is grace for that place. There's peace there. There's confidence. There's fruit.

This chapter is about clearing out the clutter, mentally, emotionally, and spiritually, and coming back to that divine simplicity where the voice of God is louder than the chaos. It's about realigning your vision, reclaiming your time, and rediscovering that the abundant life isn't a future dream or a financial number; it's a mindset rooted in who God is, what He's already done, and who you already are in Him.

Let's take some time together to clarify the chaos.

Fix Your Focus

1. Don't Live Enslaved to Others' Agendas

When your schedule is dictated by everyone else's demands, you may end up wearing someone else's yoke, and it won't fit. God never called you to serve at the expense of your health, your joy, or your time with Him. When the loudest voice in your life isn't the Holy Spirit, you can start performing for people instead of walking in faith. This chapter will explore how to break free from that pressure and reclaim your God-given authority to say no to busyness and yes to rest-filled obedience.

2. Right Place, Right Time, Right You

When you're in the place God has called you to be, doing what He's asked you to do, you're not exhausted, you're energized. You're not performing, you're flowing. There's a "rightness" to your life that can't be duplicated through effort. We'll talk about how being led by the Spirit positions you for divine appointments, favor, and fruitfulness, and how resisting His leading brings you to burnout, confusion, and regret.

3. Abundance Is a Mindset, Not a Budget

Abundance isn't measured in bank accounts; it's measured in revelation. If we think lack, we live in lack, even when we have more than enough. But when we know who our Father is and what Jesus has already made available to us, we begin to walk in a mindset of "more than enough" in every area: finances, relationships, peace, joy, and purpose. This chapter will challenge you to see abundance, not as something you chase, but as something you already carry.

The World Will Always Want More of You

You were never created to live enslaved to the world's expectations. The world will always want more of your time, more of your energy, and more of your agreement. But when your day belongs to God, the chaos loses its control. Here is a powerful truth: There is always something or someone ready to steal your time. That's why you must decide whom you serve; your time doesn't get to make the decision for you. You're not called to be enslaved by others' agendas.

> *God never called you to serve at the expense of your health, your joy, or your time with Him.*

If you've ever looked at your week and felt like there was no room for God, no room to pause, to reflect, even to breathe, that's a red flag. That means you've allowed the world's assignments to crowd out heaven's direction. But when you surrender your time to the Spirit of God, you start to clarify the chaos. Suddenly, not everything feels urgent. Suddenly, not everyone gets to demand your yes.

You can find yourself so driven by the needs of others and the desire to do good that you say yes to everything. Every time you say yes to a new request, it's actually saying no to something else, and sometimes, that "something else" was time with the Lord. You have to learn that not every good thing is a God thing.

The world will say, "Just keep doing, keep proving, keep climbing," but that's not the way of the kingdom. The Gospel is abundance, yes, but it's not abundance of busyness. It's an abundance of grace, clarity, and presence. Religion presents God as way up here, and you and I as way down here, with so many steps to climb to get to that place of blessing. But Jesus closed the distance. He brought the blessing to us. Look at this powerful verse,

First Chronicles 29:11–12 says, "*Yours, O Lord, is the greatness, The power and the glory, The victory and the majesty; For all* that is *in heaven and in earth* is Yours; *Yours* is *the kingdom, O Lord, and You are exalted as head over all. Both riches and honor* come *from You, and You reign over all. In Your hand* is *power and might; In Your hand* it is *to make great And to give strength to all.*"

If all greatness, strength, riches, and honor come from Him, then why do we run around trying to earn them from everyone else? Why are we chasing approval from people when the King has already spoken His favor over us?

That's where vision comes in. You're not created to carry everyone's needs. You're created to carry the assignment He's placed inside of you.

When you stop running to meet everyone else's expectations and start listening to God's voice for your day, that's when peace enters. That's when focus replaces frantic. And that's when you can boldly say, "No more chaos, I'm following the Lord."

This isn't about becoming rigid or unkind. It's about becoming faithful. Because when you're living by God's vision for your life, people may not always understand, but heaven will always rejoice.

Vision Brings Clarity

The more you walk with the Lord, the more your life begins to align, not scatter. Vision doesn't crowd your calendar; it clarifies it. That's why intimacy with God is never a luxury; it's your lifeline. When your time with God is in place, your yes becomes intentional. You're not just reacting anymore; you're responding.

So many people don't realize they're living without clarity, not because they don't love God, but because they haven't been quiet enough to hear Him.

You may love God deeply and still be confused. That's because the enemy doesn't attack your love; he attacks your focus. Remember when I shared with you that distraction is one of his favorite weapons. Do you remember why? Because if he can't make you sin, he'll make you busy! He'll make you doubt your next step by offering ten different alternatives, all of them "good," but none of them "God."

I remember years ago, I was juggling ministry, motherhood, missions, and managing a home, and I was doing it all with joy ... until I wasn't. I realized I had taken on burdens that God never asked me to carry. My schedule was full, but my heart was divided. That's when the Lord said to me, "Carrie, I didn't call you to do everything. I called you to do what I placed in your heart, and I'll give you grace for that." It was like scales fell off my eyes.

We often confuse being busy with being fruitful. But Jesus said in John 15:5, "*I am the vine, you* are *the branches. He who abides in Me, and I in him, bears much fruit; for without Me you can do nothing.*" This truth bears repeating and helps keep us from the trap of chaos.

So many people don't realize they're living without clarity, not because they don't love God, but because they haven't been quiet enough to hear Him.

See, fruit doesn't come from frenzy; it comes from abiding. And abiding gives you vision. It strips away distractions and false responsibilities. Vision gives you permission to stop chasing everything and start stewarding the one thing God is asking of you right now.

Let me explain it this way: you're not supposed to accept your life; you're supposed to lead it. And when I say lead it, I mean that you are in hot pursuit of Jesus Christ.

That pursuit births clarity. And clarity produces peace. You no longer wake up asking, "What do I need to do today?" Instead, you wake up saying, "Lord, what are You doing today, and how do I walk with You in it?"

The psalmist said it beautifully in Psalm 37:23, "*The steps of a good man are ordered by the* L*ORD*, *And He delights in his way.*"

That means your vision isn't up to chance; it's divinely directed. And when you walk in vision, you walk in rhythm with the Spirit, not the pressure of people.

Friend, you don't need more time. You need more clarity. And clarity comes from being with Jesus, hearing His voice, and knowing that vision simplifies your life instead of complicating it.

Let the Word Order Your Steps

So often, we pray for clarity while still clinging to the clutter. We ask for direction, but our hearts remain tangled in the opinions, expectations, and distractions of this world. One of the most freeing revelations I ever had was that God is not the author of confusion. His Word is clear. His Spirit leads with peace. But it's up to us to submit to that order and allow the Word of God to be our organizing compass.

When your thoughts feel like a whirlwind and your days are overrun with other people's agendas, it's a signal, not of failure, but of misalignment. I've seen this in my own life. There have been seasons when my yes came too easily. Not because I wanted to disobey God, but because I hadn't taken the time to ask Him first. And when your schedule is full of things God never told you to do, your energy, your joy, and your peace get stolen.

This is why time in the Word is not optional; it is essential. It's not just for learning theology; it's for learning rhythm. The Word of God is the divine tool that helps us discern "*what is good and acceptable and perfect*" (Rom. 12:2, *ESV*). If we don't know the Word, we'll fill our time with "good" things that actually distract us from the "God" things. We'll get caught up in the false urgency of others, constantly pulled into causes and crises that were never meant to be our own battles.

In Psalm 119:133 (*NIV*), it says: "*Direct my footsteps according to your word; let no sin rule over me.*"

That one verse sums up what it means to clarify chaos. When you let the Word guide your footsteps, your time becomes sacred again. Your energy is restored. And you walk with purpose, not pressure.

You don't have to chase productivity to feel valuable. God isn't impressed by hustle. What pleases the Father is faith, "*and faith* comes *by hearing, and hearing by the word of God*" (Rom. 10:17). That means the more you are in the Word, the more confidence you have to walk in God's timing and not be shaken by circumstances or the pace of others.

When your thoughts feel like a whirlwind and your days are overrun with other people's agendas, it's a signal, not of failure, but of misalignment.

I remember teaching this once at a Bible study where someone came up afterward in tears and said, "I never realized how much pressure I've been living under because I thought saying yes to everything meant I was being loving." But the Lord doesn't ask us to please people; He asks us to obey Him. And when the Word is your filter, you begin to say no without guilt and yes with confidence. That's the fruit of your no.

And let me tell you, when the Word becomes your compass, you become unshakable. You don't have to keep asking, "What am I supposed to do?" because the Word is already answering that. You start recognizing His voice faster. You say no to distractions more quickly. And you sense His peace before you ever step into a commitment.

In 2 Corinthians 9:8 (*Amplified Bible*), it says: "*And God is able to make all grace [every favor and earthly blessing] come in abundance to you, so that you may always [under all circumstances, regardless of the need] have complete sufficiency in everything [being completely self-sufficient in Him], and have an abundance for every good work* and *act of charity*."

Notice what it doesn't say: "Do everything and then maybe God will bless it." It says that as you walk in sufficiency in Him, grace and abundance will come to you. You don't have to chase it. You don't have to earn it. You just need to follow the Word.

Friend, when your calendar starts to reflect the Word of God, your life will reflect the peace of God.

Religion Blocks, but Relationship Builds

Religion paints a picture of distance, of God way up there and us way down here, left with an exhausting list of spiritual tasks to earn worthiness. But Jesus didn't come to give you a ladder of performance; He came to become the bridge. That's what grace is: it's Jesus closing the gap completely, not just spiritually, but in every area of life.

Many people still approach life as though God is holding back, and that if they do more, give more, read more, and pray more, then maybe, just maybe, they'll qualify. But abundance is not reserved for the religious elite. Grace is not a paycheck for good behavior. It's the gift of God's presence, peace, and provision, given through Christ.

In the natural, we've all looked at where we are and where we want to be and thought, "There's such a chasm between them." But Jesus didn't say,

"Climb the mountain to get to me." He laid down His life as the bridge to get you to the life you were always meant to have.

That's why John 14:6 is so powerful: "*Jesus said to him, 'I am the way, the truth, and the life. No one comes to the Father except through Me.'*" He didn't say, "I am one of the ways." He said, "*I am the way.*" That way is an intimate, abundant, grace-filled life in relationship with God.

Many people still approach life as though God is holding back, and that if they do more, give more, read more, and pray more, then maybe, just maybe, they'll qualify.

We misunderstand abundance when we think it's selfish or materialistic. But the truth is, abundance is the natural result of being rightly connected to the Father.

In 1 Chronicles 29:11–12, the Bible declares: "*Yours, O Lord,* is *the greatness, The power and the glory, The victory and the majesty; For all* that is *in heaven and in earth* is *Yours ... Both riches and honor* come *from You, And You reign* over all. In Your hand is *power and might; In Your hand* it is *to make great And to give strength to all.*"

This is the God of abundance, not lack, and He is your Father! He takes pleasure in making you strong, giving you purpose, and calling you "My child."

This understanding breaks the religious mindset that says, "I have to do more to be enough." Religion always demands performance before blessing. Relationship says, "Because you belong to Me, all I have is yours." And that's the Father's heart: to say, "Welcome home. It's clearly all yours. Come and live from abundance."

But let me be clear, this isn't about us being great so we can boast. It's about His greatness showing through us. That's what 1 Chronicles 29 makes so beautifully clear: all greatness, all power, all ability flows from Him.

So, we stop striving. We stop climbing. We stop trying to impress God or people. And we receive because relationship is the only real access to abundance.

Whose Agenda Are You Living On?

When your life is dictated by others' expectations, needs, and demands, you end up living someone else's version of purpose. That's not vision; that's chaos. But here's what I learned: clarity doesn't come from fulfilling people's agendas; it comes from surrendering to God's.

"Whose time are you living on?" That question might feel confronting, but it's necessary. If you're not aware of how your time is being used, someone else will use it for you. And in today's world, with constant demands, social pressure, and busyness disguised as productivity, the enemy would love nothing more than to keep you distracted from God's purpose.

You may have been saying yes out of obligation, guilt, or a fear of missing out. But the Holy Spirit isn't leading you to burn out. He's leading you into fruitfulness. If you say yes to everything, you'll never have room for the one thing God is asking of you.

That's why Galatians 1:10 says: "*For do I now persuade men, or God? Or do I seek to please men? For if I still pleased men, I would not be a bondservant of Christ.*"

You can't follow the crowd and follow Christ at the same time. Living enslaved to others' agendas will always rob you of the divine calendar God has designed just for you.

Let me share something with you: busyness doesn't always mean productivity; it can actually mask disobedience. The Israelites in Exodus 5:9 were literally given more bricks to make with less straw. Their workload increased, and their focus shifted from promise to survival. Pharaoh's tactic was clear: "*Let more work be laid on the men, that they may labor in it, and let them not regard false words.*"

That's what the enemy does today: he loads you down with bricks. More tasks, more performance, more pressure. Why? To keep you so overwhelmed, you start listening to "false words" instead of God's promise, His vision, and His leading.

The world celebrates hustle. But the kingdom calls us to hearing, abiding, and following. And here's the beautiful thing: when you choose God's pace, it often looks like rest to others. But that rest is full of precision, peace, and power.

Busyness doesn't always mean productivity; it can actually mask disobedience.

You are not responsible for every outcome. You are responsible for obeying the voice of God. And His voice never leads you into bondage. He leads you into freedom, clarity, and overflow.

So stop living to impress. Start living to obey. Let the Holy Spirit clarify your time, your purpose, and your path.

Lead Your Life, Don't Just Accept It

It's so easy to fall into the trap of settling. You look around at your life, your job, your routine, your limitations, and you silently agree with the lie: "This is all there is." Let me remind you of something straight from God's heart: You're not called to stay where you are. You're not called to have the same mentality as the world.

That's not self-help. That's a Spirit-led mentality.

A key to clarifying the chaos is pursuing Jesus above everything else. Because when you follow Him, you don't settle. You rise. And the more you pursue intimacy with Him, the more you realize: abundance isn't about getting more; it's about becoming more aware of what you already have in Him.

Many people feel stuck, not because they're lazy or disobedient, but because they've adopted a deficit mindset. They believe the lie that their season has expired, that their mistakes disqualified them, or that it's too late to step into purpose.

But here's the truth: When you get ahold of who you really are in the Spirit, you start to say, "Devil, who do you think you are? Do you know what I have? Do you know what I possess?" That's when you stop walking in fear and start walking in authority. That's when you lead, rather than react. That's when you start to overflow in joy, not exhaustion.

Let's look at what the Word says. In Philippians 4:19, it declares: "*And my God shall supply all your need according to His riches in glory by Christ Jesus.*"

That's not a someday promise. It's a right now reality. It's not based on your paycheck or performance; it's based on His riches in glory. And guess what? He's not running out.

We also read in Psalm 35:27: "*Let the Lord be magnified, Who has pleasure in the prosperity of His servant.*" That's you. He's not pleased when you're defeated and constantly striving. He's pleased when you prosper in your spirit, soul, and body and walk boldly into the plans He has for you.

You have the ability to prosper in everything that you do today. Why? Because the cross was that big. Amen!

When you lead your life from a place of knowing who you are in Christ, the chaos starts to clear. You stop making decisions out of fear. You stop living off someone else's opinion. You stop dragging yesterday's regret into today's opportunity. And you step into your calling with clarity, confidence, and kingdom abundance.

So I'll ask you: Are you leading your life, or just reacting to it? Are you shaping your days with the Holy Spirit, or surrendering them to distractions?

Abundance is not something you chase. It's something you walk in—one surrendered, Spirit-led step at a time.

You're Not Meant to Settle for Survival

You weren't created just to cope; you were created to flourish. But if you're constantly surrounded by pressure, busyness, and unmet expectations, it's easy to shift into survival mode. You wake up, do your job, meet your obligations, and go to bed exhausted, only to repeat it all again the next day. But let me tell you something, this is not your portion.

When you lead your life from a place of knowing who you are in Christ, the chaos starts to clear.

So many believers today are just existing in the "normal." They're living small, dull lives, not because God made them that way, but because somewhere along the way, they got stuck. Maybe it was the job that was meant to be temporary, but turned into a rut. Maybe it was fear of failure, or fear of man, or fear of being called crazy for obeying God. Whatever it is, when chaos becomes your default setting, clarity starts to feel like a luxury.

But God never called you to manage chaos. He called you to lead your life with clarity and confidence, by walking in His presence.

You're not supposed to accept your life; you're supposed to lead it. I've said this before, but let me reframe it for you: You weren't saved to survive. You were saved to shine. You were saved to radiate with the joy of the Lord, to be light in the darkness, and to carry a mindset that reflects the abundance of your Father.

You see, abundance isn't a bank balance; it's a belief system. It's not how much money you make or what job you hold. It's knowing who your source is. When you're rooted in the truth that God is your Provider, your Shepherd, and your Strength, you stop being swayed by the world's measurements of success.

Psalm 35:27 says, "*Let them shout for joy and be glad, Who favor my righteous cause; And let them say continually, 'Let the* Lord *be magnified, Who has pleasure in the prosperity of His servant.'*"

God delights in prospering you. When you carry that truth in your spirit, everything begins to change. You don't talk like a victim anymore. You don't pray like a beggar. You don't plan your life around lack or limitations. Instead, you show up with boldness. You step into rooms knowing, "I'm here on assignment. I carry the Spirit of God. I'm not a thermometer measuring the atmosphere, I'm a thermostat changing it."

There's a reason why I get passionate about this, especially when I see people settle. I've watched people walk away from twenty- and thirty-year careers, not because they were failures, but because they had the courage to follow God into the unknown. They gave up titles, pensions, comfort zones, because they finally saw that chaos wasn't from God. They weren't crazy. They were clarifying the chaos so they could step into the calling. And the world thought they were wasting their lives. But the truth is, they were finally starting to live.

Maybe that's what you need today, not another promotion, not another strategy, but a revelation. A moment of clarity where you see: you're not where you're supposed to be, and that's why it feels like survival. The good news is, you're not stuck. The cross made a way.

"*And my God shall supply all your need according to His riches in glory by Christ Jesus*" (Phil. 4:19).

That's not just about financial need; it's about vision, direction, peace, confidence, healing—all your needs. When you believe that God supplies out of His glorious riches, you stop being reactive and start being prophetic. You begin to build a life that aligns with heaven's agenda, not man's expectations.

Abundance isn't a bank balance; it's a belief system. It's not how much money you make or what job you hold. It's knowing who your source is.

And let me say this as plainly as I can: Don't let "normal" keep you numb. Don't let survival steal your song. God has called you to live with clarity, joy, and power.

So if you've been surviving chaos, today is your invitation to step out and step up. The Holy Spirit is not confused, and He's not chaotic. He brings fullness. He brings peace. He brings divine order that overrides every fear-based calendar and every guilt-driven decision. You're not here to fade into the background. You're here to reflect a Father who takes pleasure in your prosperity.

Stop Waiting for Worthiness; You're Already Qualified

So many believers delay their calling because they're waiting to "deserve" it.

They think, "Well, I've got some things to fix first. I need to be more spiritual, more mature. Maybe in five years, when I'm more ready." But that mindset is chaos. It's religious striving disguised as humility.

The enemy loves this tactic. He keeps believers waiting for worthiness instead of walking in what Jesus already paid for. But the truth is, you're already qualified because of Christ. That's not arrogance; that's alignment with the Gospel.

All we had to do was recognize our need, that we were sinners and completely unable to cross the great chasm on our own. But then we turned to Jesus and said, "I accept You. You are the only way to eternal life." And through Him, every bit of God's goodness, His abundance, His promises, His presence, it all became ours.

The moment you accepted Christ, He brought you into abundant life. Not just eternal life, but life now. Full life. Purposeful life. Your calendar doesn't need to be filled with steps to become worthy. Your calendar should reflect the fact that you already are.

And listen, this isn't just a feel-good message. This is the truth that breaks chains. It breaks the lie that says you have to earn what Jesus already gave. You're not climbing stairs to blessing. You're standing on the solid foundation of a finished work.

It's not "way out there" beyond reach, where you've got to earn it, work for it, or deserve it. No. It is fully on our playing field because of Jesus.

You don't need to "arrive" before you obey God. The reason many people live in chaos is because they're trying to earn a future instead of receiving the present. But the abundant life isn't waiting for you five years from now. It's available the moment you believe.

You can live free from that religious rat race. You can live in clarity because you know who qualified you. And when you do, you'll stop asking permission from people who never called you in the first place.

God says, "I'm the One who made the way. I am the truth that reveals to you who you are and what you can become. And through Me is life" (adapted from John 14:6).

This is why you can't afford to compare your journey to someone else's. When you start to look around and measure yourself by other people's standards or timelines, you lose your clarity. You start performing instead of obeying.

But God didn't call you to be a carbon copy. He called you to be you, at the right place, at the right time, as the right you. That's what Jesus paid for. And if He paid for it, it's already in your account.

It is important that you remember 2 Corinthians 9:8 (AMP): "*And God is able to make all grace [every favor and earthly blessing] come in abundance to you, so that you may always [under all circumstances, regardless of the need] have complete sufficiency in everything.*"

The reason many people live in chaos is because they're trying to earn a future instead of receiving the present.

That's a promise. You're not underqualified. You're not late. You're not underdeveloped. You're not waiting on a spiritual promotion. You're not stuck in "someday." You are sufficient in Him today.

The chaos that tells you to keep striving? That's not the voice of the Spirit. That's the whisper of religion, trying to keep you from walking boldly in your identity. But you know what God says? "*You are complete in Him, who is the head of all principality and power*" (Col. 2:10).

So, what do you do? You stop striving. You stop measuring. You stop comparing. You say yes to God's invitation to live from abundance, not for it. You look at your calendar and instead of filling it with pressure, you fill it with purpose.

You are not a project God is trying to fix. You are His child, fully equipped, perfectly loved, and eternally called. Let that truth clarify the chaos. Let it quiet the noise of shame and the pressure to perform. Because today, you don't have to wait for worthiness. You just have to believe it's already yours.

I Don't Have to Stay Stuck

I've seen it again and again, people who know Jesus, who love Him, but are living like they're trapped. They've given up hope that anything can be different. And sometimes, they don't even realize it. They've stopped dreaming, stopped moving, and settled into survival-mode living. But here's what I've come to know: I don't have to stay stuck, and neither do you.

There have been seasons where I found myself going through the motions, and inside, I was stuck. And if I'm honest, I realized the enemy doesn't need some big issue to trip us up. He just needs us to believe that change isn't possible, that what we see is all there is, and that we settle for whatever version we're at in many of our spheres of life.

Isaiah 58:11 says: "*The Lord will guide you always; He will satisfy your needs in a sun-scorched land and will strengthen your frame. You will be like a well-watered garden, like a spring whose waters never fail.*"

This is a beautiful verse that encourages us not to stay stuck, even in dry, unclear, or discouraging seasons. It also reinforces God's promise to guide, strengthen, and provide, all in one encouraging verse.

The fog clears the moment we remind ourselves who our Father is. "Do you know what I have? Do you know what I possess? Do you know who my God is?" Those declarations shift our posture from helpless to hopeful. We learn not to base our faith on what we see but on what He has already said.

I remember having a conversation with my daughter as we were doing some things around the house. We were talking about movie stars and people in high positions who had taken their lives. My daughter asked, "Why would they do that? They had everything." She saw it through the lens of success: fame, achievement, and power. But I got to explain to her that you can gain the whole world and still lose your soul. Real prosperity, real abundance, doesn't come from what the world hands you. It comes from what Jesus already gave you. Some people get stuck in wrong thinking and become deceived by worldly values, but we must let God clarify what truly matters,

You're not stuck because God isn't speaking. You're not confused because there isn't a path forward. The truth is, the Holy Spirit is constantly revealing, reminding, and inviting. When we pause long enough to listen, He always shows us the next step. Always.

You were never meant to live beneath your circumstances. You've been raised with Christ, above the noise, above the fog, above the opinions. The enemy would love to trap you in indecision or fear, but the Spirit leads you into boldness and clarity.

So, if you feel stuck today, take heart. Your Father isn't panicked. He's not confused. And He certainly hasn't left you without direction. You're not on your own. You are led. You are loved. And the way forward is filled with His peace.

Let Praise Become Your Overflow

When life gets chaotic, it's tempting to let our mouths mirror the mess. Complaining becomes normal. Worry gets loud. And before we know it, our words are fueling confusion rather than anchoring us in truth. I've seen it in my own life, and I've had to repent for it more than once.

But here's what I've learned: Praise is a prophetic weapon. It lifts us out of the chaos and into clarity. It reminds our souls who is really in charge, and it isn't fear, confusion, or pressure.

"Through Jesus, therefore, let us continually offer to God a sacrifice of praise, the fruit of lips that openly profess his name" (Heb. 13:15).

Praise is a prophetic weapon. It lifts us out of the chaos and into clarity.

I love that phrase: "*the fruit of lips.*" That tells me praise isn't always automatic; it's cultivated. Sometimes it's a sacrifice. But even when we don't feel it, we can still choose it. And that choice silences the enemy every single time.

There was a season in Russia when nothing seemed to be going smoothly. Ministry deadlines, visa issues, and team tensions were piling up. I remember walking outside one day in the freezing cold, and I just started singing loudly. Not because everything was fine, but because I needed to remind myself who my God was. I started declaring the goodness of God out loud, stomping through the snow, praising my way through the pressure. And something shifted, not outside of me, but inside.

I made a change. I chose praise. I chose to lift up God's Word instead of my worry. And the chaos around me didn't magically disappear, but my perspective did. Peace came. Solutions came. Vision came. Praise clarifies, multiplies, and shifts the atmosphere because it's rooted in truth, not feelings.

Praise aligns your mouth with heaven. It doesn't deny the problem, but it elevates the promise. I've learned that the more I speak life, the more I see it. The more I magnify God, the smaller the chaos feels.

Praise isn't reserved for when the victory is obvious. It's often what produces the victory. Praise is not a personality trait; it's a powerful tool of intimacy and identity. And when you step into it, everything changes, and clarity comes.

That's the beauty of a life aligned with divine order. You don't need everything to be perfect to start rejoicing. You don't have to wait until the breakthrough shows up before you start declaring God's goodness. You're not waiting for a reason to celebrate; you *are* the reason. You've been redeemed. You've been filled with the Spirit. You've been given every spiritual blessing in Christ. What more clarity do we need?

So let the chaos drown out, not by noise, but by praise. Let your words align with heaven's narrative. Let the joy of the Lord rise up and become your strength. And when you do, you won't just walk through the chaos, you'll walk above it.

Reflection

The chaos of life may swirl, but it doesn't have to take over. The world may shout its expectations, but you don't have to answer. I've learned, sometimes the hard way, that clarity doesn't come from trying to control everything. It comes from trusting the One who already sees it all.

Praise aligns your mouth with heaven. It doesn't deny the problem, but it elevates the promise.

When I look back at my journey, through the missions field, through transitions, through ministry demands and personal losses, I don't see someone who figured everything out. I see a woman who learned to let go. A woman who handed God her calendar, her plans, her reputation, and her fears and found something far better in return: peace.

You don't have to live reactively. You don't have to spend your days cleaning up the messes of yesterday or scrambling to meet the demands of today. You can live led, not pushed. You can live rooted, not scattered. You can live free, not frantic.

God is not the author of confusion; He's the author of peace. And when we let Him take His place at the center, the chaos begins to untangle. He knows how to bring beauty from the busiest places. He knows how to lead you into the "right place, right time, right you" kind of life.

And here's the best part: abundance isn't waiting for you at the end of your performance. It's here now. In the clarity of obedience. In the joy of intimacy. In the confidence that you've been placed by God Himself, on purpose and for a purpose.

Pause. Breathe. Listen.

The Holy Spirit is speaking. He's not shouting. He's not demanding. He's gently leading you. And when you follow, the chaos doesn't win. You do.

My Challenge to You

- Pause Before Planning: Don't rush to fill your calendar. Take a quiet moment first.
- Ask the Holy Spirit for Clarity. Pray: "Lord, what's truly essential for me today?" and listen for His leading.
- Lay Everything Before Him: Bring your schedule, emotions, expectations, and even your "good Christian busyness" to God.
- Release the Weight: Allow Him to lift off the pressure of things He never asked you to carry.
- Reorder Your Heart, Not Just Your Schedule: Let Him redefine what truly matters most.
- Walk in Confidence: Step into each day knowing you are right where He's placed you on time, with purpose, and full of His abundance.

Scripture Reference

1 Chronicles 29:11–12
John 15:5
Psalm 37:23
Romans 12:2
Psalms 119:133
Romans 10:17
2 Corinthians 9:8
John 14:6
Galatians 1:10
Exodus 5:9
Philippians 4:19
Psalm 35:27
Colossians 2:10
Isaiah 58:11
Hebrews 13:15

Chapter Eight

Stay on God's Path

Introduction

There's a path God has designed for your life, a path of peace, provision, and purpose. But in the middle of a busy world, that path can feel hard to see. Distractions pull at your time. Pressures cloud your decisions. And if you're not careful, you can find yourself just surviving, reacting to the chaos around you instead of walking in the vision God has placed within you.

But friend, God never called you to just survive. He's called you to abide. To know His Word. To follow His leading. To walk in the finished work of the cross and experience His abundance in every area of life. Staying on God's path doesn't start with a plan; it starts with a Person. It starts with Jesus.

I've lived this journey. I've walked through seasons where it felt like everything was screaming for my attention: ministry, needs, expectations, bills, opportunities. But every time I've stopped, realigned my heart with His Word, and remembered who I am in Christ, something powerful happens: peace returns, clarity breaks through, and provision shows up in ways I never expected.

This chapter is about that alignment. It's about shaking off the confusion and distractions, and choosing to walk fully on God's path, not just with your feet, but with your heart, your time, and your trust. We'll look at what it means to know your vision, abide in the living Word, and live from the abundance that was secured for you at the cross. Not someday. Today.

So let's dig deep. Let's remove what hinders, receive what empowers, and stay on the path that leads to life. God's not hiding His best from you. He's inviting you into it.

Fix Your Focus

I want to help you get anchored in three life-giving truths that keep you aligned with heaven's direction and free from earthly distraction.

1. Know Your Vision and Eliminate Distraction

Vision isn't just about big dreams or lofty goals; it's about knowing what God has spoken over your life and choosing to walk it out. You were designed with purpose, and the enemy knows it. That's why he fights to keep you distracted, busy with everyone else's agendas, burdened by needs, or overwhelmed by too many options. But when you know your God-given vision, it becomes easier to say no to distractions and yes to divine appointments. I want us to unpack how staying focused on God's leading helps you walk in confidence, peace, and authority.

2. Abide in the Living Word

God's path isn't discovered through striving; it's revealed through abiding. As you spend time in His Word and allow truth to saturate your thinking, clarity begins to rise and chaos loses its power. Abiding means staying close to Jesus, who is the Word made flesh. Let's explore what it looks like to keep your heart tethered to the Word, so you can discern God's leading, even in the noise of everyday life.

3. The Cross Is God's Abundance to You

When Jesus went to the cross, He didn't just forgive your sins; He gave you access to every promise of God. That includes provision, peace, direction, and freedom from lack. You're not walking an uncertain path; you're walking a path paved by the finished work of Christ. And finally, let's focus on what it means to live from a place of abundance, not lack, and how to approach every step of your journey with confidence that His will is His bill.

The Word Keeps You on Course

One of the greatest lessons I've learned is that when I stay in the Word of God, I don't just get guidance; I get anchored. I'm not swayed by fear or seduced by the urgency of life. When I abide in His Word, I don't have to manufacture clarity; I receive it.

There will be times in your life when you desperately want to know, "God, what am I supposed to do next?" You can get so busy trying to figure things out that you actually move away from the one thing that brings clarity: time in the Word. That's why John 15:7 is a verse I return to again and again: "*If you abide in Me, and My words abide in you, you will ask what you desire, and it shall be done for you.*"

> *God's path isn't discovered through striving; it's revealed through abiding.*

There's such power in abiding. It's not about checking off a devotional list or trying to prove to God how spiritual we are. It's about living connected to truth, even when everything around you feels chaotic or uncertain. The Word keeps your heart aligned and your vision clear.

I've had moments where I felt the pull of distraction, where my mind was racing with all the "what ifs" and "how-tos." But I've learned that if I go to the Word first, I find rest before answers, and in that place of rest, clarity comes. Psalm 119:105 tells us, "*Your word is a lamp to my feet And a light to my path.*" That verse doesn't say the Word is a spotlight revealing the whole journey. No, it's a lamp. Step by step, day by day, God's Word guides us. He doesn't tease us with confusion; He leads us with light.

See, when you stay in the Word, you're not chasing clarity; it starts chasing you. When you open your Bible with a heart that says, "Lord, show me Your way," the Holy Spirit begins to highlight truths that specifically apply to your moment, your question, your calling.

One of the biggest distractions to staying on God's path is the pressure to know it all up front. But the Word doesn't always give us a five-year plan; it gives us the wisdom for today. And if you follow God today, guess what? You'll end up where you're supposed to be tomorrow.

When I was a young missionary in Russia, I didn't always have a full picture of what God was doing. But I had the Word, and that was enough. I would open my Bible and find promises that told me He was with me, He was my provider, and I had not been forgotten. In those moments, peace would come, and direction would follow.

Do you want to stay on God's path? Stay in God's Word. Don't let the world, or even well-meaning people, pull you into their version of purpose. Let His Word speak louder than your fears, your to-do list, or your circumstances.

The Word Stabilizes Your Vision

When you don't know where you're going, you will grab onto anything that looks stable. But the truth is, the only stable foundation for your life is the Word of God. That's why it's not just about having a vision; it's about building your vision from the Word. I've seen so many people try to run with a good idea or a well-meaning ambition, but if it didn't come from the Word, it didn't have the power to be sustained. That's why I constantly go back to what God said. I don't want to be chasing shadows; I want to stay on His path.

I remember in Russia, sitting with people who had big dreams, but their dreams were often shaped by survival and desperation. It's easy to craft a vision out of fear, and what you don't want to happen, rather than out of the promises of God. But the Word recenters us. When I would open my Bible and read about who I was in Christ, it reminded me I wasn't alone in that frozen country. The Word was my direction and my compass when everything else felt uncertain.

When you stay in the Word, you're not chasing clarity; it starts chasing you.

Isaiah 30:21 says, "*Your ears shall hear a word behind you, saying, 'This is the way, walk in it,' Whenever you turn to the right hand Or whenever you turn to the left.*" His voice gives us course correction, but it's often a whisper, not a shout. And that whisper will never contradict His Word.

If your "vision" doesn't line up with the Word, then it's not from God. That's why we must stop asking God to bless our plans and instead start asking Him to reveal His. I've had to do this personally. There were seasons when I was so busy with ministry, I wasn't being fed by the Word, I was feeding others, but neglecting the very anchor that kept me aligned. Do you know what happens when you drift from the Word? You start making decisions from stress, pressure, and human reasoning. That's not the abundant path God has for us.

Proverbs 4:25–27 gives us a powerful picture of how to stay focused: "*Let your eyes look straight ahead, And your eyelids look right before you. Ponder the path of your feet, And let all your ways be established. Do not turn to the right or the left; Remove your foot from evil.*" That's the kind of intentionality the Word produces. You're not just moving for movement's sake. You're walking with purpose because you've been in the Word and the Word is in you.

That's why we must stop asking God to bless our plans and instead start asking Him to reveal His.

If you feel like your vision is fuzzy or your path unclear, go back to the Word. Let it cleanse your thinking, ignite your spirit, and anchor your feet. Because when your vision is shaped by the Word, you can walk in confidence, even if you don't see the full picture yet. He'll guide you step by step.

Surrender to God's Leading, Not the Noise

Sometimes the greatest battle in staying on God's path isn't the enemy; it's the noise. The voices of pressure, culture, comparison, and even well-meaning people can drown out the still, small voice of God. That's why surrender isn't weakness—it's wisdom. When I let go of my need to have all the answers and simply say, "Lord, lead me," I find clarity in the moment.

There have been times when people questioned my decisions. Especially as a young missionary, moving to Russia at twenty-one, people didn't understand. They thought I was throwing away my future. But I wasn't following their vision, I was following God's, and I had peace.

You can't explain that kind of peace to the world. It's the kind that passes understanding and anchors your spirit when nothing else makes sense.

Jesus modeled this perfectly. In John 5:30, He said, "*I can of Myself do nothing. As I hear, I judge; and My judgment is righteous, because I do not seek My own will but the will of the Father who sent Me.*" That's surrender. That's staying on the Father's path, not creating your own.

So many of us want to run after the next opportunity, the next platform, the next big idea. But if God's not in it, it's not worth it. Even ministry can become a distraction if it's not birthed from relationship. That's why you need to ask yourself regularly, "God, is this You or is this just a good idea?" Because only His path is covered in His grace.

In Proverbs 3:6, we're reminded: "*In all your ways acknowledge Him, And He shall direct your paths.*" Not some of your ways. *All.* That means we don't get to segment our lives—God over here on Sundays, our career over there, our family over here. He wants to be Lord of *all.* And when we acknowledge Him in everything, He gets to guide everything.

Distraction doesn't always look evil. Sometimes it looks like busyness, success, or even ministry. But if it pulls you off God's path, it's not from Him. The solution isn't to try harder, it's to surrender deeper. The more you abide in Him, the more you'll hear His voice and recognize when you're veering off course.

The world is noisy. But the path of God is peaceful, purposeful, and sure. If you feel surrounded by voices or pulled in a dozen directions, pause. Surrender. Ask the Holy Spirit to recenter you. He will. And when He does, you'll find yourself exactly where you need to be—on God's path, in God's timing, for God's purpose.

Your Crossroads Are Covered by the Cross

Every believer eventually comes to a crossroads, those moments where the future feels foggy and the pressure to choose "right" feels heavy. But I've learned that God's path is never discovered through pressure. It's discovered through peace. And that peace comes when we recognize that the cross has already provided everything we need to move forward

One of the most powerful revelations I ever had was this: I'm not trying to get God to bless my future. I'm walking in the blessing that's already been secured by Jesus. His finished work is not just for salvation; it's the gateway to provision, guidance, identity, and abundance—right now—for today's decisions.

In 2 Corinthians 9:8 (*KJV*), Paul says, "*And God* is *able to make all grace abound toward you, that ye, always having all sufficiency in all* things, *may abound to every good work*." While this verse is often applied to finances, it also speaks to the sufficiency of God's grace in every area of life—to make decisions, to take bold steps, navigate difficult seasons, and do it all with confidence that God is with you.

I remember sitting on a freezing trolley in Russia. I had no idea how the next rent payment would be made. I had translator salaries due, and I had no visible plan B. But I had peace because God reminded me, "Carrie, My will, My bill." That phrase has anchored me through so many situations. When you're walking in obedience, the provision will meet you on the path. It's not your job to orchestrate every detail; it's your job to stay surrendered and trust Him to lead.

God's path is never discovered through pressure. It's discovered through peace.

That is exactly what Romans 8:32 declares: "*He who did not spare His own Son, but delivered Him up for us all, how shall He not with Him also freely give us all things?*" If God gave you Jesus, how could He possibly withhold clarity, direction, peace, or provision? He's already given the greatest gift—His own Son. Everything else, no matter how significant it seems, is secondary in comparison.

That's why I can confidently say: Your crossroads are covered by the cross. You're not stepping into the unknown; you're stepping into territory already claimed by grace. You're not begging for breadcrumbs; you're walking in the inheritance as a child of God.

As we've discussed already, the enemy wants to make you feel stuck. He wants to whisper, "What if you mess this up?" But God says, "I'm leading you. I'm with you. I've already gone before you." Don't let fear dictate your decisions; let the cross be your compass.

Staying on God's path doesn't mean you'll never face uncertainty, but it does mean you'll never face it alone. The same grace that saved you is the same grace that will lead you forward—one obedient step at a time.

The Word Is a Lamp to Your Real Life

When people talk about God's Word being a lamp to our feet, they sometimes treat it like a poetic idea, something symbolic, beautiful—but distant. But I'm here to tell you: God's Word is the most practical thing you'll ever carry. It's not just for church services or devotional time. It's for boardrooms, backyards, busy schedules, and big decisions. The Word works in real time, for real life.

Let's look again at Psalm 119:105. I want to expand on the truth we discussed earlier. In Psalm 119:105, it says, "*Your word* is *a lamp to my feet And a light to my path.*" Notice how personal that is? It doesn't say, "a lamp to the world" or "a light for history." It says: **my feet**, **my path**. That means the Word of God is designed to illuminate your exact next step.

I've had so many moments where I've been unsure of what to do. There have been times I was balancing a lot of things in every area of my life, and I couldn't see the full picture. But I would get in the Word, and suddenly a verse would stand out. A phrase would leap off the page and I would know—this is my next step.

One of the biggest distractions from staying on God's path is simply trying to figure things out in our own reasoning. We get tempted to create strategy instead of receiving revelation. But remember, Proverbs 3:6 gives us this promise: "*In all your ways acknowledge Him, And He shall direct your paths.*" When we make a habit of turning to God in everything, even the small stuff, we get clarity we could never manufacture on our own.

Staying on God's path doesn't mean you'll never face uncertainty, but it does mean you'll never face it alone.

I remember teaching a group of people who were eager to hear God's voice, but many of them were afraid they'd somehow miss His will. I would remind them: You're not following a distant God, you're following a Shepherd who speaks. If you're in the Word daily, if you're meditating on what He's already spoken, then guess what? You're not in danger of missing Him. You'll hear His voice. The lamp is on.

We're living in a world that wants to replace the voice of God with the noise of culture. Social media, trends, people's opinions—they try to shape your decisions. But when you stay anchored in the Word, you walk in clarity that confuses the world. You make decisions that don't always make sense on paper, but they align with heaven's plan.

The Word isn't just spiritual; it's directional. It doesn't just teach; it leads. And if you want to stay on God's path, then make it your daily habit to get into the Word before the world gets into you.

The Cross Is the Anchor of Abundance

Abundance doesn't begin with a job, a paycheck, or a spreadsheet—it begins at the cross.

When Jesus laid down His life, He didn't just secure our salvation. He secured our access to everything we would ever need to fulfill our calling. That's why you can't separate the cross from your vision, your provision, or your peace. If you're going to stay on God's path, you must understand this: The cross is not just about forgiveness—it's about fullness.

When you look at the chaos of lack, whether it's bills, broken dreams, or burned-out hope, it can feel like you're drowning. But the cross isn't just a historical moment—it's your present anchor. It's the eternal transaction that settled every debt, spiritual, emotional, relational, and yes—even financial.

Jesus wiped out everything that tried to stand in the way of your fullness. This is a spiritual reality backed by covenant. Colossians 2:14 (*NLT*) says, "*He canceled the record of the charges against us and took it away by nailing it to the cross.*"

When you stay anchored in the Word, you walk in clarity that confuses the world.

That record wasn't just moral failure; it was everything that accused you of being unworthy, of never being enough, of always falling short. The cross put an end to that narrative. What the enemy meant to use as a permanent stain, Jesus turned into a receipt stamped "Paid in Full."

That means lack doesn't get the last word; debt doesn't get to define your limits. The cross redefined your reality.

There have been days when it looked like I didn't have enough on paper. But I had something greater than paper. I had the cross. And in those moments, I've spoken to needs, not as a desperate beggar, but as a daughter standing in covenant. My declaration wasn't based on what I saw in the natural; it was rooted in what I believed about the cross. That I've been made complete in Christ and the accusations of "not enough" were already nailed there. That His resurrection secured my new name: Lacking Nothing.

The cross is abundance secured by blood. You don't have to strive for it, you just have to anchor yourself in it.

Trust Invites the Supernatural

Living on God's path doesn't mean we'll never face need, but it does mean we'll never face it by ourselves. Abundance isn't the absence of challenge; it's the presence of supernatural provision right in the middle of it. God doesn't wait until everything's perfect to provide. He provides because He is perfect.

When you look at what's ahead—tires to replace, bills that just jumped—you can respond with worry, or you can respond with trust. Trust brings a supernatural peace that opens the door for God to move.

You'll always have a choice. When life presses in and there's more demand than you have in supply, whether it's financially, emotionally, or mentally, you can lean into your own understanding and spiral into stress, or you can lean into grace.

There's power in how we respond. Our response reveals our source. Are we leaning on our calculations, our backup plans, our hustle—or on the One who promised to never leave us, never forsake us, and supply all our needs?

God is not asking you to pretend you don't see the bills or the challenges. He's asking you to bring them to Him and then rest. Not because you've figured it out, but because you trust that He has. That's supernatural.

In Philippians 4:19, Paul declares: "*And my God shall supply all your need according to His riches in glory by Christ Jesus.*"

Abundance isn't the absence of challenge; it's the presence of supernatural provision right in the middle of it.

Paul doesn't say "according to your budget." He doesn't say "according to your careful planning" or "based on your behavior." He says, according to His riches in glory—that's supernatural. That's not from this world; it's from the heart of the Father who takes pleasure in revealing Himself as your source.

The world says lack is a wall. But when you trust God, lack becomes a doorway to a miracle. When you begin to prophesy to the unpaid bills on your counter, to the gaps in your bank account, and you say, "God is my sufficiency. I'm not stuck. I'm covered. I'm kept. I'm not limited to what I see; I live by who He is."

This is where abundance lives, in trust. Trust doesn't deny need; it declares who your Provider is, and in that declaration, the supernatural shows up.

Guard Your Heart from Financial Manipulation

If God is your source, then He is also your provider. That means we don't have to angle or strive to get the help of man. When we truly walk in abundance, we don't manipulate; it's beneath the dignity of our identity as sons and daughters of God. Manipulation stems from fear and pride: fear that God won't come through, and pride that refuses to appear needy or weak.

Abundance shifts our posture from "I must be seen and helped" to "God sees me, and He helps." As Paul wrote, "*Let your requests be made known to God*" (Phil. 4:6), not broadcast as subtle cues to those around us. Our trust is to be vertical, not horizontal.

The beauty of abundance is that it removes both manipulation and shame from the equation. We don't have to hide our needs, nor do we have to beg for them to be met. We simply cast our cares on Him, knowing He cares for us (1 Pet. 5:7). That includes every financial care.

Trust doesn't deny need; it declares who your Provider is, and in that declaration, the supernatural shows up.

We also don't need to spiritualize lack. Poverty is not a fruit of the Spirit. Being in debt or going without isn't a badge of righteousness. God doesn't use financial struggle to teach lessons or prove love. His Word already does that. He's a Father who gives good gifts and knows what you need before you ask Him (Matt. 6:8). That's who He is.

True abundance includes the integrity of your walk with God. You don't give your finances, time, or energy to be seen, and you don't receive through manipulation. You live open-handed and openhearted because you trust Him fully. This is the life we walk when we stay on God's path.

Humility Makes Room for God's Provision

Abundance isn't just about learning to give; it's also about learning to receive. For some of us, that's the harder part. And often, what gets in the way isn't a lack of faith; it's pride.

Sometimes the greatest obstacle to living in abundance isn't what we don't have—it's what we won't admit. We don't want anyone to know we're struggling. We don't want to appear weak, needy, or imperfect. But when we cling to that image, we push away the very help God wants to send.

Some of you are so prideful that you refuse to let anyone see your struggles because of this image issue. That hits close to home for many, as pride often wears a mask of strength. But God doesn't respond to masks; He responds to hearts.

James 4:6 tells us clearly: "*God resists the proud, But gives grace to the humble.*" Grace is the fuel of abundance. It's unearned, undeserved, and more than enough. But it only flows where humility opens the door.

Humility says, "Lord, I can't do this alone, I trust You." It doesn't manipulate or perform—it simply receives. And when we walk in that place of dependency, we begin to see provision flow into areas we've tried for years to manage on our own.

I want to encourage you not to be the person who just works harder and tries to "make it happen" in your own strength. Cutting corners, juggling stress, skipping rest, and refusing help are all signs of pride in disguise. But when you pause and say, "God, I surrender this area of lack to You," He steps in.

Let's be clear: that doesn't mean you stop stewarding well—it means you stop trying to control everything. You stop striving. You begin to walk in grace. You're confident that your Father sees you and loves to provide for His children.

We were never meant to walk the path alone. Staying on God's path means walking in humility because that's the place where provision flows.

True Abundance Flows from a Surrendered Life

A clear lesson I've learned over years of ministry, missions, and daily life is this: Abundance doesn't come from chasing what you want. It comes from surrendering to what God wants.

So many believers want God to fund their dreams, back their plans, and provide for their version of success but they haven't asked Him what He's actually calling them to do. We want God's abundance, yet too often we want Him to pay for all that we want to accomplish. That's a truth that both stings and heals.

The real joy of staying on God's path is not that we get everything we want; it's that we receive everything we need for His will to be fulfilled through us. When our hearts are aligned with His, lack becomes irrelevant. We begin to experience peace even when the numbers don't make sense, and joy even in the face of uncertainty. That's the supernatural rhythm of surrender.

Cutting corners, juggling stress, skipping rest, and refusing help are all signs of pride in disguise.

Proverbs 16:3 (*NIV*) says, "*Commit to the Lord whatever you do, and he will establish your plans.*" There's a divine exchange that happens when we let go of our agenda and pick up His. Our path straightens. Our steps are ordered. Our provision is released, not because we earned it, but because He promised it.

We want to be the kings of our own lives but still expect kingdom provision. It doesn't work that way. The path of surrender is the path of supply.

This is why intimacy with God is not a luxury; it's the source. When you abide in Him, you're not just checking boxes or hoping for blessings; you're walking in rhythm with the One who already authored your provision.

You start to notice how His timing protects you, His voice redirects you, and His grace empowers you.

That's the secret: staying on God's path is less about getting it all right and more about being willing to yield to Him every step of the way. That's where confidence grows. That's where abundance flows.

Reflection

I've learned that God doesn't just want to guide you occasionally; He wants you to live on His path. He wants His Word to be the compass, His Spirit to be the rhythm, and His abundance to be your portion, not as something you chase, but something you carry. Staying on God's path isn't just about obedience; it's about trust. It's about living from a place of daily surrender where your yes to Him is louder than the noise of the world.

We started this chapter talking about knowing your vision and eliminating distraction. Now you've seen how clarity is a gift that flows from intimacy. You don't need to force your future. You need to fellowship with the One who already holds it. And in that place of intimacy, the living Word becomes more than pages; it becomes your light, your anchor, your daily bread. Staying in the Word isn't religious duty; it's relational depth. It's how you discern, how you stay rooted, and how you recognize the counterfeit paths that try to lure you away.

He wants His Word to be the compass, His Spirit to be the rhythm, and His abundance to be your portion.

And finally, let's not forget this unshakable truth: The cross is God's abundance to you. There's no lack in His sacrifice. There's no striving in His provision. You don't earn this life, you receive it. When you truly receive what He's done, you stop begging for direction and start walking in divine assurance.

I don't know what distractions you've faced lately. I don't know what paths you've wandered or what pressures are demanding your attention. But I do know this: You were never meant to walk without Him. His Word will guide you. His Spirit will empower you. And His path will always lead to more than you imagined.

Stay on it. Not just because it's right, but because it's rich. Because it's where peace lives, where purpose flows, and where God's abundance meets you every single step of the way.

My Challenge to You

- Begin with Abiding, Not Scrolling: Each day, give God the first 10–20 minutes. Open the Word before you open your phone.
- Invite the Holy Spirit in Before Making Decisions: Pause and pray: "Holy Spirit, what do You want me to do here?" Wait long enough to sense His nudge.
- Speak Faith over Lack: Over your bills, needs, or deadlines; declare: "My Father supplies and leads; I will not fear."
- Create a Distraction Reset: When you notice you've drifted—stop, breathe, look up, and realign: "Jesus, I return my attention to You."
- Choose One Uncompromised Obedience: Identify one area where you've been wavering and obey today, no delay, no excuses.
- Walk the Narrow Path on Purpose: Remove one habit, input, or commitment that consistently pulls you off-course.
- Keep Your Eyes on Jesus: Place a reminder where you'll see it (sticky note, phone lock screen): "He is the Way."
- Review Your Steps Nightly: Ask: Where did I abide? Where did I hurry? What will I realign tomorrow? Jot two sentences in a journal.

- Measure Fruit, Not Frenzy: Look for peace, clarity, favor, and grace in your day—these are signs you're on His path.
- Give Thanks Out Loud: End the day by thanking Him for one leading and one provision you noticed.

Scripture References

John 15:7
Psalm 119:105
Isaiah 30:21
Proverbs 4:25–27
John 5:30
Proverbs 3:6
2 Corinthians 9:8
Romans 8:32
Colossians 2:14
Philippians 4:19
Philippians 4:6
1 Peter 5:7
Matthew 6:8
James 4:6
Proverbs 16:3

Chapter Nine

Realign, Refocus, Reignite

Introduction

Have you ever had that moment where you realize something just isn't right? You've been doing all the things, following the plan, keeping busy, and yet something inside of you feels unsettled. You're managing life, but you're not flourishing. You're active, but you're not aligned. I've been there too. And I've learned that when your spirit starts whispering, "Something needs to shift," it's often the Lord lovingly inviting you to realign, refocus, and reignite.

This chapter is for those of us who know God has more. It's for the weary, the overextended, the distracted, and the dreamers who've lost sight of what first stirred their hearts. Whether it's the demands of time, the pressure to provide, or the slow drift of striving in our own strength, God is calling us back. He's not condemning us; He's inviting us into clarity, into vision, and into peace.

There's a path marked by divine order, and it leads to overflow. But we don't arrive there by pushing harder. We arrive there by coming back to relationship. We realign with God's priorities. We refocus our vision through His eyes. And we reignite our purpose in the simplicity of saying yes again—yes to His voice, His way, His timing.

You may not have all your ducks in a row. You may feel like your time, finances, or even your faith are hanging by a thread. But I want to tell you, the thread of God's faithfulness is stronger. In fact, it's holding you even now.

We're going to explore what it means to walk away from pressure and step into peace. You'll discover how vision flows from relationship—not striving. And you'll learn how financial peace isn't about having more—it's about surrendering all.

Let's take this journey together. Let's get back on the right path; not by guilt or fear, but by grace. Because God isn't asking for your perfection, He's asking for your attention.

Fix Your Focus

Divine order always begins in the heart. Before we can walk in abundance, we must allow the Holy Spirit to gently expose where we've veered off course. It's easy to get caught up in the whirlwind of busyness or consumed by our own efforts to make life work. But God never asked us to carry it all. He's not impressed by how much we do; He's moved by how much we trust.

This chapter explores three vital areas where divine realignment takes place:

- Realign: We shift from self-effort to Spirit-led surrender. We recognize where we've been running ahead or lagging behind and return to the rhythm of His grace. This isn't about doing more; it's about being yielded to the One who already knows the way.

- Refocus: We clear the clutter and recenter our vision on Jesus. Relationship always precedes assignment. The moment we fix our eyes back on Him, clarity follows. We stop striving to figure it all out and start listening for what He's already speaking.
- Reignite: When we yield our time, talents, and trust, God breathes fresh fire into our lives. Dreams that felt dormant come alive. Confidence replaces confusion. Peace floods the areas that once caused panic. And our faith is no longer about surviving; it's about sowing, building, and overflowing.

Realignment is not a punishment—it's a rescue. Refocusing isn't shame—it's clarity. And reigniting isn't about performance—it's about purpose. As we walk through this chapter, let the Lord gently highlight where your heart has grown tired, where your hands have grown heavy, and where your hope may have flickered. Because His invitation remains: Come back to Me, and you'll find that everything you need is already waiting there.

Get Back on the Right Path

There comes a point in every believer's life where the Lord gently taps your heart and says, "Come back to Me, realign." It's not a shout of condemnation; it's a whisper of invitation. And the truth is, the longer we stay out of sync with Him, the easier it is to keep moving on autopilot, disconnected from the source.

For me, the moment I start to drift in my priorities, the Lord will show me, and I'll feel something unsettled. It's like I know I'm veering, and I have a choice: realign, or keep drifting. That moment of recognition isn't meant to shame you. It's the Spirit's way of calling you back to the better path. It's the voice of God showing His love for you.

So many believers live in a cycle of burnout and blame. They think, "If I just try harder, I'll get there." But divine order doesn't begin with doing—it begins with being. Being with Him. Abiding. When we're with Him, He doesn't hand us a checklist; He offers us peace. Clarity returns. Strength flows. Vision reignites.

God is not looking for a polished version of you; He's looking for a surrendered heart. A realigned spirit. One that says, "Lord, I'm coming back to the place where Your voice leads me, not my schedule." That's where everything changes.

The longer we stay out of sync with Him, the easier it is to keep moving on autopilot, disconnected from the source.

And the beautiful part is that His path is not hidden. He's not making you search for it in the dark. Psalm 32:8 says, "*I will instruct you and teach you in the way you should go; I will guide you with My eye.*" That's personal guidance. That's a Father saying, "I see what you can't see, let Me lead."

If you've felt distracted or discouraged—this is your moment. He's not angry; He's just waiting. Realignment is always available, and His path is always better than ours.

The Indicators of Drift

Spiritual drift doesn't always look dramatic. It often starts subtly, with busyness, distraction, or the weight of responsibility. You're still serving, still showing up, but something's off. You begin to react in the flesh instead of responding from the Spirit. You find yourself blaming others, avoiding quiet time, or even resenting the very things God once called you to.

I've seen this pattern again and again, not just in others, but in myself. That's why I've learned to ask, "Where am I right now? Am I walking in divine flow, or have I taken the reins back into my own hands?"

One of the greatest indicators that you're drifting is when pressure replaces peace. See, a driven life and a Spirit-led life look very different. The driven life runs on adrenaline, deadlines, and fear of failure. The Spirit-led life runs on joy, clarity, and grace.

You'll also know you're drifting when everything starts to feel like a chore instead of a calling. Your passion gets buried under performance. You feel exhausted, but that kind of exhaustion sleep doesn't fix. That's not just physical tiredness; that's soul tiredness. And that's your red flag.

It's in these moments that we must pause and listen, not for more instruction, but for an invitation back into intimacy. One of the most powerful indicators of misalignment is that we stop hearing God clearly, not because He stopped speaking, but because we stopped sitting still.

That's why we're reminded in Isaiah 30:15, "'*In returning and rest you shall be saved; In quietness and confidence shall be your strength.' But you would not.*" What a sobering reminder. It's not that strength wasn't available; it's that they wouldn't receive it God's way. They chose striving over stillness.

God doesn't reveal drift to condemn you; He reveals it to restore you. When you realize you've drifted, don't panic. Don't strive to fix it. Just return. Rest. Listen. Reignite the relationship. Because vision without relationship becomes striving, and striving always leads to burnout.

A Lifestyle of Constant Growth

God never calls us to settle. Growth in Him isn't seasonal; it's a lifestyle. It's what keeps our hearts tender, our ears tuned to His voice, and our lives available for His glory. When we stop growing, we start stagnating, and stagnation is a silent killer of vision.

If you're not growing in Christ, you're becoming more conformed to the world. There's no neutral ground. That might sound intense, but it's true. Kingdom living is progressive. There's always more of Him to know and more of you to surrender.

You can't just coast on yesterday's obedience. Real transformation comes when you pursue Him today, when you lean into truth even when it's uncomfortable, when you invite correction, and when you resist the temptation to perform instead of abiding. That's maturity. That's growth.

See, surrender is a daily choice. You surrender when you forgive, when you wait instead of rushing, when you let the Spirit speak before your emotions do.

Second Peter 3:18 says, "*But grow in the grace and knowledge of our Lord and Savior Jesus Christ.*" That word "grow" is present tense; it's active and ongoing. It doesn't say, "have grown." This means there's grace for where you are, but there's also a call to keep going. No matter how long you've walked with the Lord, there's still more.

Let me remind you that growth doesn't happen in chaos. It requires clarity, and clarity comes from abiding. John 15:5 reminds us: "*I am the vine, you* are *the branches. He who abides in Me, and I in him, bears much fruit; for without Me you can do nothing.*" True growth comes from staying connected. Not from striving. Not from comparing. From abiding.

If you're not growing in Christ, you're becoming more conformed to the world. There's no neutral ground.

A lifestyle of growth also transforms how you handle correction. When you're truly growing, correction isn't rejection—it's refinement. God disciplines those He loves, not to shame them, but to shape them into vessels that carry more of His presence.

So if you've felt stuck or plateaued, don't get discouraged. Just ask the Lord: "Where are You calling me to grow next?" It might be in patience. It might be in boldness. It might be in trust. But wherever He leads, growth is waiting, and with it comes fresh fire, fresh vision, and fresh abundance.

Discipline and the Spirit-Led Life

There's a misconception in the body of Christ that discipline and the Spirit don't go together, that if you're truly Spirit-led, everything will just "flow" without effort. But the truth is, a Spirit-led life requires discipline. Not the kind born of striving, but the kind forged in surrender.

Discipline doesn't compete with the Spirit; it clears space for the Spirit to lead. When you make choices ahead of time about what your priorities—what you'll say yes and no to, how you steward time, finances, and relationships—that's not legalism. That's spiritual maturity.

One of the things I've learned in years of ministry and missions is that the Holy Spirit has a calendar, but it doesn't look like ours. We fill our lives with appointments, demands, and expectations, then wonder why we feel burned out. But God calls us to live led, not driven. That requires intention.

You can't expect a Spirit-led life without choosing a disciplined one. If we're constantly reacting to life instead of responding to God, it's usually because we've let distractions take the driver's seat.

Discipline creates space for God to speak. It quiets the noise and brings focus back to what matters. That doesn't mean you become robotic or rigid; it means you give God your first and best, not your leftovers.

Discipline doesn't compete with the Spirit; it clears space for the Spirit to lead.

Hebrews 12:11 (*NIV*) reminds us, "*No discipline seems pleasant at the time, but painful. Later on, however, it produces a harvest of righteousness and peace for those who have been trained by it.*" Did you catch that? Discipline doesn't just bring peace; it trains us to receive it.

Discipline is what empowers you to say yes to your calling when comfort begs you to say no. It's what helps you steward your finances when fear says, "You don't have enough." And it's what gives you spiritual stamina when the assignment is long or the fruit seems delayed.

Being Spirit-led means being sensitive, but sensitivity requires stillness, and stillness requires discipline. It all connects. If you want to walk in vision that lasts, if you want to avoid burnout and bear fruit in every season, then let the Lord teach you discipline, not as a burden, but as a gift.

You don't have to do it in your own strength. You've got the Spirit of the Living God inside of you, and with Him, even your daily schedule can become an altar.

Vision Follows Relationship

We live in a world that constantly tells us we need a five-year plan, a backup strategy, and a social media rollout before we ever dare to take a step. But in the kingdom of God, vision doesn't come from spreadsheets; it flows from intimacy. I've learned that real vision for where I'm going never comes from working harder. It comes from being with the One who already knows the way.

When I was stepping into full-time missions, there were plenty of unknowns. I didn't have a marketing plan. I didn't have a fundraising team, but I had a deep relationship with the Lord, and that became my compass. Every time I paused to be with Him, He would realign my heart, open my eyes, and show me where to go next. I wasn't chasing opportunities; I was following peace.

The problem with just working harder is that it always places the burden of outcome on your own shoulders. You start thinking vision is something you have to manufacture rather than something you receive through abiding. But the Holy Spirit doesn't need your hustle; He needs your attention.

I remember during my years in Russia, there were moments when I felt the pressure to produce, to prove the mission was "working." But the Lord constantly reminded me that His pleasure wasn't in my performance, it was in His presence. When I stayed close to Him, provision came. Direction came. The right people showed up. The right doors opened. Not because I was trying to make it happen, but because I was aligned with the Lord.

"*Trust in the Lord with all your heart, And lean not on your own understanding; In all your ways acknowledge Him, And He shall direct your paths*" (Prov. 3:5–6).

This scripture has become a lifeline for me. Every time I've felt the pressure to "figure it all out," I return to this truth: My job is not to engineer the future. My job is to trust. And as I acknowledge Him in every step, He aligns the path under my feet. He directs it. He clarifies it.

Your vision doesn't need to be perfect; it just needs to be planted in His presence. You don't need to strive to get there. You just need to trust that He's already there.

Let God Be the Source, Not the Back-Up Plan

There's a temptation in all of us to treat God like our emergency contact. We want to chase our dreams, make our plans, secure our finances, and then check in with God if things don't work out. But that's not relationship. That's backup planning. The truth is, God was never meant to be our Plan B. He is the source.

We can say God is our provider but still live like we're our own savior. That's what pride does. It makes you feel like everything depends on you: your performance, your paycheck, your ability to fix what's broken. That pride is what keeps so many people locked out of God's abundance. They're praying for provision but still holding the reins.

I remember those moments early in missions when I was tempted to figure it all out myself. Fundraising, logistics, visas, it felt like I had to make it happen. But the Lord would gently remind me, "Carrie, I'm not here to fill in the gaps. I'm here to lead." When I surrendered, that's when provision flowed because I didn't force it; I chose to follow Him.

"*But seek first the kingdom of God and His righteousness, and all these things shall be added to you*" (Matt. 6:33).

God never said you had to take care of everything and then squeeze Him into the cracks. He said to seek Him first, and then He would take care of what you need. It's not about being irresponsible or pretending bills don't exist. It's about knowing that when you put Him first, you're no longer walking alone. You're walking with the One who sees the end from the beginning.

Stop asking God to support your plan. Start asking Him to lead it. Make Him the starting point, not the safety net. His abundance isn't reserved for your moment of desperation; it's available when you align with Him from the beginning.

Seed and Bread: Understanding God's Economy

God's provision is not random, and His economy doesn't work like the world's. In our own logic, we tend to think in terms of survival: pay the bills, stretch the budget, and maybe give if there's anything left. But God's economy functions on generosity, trust, and multiplication. When we understand the principle of seed and bread, it transforms how we live, give, and expect.

"*Now may He who supplies seed to the sower, and bread for food, supply and multiply the seed you have* sown *and increase the fruits of your righteousness*" (2 Cor. 9:10).

This verse was a game changer for me. For years, I believed that every dollar I received had to be either spent or given. But 2 Corinthians 9:10 helped me see that some of what comes into our hands is bread, daily provision for what we need, and some is seed, given to be sown, not consumed. That distinction set me free.

God never said you had to take care of everything and then squeeze Him into the cracks. He said to seek Him first, and then He would take care of what you need.

When you understand this, you stop being guilted into giving and start partnering with God in faith. You're not reacting to emotional pressure or fear. You're walking in relationship, asking, "Father, what is seed and what is bread?"

When I lived in Russia and couldn't work as a missionary, I had no paycheck, no guaranteed income. Yet, I saw supernatural provision for sixteen years. Why? Because God moved on people's hearts to sow, and He gave me seed to sow too. I wasn't just receiving, I was giving, even in the lean seasons. And it multiplied.

"*And you shall remember the* L*ORD* *your God, for* it is *He who gives you power to get wealth …*" (Deut. 8:18).

We often forget that even the power to produce income, your talent, strength, and energy, are a gift from Him. So, when that paycheck comes in, it's not yours to clutch. It's His. That's why we ask, "Lord, what part of this is bread to nourish what You've entrusted to me? And what part is seed to sow into what You want to grow?"

"*Give, and it will be given to you: good measure, pressed down, shaken together, and running over will be put into your bosom*" (Luke 6:38).

God's economy works on overflow, not lack. He's not interested in scraping by. He's a multiplier, but He multiplies what is sown, not what is hoarded. When you give by faith, trusting that He knows your needs, you release heaven's increase.

Don't be afraid of generosity. Be led by it. Let the Holy Spirit show you what's bread and what's seed. Don't spend what's meant to be sown, and don't sow what's meant to be eaten. It's not about formulas; it's about fellowship.

When we get this revelation, we step into peace. Financial stress lifts. Guilt lifts. Compulsion lifts. And what remains is the joy of walking in God's abundant, supernatural, relational provision.

Provision Lives in the Place of Obedience

We all want God's provision, but often we want it on our own terms. We want to keep our preferences, stay in our comfort zones, and still expect heaven's abundance. But God's provision doesn't follow our plan; it follows our obedience. Provision lives in the place where God told you to go.

Let's look back at a moment when God told Elijah to go to the brook Cherith during a famine: "*Then the word of the Lord came to him, saying, 'Get away from here and turn eastward, and hide by the Brook Cherith, which flows into the Jordan. And it will be* that *you shall drink from the brook, and I have commanded the ravens to feed you there*'" (1 Kings 17:2–4).

He's a multiplier, but He multiplies what is sown, not what is hoarded.

God had already commanded the provision but notice something important: it was located there. Not where Elijah wanted to be, not where it made sense, but at a specific location God appointed. The provision wasn't promised everywhere; it was promised there, in the place of obedience.

How many times have we found ourselves frustrated, wondering where God's provision is, while standing somewhere He never told us to be? Sometimes we drift into self-reliance. We step outside of God's instruction and then wonder why it's dry. But the Word says: "*If you are willing and obedient, You shall eat the good of the land*" (Is. 1:19).

Obedience isn't just about righteousness; it's about alignment. It positions you under the flow of God's blessing and it doesn't always look logical. Sometimes obedience means staying when you want to leave. Other times, it means stepping into something new when fear says you're not ready. But on the other side of obedience you'll find provision, not just financially, but in relationships, opportunities, clarity, peace, and your schedule.

I've seen this again and again. Even in missions, the provision didn't show up until I said yes. And it wasn't just about money; it included the grace, stamina, and divine connections that met me as I walked in what He said.

In Philippians 4:19, it says, "*And my God shall supply all your need according to His riches in glory by Christ Jesus.*"

Yes, He supplies—but according to His riches and not your plan. His riches are found in the place of surrender.

So if it feels dry, check your location. Are you where He told you to be? Or have you drifted into comfort, distraction, or control? The good news is—it only takes one decision to return. Realign your heart. Refocus your steps. Reignite your obedience, and the provision will meet you there.

Return to the Source

Sometimes the clearest sign that we are not where we should be is not open rebellion; it's exhaustion. It's the weariness that sets in when we've tried to carry too much, plan too far, or produce too fast—all without truly drawing from the source. We might be doing good things, even godly things, but if we're doing them apart from God, we will burn out.

In Jeremiah 2:13, the Lord speaks to His people: "*For My people have committed two evils: They have forsaken Me, the fountain of living waters, And hewn themselves cisterns—broken cisterns that can hold no water.*"

This is a sobering image. The people weren't running to idols; they were just running to themselves. They were trying to store up strength and security from a source that was never meant to hold it. That's what happens when we treat God like a Sunday appointment but live the rest of the week in our own wisdom.

Real growth is returning again and again to the source. It's recognizing when you've moved off the mark and choosing to let Him refresh you and lead you. It's not just about more time in the Word; it's about coming thirsty and ready to be filled.

Yes, He supplies—but according to His riches and not your plan.

As Jesus said: "*Whoever drinks of this water will thirst again, but whoever drinks of the water that I shall give him will never thirst. But the water that I shall give him will become in him a fountain of water springing up into everlasting life*" (John 4:13–14).

When you return to the source, it leads to overflow. You don't just get enough to make it through the day. You receive rivers of living water that pour into every dry place: your vision, finances, relationships, and your purpose.

Real growth is returning again and again to the source.

David knew this when he wrote Psalm 23:1-3: "*The Lord is my shepherd; I shall not want. He makes me to lie down in green pastures; He leads me beside the still waters. He restores my soul; He leads me in the paths of righteousness For His name's sake.*"

Realignment starts with a return to the Shepherd. Not to a routine. Not to a church service. To Him. Because He restores. He leads. He satisfies. And He knows exactly where your path needs to go next.

So pause. Take inventory. Have you been drawing from broken cisterns? Have you been running on fumes? If so, don't condemn yourself, realign yourself. Reignite the flame of intimacy and let the overflow return.

Your Peace Is Proof of His Presence

Peace is not the absence of problems; it's the evidence of God's presence. When you're walking with God, you don't have to manufacture peace through control or perfectionism. True peace comes when you're aligned with the will of God and yield to His provision, His timing, and His grace.

There's a temptation, especially when life feels chaotic, to wait for everything to settle before we feel peace. But that's not how peace in the kingdom of God works. The peace of God is not circumstantial; it's positional. You need to refocus on the truth, which is, you're seated in Christ. You're hidden in Him. And His peace is a fruit of that relationship, not a result of your effort.

There have been times when I faced real uncertainty. I remember one season in Russia when my visa situation was in limbo. I had done everything I knew to do in the natural. I submitted the forms, followed the process, but the doors just weren't opening. The stress was real. I knew that at any moment, I could be forced to leave the country and the people I had been called to. In the middle of that tension, the Lord reminded me that my circumstances weren't my source; He was.

I got quiet before Him, and I said, "Father, You didn't bring me this far to drop me now. I'm not going to let fear drive me. I choose peace." And in that place of trust, peace flooded my heart, not because the paperwork had been approved yet, but because I knew who held the outcome. That peace carried me through the uncertainty. And yes, God moved. The visa came through in a way only He could orchestrate. But I had already received His provision the moment I trusted Him with the process.

Philippians 4:6-7 says, "*Be anxious for nothing, but in everything by prayer and supplication, with thanksgiving, let your requests be made known to God; and the peace of God, which surpasses all understanding, will guard your hearts and minds through Christ Jesus.*"

God's peace guards you. It's like a shield that surrounds your heart and mind when you choose to bring everything—your calling, finances, decisions, and your fears to Him in prayer. So many people get shipwrecked in their faith, not because they lacked calling, but because they were overwhelmed with anxiety and fear around provision. They couldn't find peace in the process, so they gave up.

But when you adjust your focus and trust that God is not only with you but ahead of you, peace becomes your guide. You can rest, knowing that even if you don't see the full answer yet, He is already working on your behalf. Isaiah 26:3 tells us where to place our focus, "*You will keep* him *in perfect peace,* Whose *mind* is *stayed* on You, *Because he trusts in You.*"

I want you to look at Colossians 3:15: "*And let the peace of God rule in your hearts, to which also you were called in one body; and be thankful.*" That's powerful.

It is peace that is supposed to rule in your heart, not fear, not pressure, not chaos. It becomes the umpire in your decision-making, the litmus test for whether you're aligned with heaven's perspective or the world's anxiety.

God's peace guards you. It's like a shield that surrounds your heart and mind when you choose to bring everything—your calling, finances, decisions, and your fears to Him in prayer.

Sometimes the most spiritual thing you can do is pause long enough to realign your heart with the peace of God. Don't ignore the check in your spirit. Don't push forward just because something makes sense on paper. If there's no peace, it may not be the right time, the right assignment, or the right path.

This is how we live, realigned and refocused, by listening to the Spirit of peace. His presence in your life is not just a theological concept. It's a daily reality that brings calm into the storm and stability into your spirit.

When you rest in that peace, you're not just surviving, you're igniting. You're walking in a revelation that your life is not random. You're not alone. You're not behind. You're exactly where your Father has placed you. And that awareness kindles a fire that overflows because you're no longer trying to carry your future—He is.

Reflection

Sometimes the path back is the path forward. There is no shame in needing to realign. I've had to do it more times than I can count. That's the beauty of a relationship with God: it's not rigid or punishing, but redemptive and full of grace. Maybe you've drifted into striving, trying to prove yourself. Or maybe you've been carrying the financial weight of your life like it all depends on you. Maybe your vision has grown dim because you've been running on empty.

The good thing is, there's a way back. And it's not complicated. It's not full of rules. It's about presence.

As we return to relationship, where the Spirit leads, we begin to see again. We begin to dream again. That's the divine order. And from that place, abundance isn't something we fight for; it flows naturally from the hand of our Father, who knows what we need and delights to give it.

Sometimes the path back is the path forward. There is no shame in needing to realign.

Every place of surrender becomes a place of peace. And every place of peace becomes proof that you are exactly where you're meant to be, under the shadow of His wings, in the fullness of His provision, and right in the middle of His plan.

If you've gotten off track, don't condemn yourself. Realign. Refocus. Reignite. He's here for you, and He's simply inviting you back into the place where His presence leads, and your peace follows.

My Challenge to You

- Pause for Inventory: Take 10 quiet minutes today and write down the areas where pressure has replaced peace, your schedule, finances, vision, or identity.
- Ask the Spirit for Clarity: Pray, "Holy Spirit, show me where I've drifted from abiding." Listen without fear of shame; He reveals truth to heal, not condemn.
- Lay Down the Weight: Identify one commitment, burden, or thought pattern you've been carrying that He never asked you to. Surrender it to Him in prayer.
- Take One Obedient Step: Choose either to release what isn't yours or to courageously say yes to something He's been nudging you toward. Keep it simple, just one step.
- Let Peace Lead: As you act, let peace be your compass. If peace increases, keep walking that way. If peace lifts, pause and realign.
- Repeat Daily: Each morning, ask: "Am I striving, or am I abiding?" Then reset your heart to follow His presence.
- Celebrate Progress: At the end of the week, note one area where peace has replaced pressure. Thank God for restoring clarity.

Scripture References

Psalm 32:8
Isaiah 30:15
2 Peter 3:18
John 15:5
Hebrews 12:11
Proverbs 3:5–6
Matthew 6:33
2 Corinthians 9:10
Deuteronomy 8:18
Luke 6:38
1 Kings 17:2–4
Isaiah 1:19
Philippians 4:19
Jeremiah 2:13

John 4:13–14
Psalm 23:1–3
Philippians 4:6–7
Isaiah 26:3
Colossians 3:15

Chapter Ten

Redefining Success

Introduction

Sometimes we treat success like a moving target, one we chase with to-do lists, ambition, and pressure. We don't stop to ask: "Who told us this was success in the first place?" If it wears us out, steals our joy, and leaves us comparing ourselves to others, maybe we've bought into the wrong definition.

The Lord has been teaching me that real success is not about doing everything; it's about doing the right thing. And the "right thing" starts with seeking Him, not just with part of our hearts, but with focus and intentionality. When we chase worldly definitions of productivity, we'll always feel behind. But when we pause and let God define success, we find peace.

Prosperity is soul-deep. It's what happens when the Word of God comes alive in you, and you start recognizing that His grace, His provision, and His wisdom already live inside of you.

This chapter is about redefining success. It's about asking better questions: "Lord, what are You doing? Where are You leading? What does success look like to You in this season?" And when you live with that kind of heart posture, you'll see that success doesn't trap you, it launches you into the joy of kingdom impact.

We're going to explore what it looks like to live from the inside out, to lead from intimacy, and to give from overflow. This kind of life doesn't happen accidentally; it happens when we realign our hearts with Heaven's values. And when we do that, we discover a kind of success that doesn't burn out, break down, or fade away. We discover a life that's abundant, eternal, and powerful.

Fix Your Focus

I want to talk about the kind of success heaven applauds. We've been taught to measure success by what we produce, how much we check off, how busy we are, and how fast we go. But heaven doesn't applaud busyness. Heaven looks for faith. Heaven looks for obedience. Heaven looks for the fruit that comes from abiding.

I want to flip the script on the world's version of productivity and prosperity. We are not called to do all things. We're called to do the right things: His things. That means you don't have to carry the weight of figuring everything out. The answers are already within you, because the Spirit of God is within you. And from that place of intimacy with Him, success will come.

Abundance, too, is often misunderstood. It's not about stockpiling wealth or proving spiritual strength by showing off what we own. True abundance is a kingdom force; it's joy, wisdom, peace, generosity, and divine provision flowing through your life to touch others. The prosperity of God is meant to go beyond your bills and budgets; it's meant to overflow into nations and generations.

As we walk through this chapter, we're going to realign our vision with God's heart, refocus our definition of success to match His Word, and reignite our faith in the provision, wisdom, and destiny already planted inside of us. You'll see that true success isn't something you achieve. It's something you walk in when your eyes are fixed on Him.

Breaking Free from the Trap of More

We live in a world that constantly tells us we have to do more, be more, have more. It's this relentless pressure to stay busy, to work harder, to keep up. But let me ask you something: Have you ever stopped and asked, "Who told me that I have to live like this?"

See, the world's version of success is loud and fast. It's jam-packed schedules, burnout masked as productivity, and a never-ending list of demands. And before you know it, you're exhausted, emotionally, mentally, even spiritually. You're running at a pace God never asked you to run. The trap of more makes it feel as if you're not constantly producing; you're falling behind. But let me tell you—that is not how God defines success.

The prosperity of God is meant to go beyond your bills and budgets; it's meant to overflow into nations and generations.

God never called you into chaos. He called you into peace. His way is marked by rest, clarity, and focus. There's a constant pull from the world to value a packed calendar as if that's proof of purpose. But our value doesn't come from busyness; it comes from abiding in Him. You can't produce spiritual fruit from a place of spiritual exhaustion.

In Isaiah 26:3, it says, "*You will keep* him *in perfect peace,* Whose *mind* is *stayed* on You, *Because he trusts in You.*"

Too many people jump into action before they've even heard from God. We run with a vague sense of "calling" but no vision from relationship. And when we don't start with Him, we end up with confusion. Vision becomes blurred, energy is wasted, and we start spinning our wheels. That's not kingdom productivity. That's worldly chaos dressed up to look like purpose.

You've got to redefine success through God's lens. And that starts with learning how to say no, not just to sin, but to anything He didn't call you to do. Even good things can become distractions if they're not God things. You weren't created to chase outcomes. You were created to walk with Him.

Prosperity isn't about piling on more tasks or pushing harder. Prosperity starts in the soul. It's peace, vision, and joy that come from knowing who you are in Him. That kind of internal abundance lets you step off the hamster wheel of performance and into Spirit-led fruitfulness.

You can't produce spiritual fruit from a place of spiritual exhaustion.

In Philippians 4:7 (*NIV*), it says, "*And the peace of God, which transcends all understanding, will guard your hearts and your minds in Christ Jesus.*"

So take a breath. You don't have to prove yourself to God. He's not measuring you by your output. Focus on the fact that God is inviting you into His presence and His peace. He wants to guard your heart and mind. And in that presence, you'll find the pace you were actually designed for.

Lay Down the Burden of Figuring It Out

I want to share with you one of the most freeing things you'll ever learn in your walk with God: you're not the author of your own success. You don't have to map out every step of your journey or carry the weight of figuring everything out. Success in the kingdom of God isn't about what you can figure out; it's about what you yield to. When you seek the Lord and invite Him into your day, His wisdom fills the gaps where your own understanding runs out.

You might feel pressure to "get it all right," to know exactly what to do, where to go, and how it's all going to work. But that's not how the Spirit leads. He doesn't expect you to have the whole blueprint. He simply calls you to seek Him. His voice will guide you one step at a time. When I'm walking with the Lord and I get into His presence, it becomes clear that my job isn't to strategize; it's to listen. His voice carries the power to direct, to correct, and to protect.

There's something so powerful about letting go of the burden of performance. That drive to strive, to impress, or to succeed by the world's standards will only lead to burnout. You can be doing many "good" things and still be completely missing God's best if you haven't taken time to be still and hear Him. We sometimes confuse productivity with obedience. But God's definition of fruitfulness is rooted in relationship, not results

Success in the kingdom of God isn't about what you can figure out; it's about what you yield to.

I remember a time in my life when I felt like I had to have all the answers. I was trying to be five steps ahead of God instead of walking beside Him. And what I learned, and what I continue to relearn, is that the pressure to "figure it all out" is a trap. It's rooted in fear, not faith. But when I turn to the Lord and say, "Okay, what's today's step?", He meets me with clarity, peace, and supernatural wisdom.

Abundance is tied to revelation. It's not just about what you hold in your hands; it's about what you see through the eyes of faith. When you're intimate with the Word, it begins to shape your decisions and your direction. You start to live with a confidence that doesn't come from having a perfect plan; it comes from knowing the Planner.

I want you to look at this verse in Philippians 4:19 (*NIV 1984*): "*And my God will* [supply] *all your needs according to his glorious riches in Christ Jesus.*"

You don't need to have it all figured out. He will supply all your needs. You just need to stay close. God is not expecting perfection; He's inviting connection. He wants to walk with you, guide you, and unfold His plans as you trust Him. And in that surrender, you'll find a kind of success that the world can't offer and a peace the world can't take away.

Prioritize His Voice over Pressure

There are times we get so used to the pressure of the world that we forget it's not our portion. Our lives begin to follow this default rhythm of deadlines, expectations, and productivity, and before long, we're led by pressure instead of presence. But success in the kingdom isn't about frantic activity; it's about intentional intimacy.

I used to come to the Lord with a long list of things I needed Him to approve or accomplish. But then He gently reminded me: "I didn't ask you to come with a plan. I asked you to come to Me." I didn't have to manufacture success; all I had to do was listen. I had to prioritize His voice over the pressure to perform.

The pressure to be productive can feel spiritual, especially when it's tied to ministry or vision. But God's voice doesn't push; it leads. You see, real success begins with intimacy. You can be working hard, even in your calling, and still be missing the voice of the One who called you. That's why pressure is never a substitute for presence.

Scripture makes this beautifully clear in 2 Corinthians 8:7, which reminds us, "*But just as you excel in everything—in faith, in speech, in knowledge, in complete earnestness, and in the love we inspired in you—see that you also excel in this grace of giving*" (*Berean Standard Bible*). The grace of giving is about more than just finances; it's about surrendering your pace, priorities, and the pressure to perform to His leading. When we learn to excel in earnestness and wholehearted passion led by the Spirit, we're actually aligning with His abundant life.

Success Isn't Found in Performance

I used to live in a place of drive. I wanted to do it all and do it all well, especially ministry and the things God had called me to. But if I'm honest, there were seasons where it became more about performing than partnering. I'd measure my value by how much I accomplished. And I think many of us fall into that same trap, especially when the world constantly flashes its version of success: productivity, speed, recognition, and results.

Your value is found in your identity as a child of God. And if you don't know who you are, if you're not walking in that place of grace, you'll always be trying to prove something to God, to people, or even to yourself.

In Deuteronomy 8:18 (*KJV*), it says, "*But thou shalt remember the* L*ORD thy God: for* it is *he that giveth thee power to get wealth, that he may establish his covenant which he swore unto thy fathers, as* it is *this day*." That verse isn't about striving to earn; it's about remembering the source. He gives the power. He gives the wisdom. He gives the anointing. Our job isn't to make things happen. We are to stay connected to God, who can make things happen.

One of the greatest traps I see in the body of Christ is the idea that we have to earn God's approval or the approval of others through what we accomplish. That pressure to "do" can quietly creep into our walk with God until performance replaces relationship. And before we realize it, we're no longer walking in the joy of intimacy with God. Instead, we're managing an image, a reputation, or a goal.

I've had to unlearn that in my own journey. I remember when I felt like my value was tied to the number of meetings I led, lessons I taught, or things I built. But God, in His grace, reminded me that He didn't call me to build an empire. He called me to walk with Him. That's success. That's where abundance flows from.

God's definition of prosperity is always tied to His covenant. It's not about success for self; it's about impact through surrender. And that starts when we stop striving to perform and start living from the place of being known and loved by God.

There's a grace in knowing that you're already accepted. There's freedom in no longer needing to prove your worth through effort. The most productive thing you can do today might be to sit at His feet, listen to His voice, and let Him remind you that you are His. That's the place where real success begins.

Your Daily Path Is His Assignment

I think we often make the mistake of thinking that success is out there somewhere, in the future, in a bigger opportunity, on a better platform. But success is found right here, as we walk with the Holy Spirit right now. I don't have to stress about how I'm going to get from A to Z. My job is to stay present and in step with Him today.

There's pressure in the world to have everything figured out, to have your year mapped, your five-year vision in place, and your productivity tracked. But that's not how the Lord leads. He doesn't demand the whole plan from you. He simply asks for your heart and your yes.

We try to make everything fit perfectly on a vision board, titles, timelines, and positions. But if we're not careful, we become so focused on what the vision is "supposed" to look like that we miss the invitations of God in our daily steps. We end up idolizing the vision instead of trusting the Author of it.

There is a beautiful gift we can give the Lord, which is the stewardship of our time. And that stewardship doesn't always look flashy. It looks like asking the Lord, "What do You have for me today?" And then trusting that what He places in front of you matters.

Your time is the most powerful seed you can give to God. Because when we give Him our time, our attention, our willingness to be led, He takes it and multiplies it in ways we never could.

There were seasons when I used my time trying to prove something: that I could do it, that I could make things happen. But the more I pushed, the more I missed the peace that comes from time spent just walking with God. That's what I want more than anything now. I want to walk with Him, not run ahead of Him, not drag my feet behind Him, but truly walk with Him.

I can't tell you how many times I thought something was a small step, taking a phone call, helping a student, stopping to pray for someone, but those "small" assignments turned out to be the exact thing God was using to align everything else. That's how the kingdom works. It's often in the ordinary where the extraordinary unfolds.

I want you to think about this: God calls us to be faithful, not flashy. The world will try to define success by visibility. But in the kingdom, success is found in obedience. And often, obedience looks like giving

God your "today"—your schedule, your interruptions, your unknowns. Sometimes we undervalue our obedience because it doesn't feel strategic. But I've learned that obedience is always prophetic. He's not just giving you something to do; He's releasing His vision through you.

The Grace of Giving Is Excellence

Excellence in the kingdom isn't about wealth or applause. It's about stewardship—how we handle what has been entrusted to us. I've met believers who feel disqualified from generosity because they assume they don't have "enough" to give. But God's definition of generosity isn't measured by amount; it's measured by the heart. It's the grace to give. That's true abundance.

Prosperity is not about storing up. It's about pouring out. When we talk about the grace of giving, we're talking about more than finances. We're talking about time, energy, encouragement, leadership—whatever God has placed in your hand. That's your seed. And excellence says, "I'll sow it with joy."

There's a grace in knowing that you're already accepted. There's freedom in no longer needing to prove your worth through effort.

What I've learned over the years is that lack doesn't define generosity; obedience does. I've given in times when I didn't have overflow in the natural, but there was an overflow in the Spirit, and I responded to God's prompting. And do you know what happened? Provision followed. Not because I forced it, but because I obeyed.

Sometimes we want to give like someone else. We look at their resources and think, "Well, if I had that, I'd be generous too." But comparison kills obedience. God's not asking you to give like them. He's inviting you to partner with Him in the way He designed you.

Generosity is part of the vision. Vision doesn't exist to benefit you; it's designed to flow through you. Your calling and generosity are inseparably connected. You'll never fulfill the fullness of your purpose if you're holding back your seed.

I've seen this repeatedly on the mission field. When we gave to others, even when it seemed small, it created space for supernatural return, not just for us, but for the people we were called to serve. That's the kind of excellence God is after. Not perfect performance, but intentional, obedient generosity.

You don't need a title, a platform, or a lush bank account to live generously. You just need a willing heart. When you release what's in your hand, God releases what's in His. That's grace. That's excellence.

Prosperity Is a Funnel, Not a Trophy

The world sees prosperity as a trophy, something you win, display, and use to elevate yourself. But in the kingdom of God, prosperity is a funnel. It's not about accumulation; it's about distribution. When God blesses you, it's not just for you. It's to flow through you into the lives of others. That's how nations are reached. That's how vision becomes impact.

I remember a time when I had to decide whether to cling to what I had or release it in obedience. Every time I chose generosity, something shifted. It wasn't just about money. Sometimes it was time. Sometimes it was encouragement. Sometimes it was stepping into opportunities that seemed small but carried eternal weight. Prosperity is so much bigger than a bank account; it's about being a vessel God can trust.

In Mark 8:36–37 (*ESV*), Jesus asks, "*What does it profit a man to gain the whole world and forfeit his soul? For what can a man give in return for his soul?*" It's a sobering reminder that success without surrender is empty. You can have everything the world applauds and still miss what matters most. But when you live as a funnel of His abundance, when your life becomes a channel of His love, provision, and truth, you start to walk in success that has eternal value.

One of the lies the enemy whispers is that you have to protect what you've been given. But kingdom prosperity doesn't shrink when it's shared; it multiplies. I've seen it over and over again. We would step out to fund missions, help students, sow into nations, and somehow, we never lacked. In fact, we were more full, more alive, more clear on our purpose than ever before.

Real success is about who's being reached through your life. When you understand that prosperity is a tool for transformation, you stop measuring your life by what you have, and start asking, "Lord, what do You want to do through me today?"

Poverty Is a Lie Against Purpose

There's a lie the enemy whispers into the hearts of believers: "If you don't have enough, you don't qualify." That lie is crafted to isolate, disqualify, and discourage. But I've seen repeatedly in my life and in the lives of others that provision is not the starting line for purpose; obedience is. God never told us to wait until we had enough. He told us to trust Him.

I remember being in Russia and having a deep desire to do more, to expand, to reach more people, to pour into the church. However, I didn't always have the physical resources in front of me. What I did have, though, was a Word from God and a heart ready to obey. And every time I said yes to the call, even when it didn't make sense financially, He showed up. Money followed purpose. Provision followed faith.

Sometimes we look at our bank accounts, our resumes, or our ministry titles, and we think we're disqualified from doing something big. But God doesn't qualify us based on our wealth. He qualifies us based on our willingness to trust Him. You don't have to be wealthy to be impactful. You just have to be obedient.

When I look back at the most powerful moves of God in my life, they didn't start with financial abundance. They started with a step of faith. And many times, that step looked crazy. But here's what I've learned: God gives seed to the sower, not the keeper. He's not trying to figure out how much you have. He's looking at how much you're willing to release. He's not asking you to fund your purpose. He's asking you to believe that He already has.

Real success is about who's being reached through your life.

Jeremiah 33:3 (*NIV*) says, "*Call to me and I will answer you and tell you great and unsearchable things you do not know.*" That's not just a promise of revelation; it's a promise of divine strategy. When you call on Him, He gives you insights that no budget could plan for. He opens doors you didn't even know existed.

That's why poverty is such a demonic strategy. It's not just about a lack of money. It's about shutting down vision. It's about convincing you that you're disqualified before you even start. But the Word of God declares something completely different. In Psalm 147:11 (*NIV*), it says, "*The* Lord *delights in those who fear him, who put their hope in his unfailing love.*" That means your value, capacity, and worth are not tied to your bank account. It's tied to His love.

I've met people with very little who have had a massive kingdom impact. Why? Because they knew who their source was. And I've seen people with a lot who never moved in purpose because they were too busy trying to protect what they had. God isn't looking for people who can fund their vision. He's looking for people who will trust Him to fulfill His.

Let me encourage you: don't let lack lie to you. If you've been believing that you need to wait until you have more to do what God's called you to do, that is not the voice of God. He says, "Call to Me." He says, "I will show you great things." He says, "I am your source."

There is nothing too small for Him to use. Not your story. Not your gift. Not your finances. He multiplies the surrendered, not the stored. And if you'll trust Him, He'll take your obedience and expand your reach in ways that impact eternity.

Expand Your Vision: Nations Await

When you understand that prosperity isn't just for you, everything changes. It's not about accumulation; it's about assignment. God never gives us more so we can simply enjoy comfort. He gives us more so we can carry more, serve more, give more, and reach further. Prosperity is kingdom fuel, and its reach is global.

I've seen this firsthand through our missions. There was a time when I was doing work in a closed nation, and we were ministering in underground churches, places where Bibles were scarce and public worship was dangerous. We weren't there to just hand out money. We were there to bring the message of the Gospel, to equip leaders, and to empower believers to know their authority in Christ. But here's what I noticed: financial partnership made that trip possible. People I'd never

> *That's why poverty is such a demonic strategy. It's not just about a lack of money. It's about shutting down vision.*

met gave and prayed, and because of their generosity, the Gospel went where I couldn't go alone.

The enemy would love to keep your vision small, limited to your own bills, your own family, your own city. But that's not how the kingdom works. God's economy is always outward-facing. That's why when people say, "Well, I don't need much. I'm content," I want to gently challenge that thinking. That mindset might be noble on the surface, but it can become selfish if it stops you from stepping into what God wants to do through you for others.

In Proverbs 8:17 (*NIV*), it says, "*I love those who love me, and those who seek me find me.*" There have been so many times I've watched God connect people across nations simply because someone sought Him and said yes. They didn't have all the answers. They didn't have the resources upfront, but they had a heart to partner with heaven, and that was enough.

I took a trip to Africa, where we were ministering in a region that had been heavily impacted by poverty and religious oppression. We were able to bring resources, yes, but more importantly, we brought training. We invested in leaders, we cast vision, and those pastors went back to their churches with a fire and understanding that they could impact their communities, not by waiting for foreign aid, but by walking in kingdom identity.

That's what true prosperity looks like: it multiplies, trains, equips, and sends. God didn't bless us to hoard the blessing. He blessed us to release it into the nations.

We're told in Jeremiah 29:11–13 (*NIV*), "*For I know the plans I have for you," declares the Lord, "plans to prosper you and not to harm you, plans to give you hope and a future. Then you will call on me and come and pray to me, and I will listen to you. You will seek me and find me when you seek me with all your heart.*" That promise isn't just personal. It's generational. It's international. It's prophetic.

If you think prosperity is just about paying your bills and having a little extra, your vision is too small. God is raising up givers, partners, senders, and goers. And when your finances become an instrument of impact, not only are others changed, but you are too.

I've watched countless people step into this. They get a vision for missions. They start giving even when it stretches them. And then God begins opening doors, aligning assignments, and funding the very dreams they didn't even know how to pray for yet. That's the ripple effect of kingdom prosperity. It doesn't end with you; it flows through you into the nations.

So lift your eyes. Think bigger. Ask God how He wants to use what's in your hands. Because somewhere out there, someone is waiting on your obedience. And your yes might just be the bridge to their breakthrough.

God's Definition of More than Enough

Do you understand now that abundance isn't just about money? It's not a salary bracket or a certain number in your savings account. Abundance is a mindset, and it's the revelation of who you are in Christ, plus what you already have access to in Him. If we don't understand that, we'll keep looking for more while living like we're lacking.

That's what true prosperity looks like: it multiplies, trains, equips, and sends. God didn't bless us to hoard the blessing.

When I think about more than enough, I don't think about wealth accumulation. I think about what happens when you know your source and live connected to Him. That's the abundance I want the body of Christ to walk in. Not just the ability to pay bills or be generous, but the deep, abiding confidence that everything you need is already yours in Christ.

There's such a beautiful picture in John 10:10 (*NIV*), where Jesus says, "*The thief comes only to steal and kill and destroy; I have come that they may have life, and have it to the full.*" That word "full" isn't halfway. It's not survival. It's not just enough to scrape by. Jesus came to give us overflowing life, and that life touches every area: peace, joy, provision, direction, purpose, vision, and relationships.

You can live in a shack and walk in abundance. You can live in a mansion and still be in lack because abundance is about who's leading your life. When Jesus is your Shepherd, when you're abiding in Him, everything changes—not always externally first, but always internally.

I've experienced this so many times. There were moments where we didn't have "enough." The numbers didn't line up. The provision hadn't shown up yet. But in my spirit, I wasn't lacking anything. I had peace. I had direction. I had confidence in His faithfulness, and that's what carried us. That's what still carries us.

One of the things I love about Proverbs 4:10–13 is how it speaks to this internal posture of abundance through wisdom. "*Hear, my son, and accept my sayings And the years of your life will be many. I have directed you in the way of wisdom; I have led you in upright paths. When you walk, your steps will not be impeded; And if you run, you will not stumble. Take hold of instruction; do not let go. Guard her, for she is your life*" (*New American Standard Bible 1995*). That's abundance. A life that's directed, protected, and filled with wisdom, and it's not because you're perfect, but because you're led.

There's nothing wrong with believing for provision. In fact, we should! But the real breakthrough comes when you stop measuring God's faithfulness by what's in your bank account and start measuring it by what's alive in your spirit.

In 1 Corinthians 2:9 (*NIV*), Paul reminds us, "*No eye has seen ... no ear has heard, and ... no human mind has conceived—the things God has prepared for those who love him.*" That's what you have access to, not just survival-level grace but unimaginable goodness stored up for you in relationship with Him.

So what does redefining success really mean? It means aligning with His definition. It means recognizing that abundance starts with identity; that your inheritance isn't pending, it's present. That Jesus didn't die just to get you to heaven but to bring heaven into you now. You already have more than enough. Because you already have Him.

The Overflow Isn't Just for You

One of the most freeing revelations you can have about abundance is that it was never meant to stop with you. God's blessings are not containers; they're channels. When you receive His love, His provision, and His promises, they're designed to spill into the lives of others. The kingdom is always multiplying, always advancing, always reaching beyond one person to touch nations and generations.

Jesus said in Matthew 25:34 (*ESV*), "*Then the King will say to those on His right, 'Come, you who are blessed by my Father, inherit the kingdom prepared for you from the foundation of the world.'*" This inheritance is not just a personal comfort; it's a commissioning. The moment you receive from Him, you step into a kingdom prepared long before you were born—a kingdom where your life becomes a living invitation for others to taste and see His goodness.

I've seen this firsthand through missions, teaching, and personal ministry. Sometimes it has been in a stadium filled with people hungry for the Word; other times it's been in a small village, sitting with one family and watching the Word transform their perspective. The common thread is that what God gives you is always bigger than you, and it's never meant to stay in your possession alone.

When you walk closely with God, your life becomes an overflow point. Peace overflows into anxious hearts. Joy overflows into places of sorrow. Provision overflows into situations of need. Even your testimony becomes a seed that God plants in the soil of another person's heart. You might never fully see the harvest in this lifetime, but you can be sure that heaven keeps a perfect record of every seed sown.

We live in a culture that teaches us to measure success by what we accumulate. But kingdom success is measured by how much flows through us, not just to us. When you allow God's abundance to move unhindered through your life—your resources, your time, and your prayers—you become a vessel that carries His heart into places you could never reach on your own.

The more you give yourself away in obedience, the more room you make for God to pour in fresh supply. That's why in the kingdom, you never have to fear running out. Your overflow isn't just a blessing to others; it's the very evidence that the kingdom of God is alive and moving through you.

Reflection

If the world had its way, you'd be constantly chasing—chasing goals, validation, even your worth. But when you step into kingdom success, all that chasing stops because you finally realize it's already yours.

You don't have to run faster or do more to be seen by God. You don't have to figure it all out to be used by Him. You don't have to measure your value by numbers, platforms, or applause. Success has a new definition. It's Jesus. It's intimacy. It's obedience. It's stewardship of the small things with great trust. It's living open-handed and fully surrendered, knowing that His plans are better, bigger, and more abundant than anything you could build on your own.

I've watched God redefine my idea of success many times, not by stripping things away, but by revealing what matters most. He's after your heart, not your hustle. From that surrendered heart, true impact flows, an impact that touches families, nations, and generations.

> *The more you give yourself away in obedience, the more room you make for God to pour in fresh supply.*

This journey isn't about perfecting that five-year plan. It's about walking with our perfect God today. Real success isn't earned; it's inherited. And you've already received it in Christ.

My Challenge to You

- Ask the Lord to Redefine Success: In prayer, invite Him to show you if your definition of success has been shaped more by pressure, performance, or worldly expectations than by His Word.
- Identify Where You're Striving: Write down the areas of your life where you feel you're "managing" in your own strength rather than abiding in His presence.
- Listen for His Correction: Let the Holy Spirit expose what is distracting or draining you. Be willing to hear Him as He highlights both both the subtle and obvious things pulling you away.
- Surrender the Burden: Trade the need to prove yourself for the joy of partnering with Him. Consciously lay down self-effort and invite Him to carry the weight.
- Adopt God's Definition: Ask, "Lord, what does success look like to You in this season?" Write down the words, impressions, or pictures He gives you.
- Commit to One Obedient Step: Choose one area where you will walk out His definition this week—whether it's resting when He says rest, or moving forward in boldness when He prompts.

- Celebrate Jesus in You: At the end of the week, reflect: *Did my choices look like peace, purpose, and Jesus living big in me?* Thank Him for being faithful to lead.

Scripture References

Philippians 4:7
Isaiah 26:3
Philippians 4:19
2 Corinthians 8:7
Deuteronomy 8:18
Mark 8:36–37
Jeremiah 33:3
Psalm 147:11
Proverbs 8:17
Jeremiah 29:11–13
John 10:10
Proverbs 4:10–13
1 Corinthians 2:9
Matthew 25:34

Chapter Eleven

Rest Is a Strategy

Introduction

When we think about strategies for success, most of us picture action, plans, deadlines, and constant motion. The world applauds busyness, equating movement with progress. But in the kingdom, one of the most powerful strategies you can embrace is rest. Rest isn't laziness, passivity, or a lack of ambition. It's a deliberate choice to step out of the noise and into the presence of God, letting Him set the pace and direct your steps.

I've learned that rest is where clarity is born. In the stillness, your heart becomes quiet enough to hear His whisper. Rest is where striving ends and trust begins. It's the posture that says, "Lord, I believe You can lead me better than I can lead myself."

When you rest in Him, you're not falling behind; you're actually arriving prepared. You enter your assignments already full, already anchored, already clear on your direction. And because your heart is established in His promises, you carry an authority and peace that no schedule, meeting, or deadline could ever produce.

Rest isn't wasted time; it's seed time. It's the space where God plants wisdom, renews vision, and strengthens your faith so that when you step into action, you're moving with precision and purpose. This is how you prosper through the Word, by letting it saturate your heart until it shapes your decisions, your pace, and your very definition of success.

In this chapter, we're going to discover that rest is more than a pause in the action; it's the very strategy God uses to release direction, prepare you for purpose, and cause you to flourish.

Fix Your Focus

Rest is not a reward you get after you've done enough; it's a position you live from in Christ. In the world's system, rest is often the opposite of productivity. But in God's kingdom, rest is the foundation for it. True rest is rooted in trust. You must trust that God's timing is perfect, that His Word is enough, and that His Spirit is faithful to lead you into every good work prepared in advance for you. When you embrace rest, you quiet the competing voices that demand constant activity and make room to hear the one voice that matters most, which, of course, is His voice. This rest positions you to receive direction before you take a single step, to arrive fully prepared when opportunity comes, and to prosper in every assignment because you're walking in the wisdom and strength of the Word. Rest is not the absence of work; it's the alignment of your work with God's pace, priorities, and power. Rest is choosing to believe that while you pause, God is still working. And often, it's in those pauses that we receive the clearest direction for our next steps.

When you rest in Him, you're not falling behind; you're actually arriving prepared.

Rest Is More than Stopping

When most people think of rest, they imagine taking a nap, going on vacation, or zoning out in front of a screen. But biblical rest is far deeper than that. It's not the absence of activity; it's the presence of God's leadership in the middle of life's demands. Rest is the clarity that comes when you've laid down the weight of running your own life and chosen to be led by His Spirit. It's the security of knowing that your steps are ordered by Him, even when the schedule is full and the pressures are real.

I used to think that if I could just get everything on my to-do list finished, then I'd finally be able to rest. But here's the truth: life doesn't stop handing you more things to do. If you wait until there's nothing left on your plate before you rest, you'll never get there. Real rest is learning to trust in the middle of the "too much." Proverbs 3:5–6 says, "*Trust in the Lord with all your heart, And lean not on your own understanding; in all your ways acknowledge Him, And He shall direct your paths.*" That kind of trust is active, and it's a daily choice to shift from relying on my own strategy to leaning into His wisdom.

There was a season when I said yes to almost everything people asked of me. I thought it was what ministry was supposed to look like, being everywhere, doing everything, helping everyone. But slowly, my peace began to drain away. I didn't realize it at the time, but I was leaning on my own understanding. I was measuring my worth by my productivity. It wasn't until the Lord stopped me in prayer and asked, "Who told you to do all these things?" that I realized I was carrying assignments He had never given me. That moment was a wake-up call.

When I started practicing true rest, it wasn't about doing less; it was about doing only what He asked. Some days that meant stepping into big, faith-filled assignments. Other days it meant saying no to good things so I could be available for the God things. Rest—along with acknowledging Him in all my ways and letting Him make my paths straight—became my heart's posture. That shift changed not just my schedule but the way I approached every decision. I began showing up to each assignment full. I was full of the Word, full of revelation, and full of grace to pour out because I was no longer running on my own strength.

Rest isn't passivity; it's power under His control. It's the confidence that comes from knowing that the outcome doesn't depend on me working harder but on staying connected to Him. When you discover that kind of rest, you stop trying to earn God's approval or keep pace with the world's demands. Instead, you learn to walk in step with the Spirit, and every step becomes a place where His peace, provision, and purpose meet you.

Rest Strengthens for Battle

We tend to think strength comes from doing more, pushing harder, training longer, and stacking one task on top of another. But in God's kingdom, strength begins in rest. David wrote, "*Blessed be the Lord, my rock, who trains my hands for war, and my fingers for battle; he is my steadfast love and my fortress, my stronghold and my deliverer, my shield and he in whom I take refuge, who subdues peoples under me*" (Ps. 144:1–2, *ESV*). Notice, the very God who teaches you how to fight is also the One who shelters you. He equips you from a place of safety.

Rest isn't passivity; it's power under His control.

I've learned this the hard way. There have been seasons in ministry and in everyday life where the battles were fierce, full of spiritual warfare, physical fatigue, financial strain, and the pressure of leading people—all happening simultaneously. My instinct was to get busier, to plan harder, to fight in my own strength. But every time I did that, I wore myself down and lost clarity. The turning point came when the Lord said, "I am your shield. Let Me train you." That training didn't happen in the chaos of constant motion; it happened in quiet moments with Him.

I remember being in Russia, and the opposition was relentless. Everything around me felt like it was pressing in. I didn't have a step-by-step strategy, but God would meet me each morning in His Word. Those mornings weren't "off days" from battle; they were my training ground. He was shaping my heart, sharpening my discernment, and teaching me which battles were mine to fight and which ones He had already won.

The world says you prepare for battle by constantly being in motion, but the Lord says you prepare by being in position close to Him. The enemy wants you exhausted, because a weary heart is more likely to surrender in defeat. But when you've been fortified in God's presence, you walk onto the battlefield already clothed in peace, carrying His wisdom, and standing on His promises. Rest is not your retreat from the fight; it's your secret weapon in it.

Guard Your Heart, Guard Your Purpose

One of the most powerful ways we protect the call of God on our lives is by guarding our hearts. Proverbs 4:23–27 says, "*Keep your heart with all diligence, For out of it* spring *the issues of life. Put away from you a deceitful mouth, And put perverse lips far from you. Let your eyes look straight ahead, And your eyelids look right before you. Ponder the path of your feet, And let all your ways be established. Do not turn to the right or the left; Remove your foot from evil.*" When you realize that your heart is the wellspring of everything you say, think, and do, you start to understand why the enemy works so hard to distract and pollute it.

For years, I thought guarding my heart meant staying away from obvious sin, and yes, that's part of it, but the Lord showed me it's also about what I allow to take root in my thoughts, emotions, and focus. If the enemy can fill our heart with worry, comparison, offense, or busyness, he can quietly drain our ability to hear God's voice. That's why guarding our hearts is really about protecting the flow of life that comes from Him.

There is a beauty in letting the Word anchor your focus. When you keep your eyes straight ahead, you're not swayed by pressure, flattery, or fear of missing out. You stop swerving into lanes that don't belong to you. Rest plays a huge role in this because you can't discern the subtle checks of the Spirit when your life is crowded with noise. But when you've slowed your pace to match His, you're able to see clearly and walk confidently.

> *If the enemy can fill our heart with worry, comparison, offense, or busyness, he can quietly drain our ability to hear God's voice.*

Guarding your heart is not about closing yourself off from people or hiding from the world; it's about staying so filled with His Word and so aware of His presence that no counterfeit can sneak in. It's choosing to remove your feet from anything that pulls you off His path and committing to let Him establish every step. When you live this way, you're not only protecting your peace, you're also protecting your purpose.

The Word Anchors Your Assignment

No matter how big the calling or how busy the season, the Word of God is what keeps us grounded. It's so easy for the enemy to pull us in a hundred different directions, but when our hearts are anchored in Scripture, our path stays clear.

When God asks me to step into something new, to learn a new skill, formulate a new plan, push a new timeline, the pull to hustle is real. But the Lord keeps bringing me back to the same anchor: His Word. If I let the pace set my heart, I drift. If I let the Word set my heart, I'm steady. That's why I don't treat Scripture like a box to check; I let it breathe over my day until it shapes my decisions.

In every fresh season of leadership or ministry, I've felt the pull of expectations. And the Spirit has nudged me to get back to what He's already spoken. I'll carry a verse into meetings, into travel, into the quiet corners of the house, and then read it, pray it, and speak it until my mind aligns with heaven again. That's when clarity returns. That's when the "what" and "when" of an assignment line up with His "how."

This is why God told Joshua, and why we remind our own hearts: "*This book of the law shall not depart out of thy mouth; but thou shalt meditate therein day and night, that thou mayest observe to do according to all that is written therein: for then thou shalt make thy way prosperous, and then thou shalt have good success*" (Josh. 1:8, *KJV*).

Did you catch that? As we keep the Word in our mouths and on our minds, our ways become clear and fruitful. Not because we muscled it into place, but because we stayed in step with what God already said. The Word guards us from drifting into man-made strategies, and it keeps us from building something He didn't ask for. When we anchor our assignments in Scripture, the fruit comes from obedience, not burnout, and the peace that follows is proof we're rooted in something unshakable.

Rest Positions You in Your Inheritance

I have learned, in my walk with the Lord, that rest is not a pause from my calling, but it is the very place where my calling is empowered. I used to think that if I slowed down, I'd lose ground. But I've learned that when I stop striving and simply abide, I'm actually stepping fully into what's already mine in Christ. As Colossians 1:13 says, "*He has delivered us from the power of darkness and ... into the kingdom of* [His dear] *Son ....*" I'm not waiting for God to move me into my inheritance, because it has already happened. Rest allows me to live from that truth. Rest isn't a reward after the work; it is the position from which the work flows.

Peter describes our inheritance in 1 Peter 1:3–4, saying it is incorruptible, undefiled, and does not fade away. That means nothing in this world can diminish it. I don't have to fear losing it if I slow down. In fact, in rest, I become more aware of what's been given to me. I begin to see how His mercy has not only saved me but equipped me with everything I need for life and godliness.

When I'm at rest in Him, my perspective shifts. I stop focusing on what I lack and start recognizing what I already possess. I can walk into a new assignment with confidence, not because I've checked every box, but because I know my identity is secure in Him. That security silences the enemy's lies that say I'm not enough or I'm not ready. Inheritance is never something I earn; it's something I receive because I belong to Him.

As we keep the Word in our mouths and on our minds, our ways become clear and fruitful.

I've found that rest also makes me more generous. When I'm grounded in the truth that I already have abundance in Christ, I'm not afraid to pour out into others because I know my supply doesn't run dry. My inheritance isn't just for my benefit; it's for kingdom impact. Rest keeps me connected to the Giver, so the giving never stops.

This is why I guard my rest so fiercely. It's where I'm reminded that my Father delights in me, that I'm already in His kingdom, and that His resources are mine because I am His child. When I stay in that place, I live out of overflow, ready for whatever He calls me to do next.

Reflection

If I could leave you with one thing, it would be this: rest is not weakness; it is wisdom. It's not the opposite of productivity; it's the foundation of fruitfulness. In every season, God has shown me that when I quiet my heart before Him, He gives me clarity, strength, and provision far beyond what I could achieve in my own effort. Rest is where I hear His strategy, where my faith is renewed, and where my steps are ordered.

I've seen it in my own life when I tried to push forward in my own strength, only to end up weary and distracted. But the moments I chose to step back into His presence—even when deadlines loomed or needs pressed in—those were the moments where direction became clear, and opportunities opened that I could never have orchestrated.

Rest will always be counter to the world's way of doing things, but it is exactly how the kingdom operates. It's in stillness that we remember we are already seated with Christ, already heirs to every promise, already equipped for every good work. The world might run itself ragged chasing more, but we walk in peace knowing we already have more than enough in Him.

It's in stillness that we remember we are already seated with Christ, already heirs to every promise, already equipped for every good work.

My Challenge to You

- Schedule Kingdom Rest First: Don't leave it for leftovers in your day; make rest with God your starting point.
- Anchor Yourself in the Word: Open your Bible at the beginning of your day and let His promises set the tone for everything else.
- Take a Walk with Him: Use creation as a place of conversation, talk to God as you move, and listen as He speaks back.
- Shut Out Distractions: Turn off social media, mute the noise, and make room for His voice to be louder than the world's.

- Choose Rest as Trust: Remember that rest is not laziness; it is an active choice to lean on God's strength instead of your own.
- Watch for Alignment: Expect Him to shift your perspective, reorder your priorities, and position you to live from your inheritance.
- Abide to Bear Fruit: Believe that your greatest effectiveness will flow, not from doing more, but from abiding more deeply in Him.

Scripture References

Psalm 144:1–2
Joshua 1:8
Colossians 1:13
1 Peter 1:3–4
Proverbs 3:5–6
Proverbs 4:23–27

Chapter Twelve

Disciplined by Grace

Introduction

When I first heard the word "discipline," I didn't think of grace. I thought of rules. Restrictions. Someone telling me no when I wanted to hear yes. But God has shown me that true discipline isn't punishment; it's grace in action. It's the empowering work of His Spirit that shapes my choices, trains my steps, and positions me for the fullness of His abundance. Grace doesn't just save us; it teaches us how to live.

We often think grace is only there to rescue us when we fail, and yes, it does that, but it also equips us before we even face the trial. Discipline led by grace is like a good coach who sees your potential, stretches your capacity, and refuses to let you settle for less than your calling. It's not about striving harder in your own strength; it's about leaning into the strength and wisdom of God so that every step forward is intentional, fruitful, and full of His presence.

I've learned that discipline is often revealed in the small, hidden moments—choosing prayer over scrolling, speaking life when I feel like complaining, saying yes to God's assignments when my flesh wants the easy way out. Each of those choices becomes a seed, and over time, grace turns those seeds into a harvest. That's why resistance is not a sign you're failing; it's often the evidence you're stepping into greatness. And it's why knowing your position in God's abundance changes the way you respond to challenges—you realize you're not fighting for victory, but from it.

This chapter is really key because it will show you how it all comes together. We're going to explore how discipline and grace work hand in hand. We'll see how God's training positions you for greater influence, how resistance actually confirms your direction, and how living in your rightful place in His abundance keeps you from shrinking back. I believe by the time we finish, you'll not only see discipline differently, you'll embrace it as one of the most loving, empowering gifts God has ever given you.

Fix Your Focus

I want you to focus on what is true: discipline isn't about earning God's favor; it's the fruit of living in it. Grace is the steady hand that not only lifts us when we stumble but also guides us, so we don't keep tripping over the same stones. It's the voice of the Holy Spirit whispering, "This is the way, walk in it," when distractions pull at our attention. Grace doesn't leave us where it found us; it develops us, trains us, and prepares us for the weight of the vision God has entrusted to us.

When we see discipline through the lens of grace, it stops feeling like pressure and starts looking like preparation. The trials we face are not punishments; they are proving grounds. The resistance we encounter isn't a signal to turn back; it's an indicator that we're advancing into new territory. And in every step of that journey, we are not operating from scarcity but from the limitless abundance of God's provision.

I want to invite you to lay down the misconception that discipline means striving in your own strength. Instead, you'll see how discipline, empowered by grace, is the very thing that keeps you steady when storms come, bold when opposition rises, and confident when God calls you into something bigger than yourself.

Grace Is Not Passive

Grace isn't God's way of forgiving us when we mess up, a safety net for our failures. In fact, the more we walk with Him, the more we realize grace isn't passive at all. It's not just a rescue; it's a teacher. Titus 2:11–12 tells us that the grace of God has appeared to all men, teaching us to say no to ungodliness and to live self-controlled, upright, and godly lives in this present age. Grace trains you. It strengthens you. It doesn't simply cover your weakness; it builds your capacity to walk in victory.

That's why resistance is not a sign you're failing; it's often the evidence you're stepping into greatness.

It's learning that when God entrusts us with something small, grace is what empowers us to steward it well. It's not our personality or our natural discipline; it's His ability in us. Jesus said in Matthew 25:21, "*Well* done, *good and faithful servant; you were faithful over a few things, I will make you ruler over many things.*" When we're faithful in the hidden, everyday assignments, God opens doors for greater responsibility, not as a reward for our performance, but because grace can shape our character to carry more.

I remember a season early in life when my role seemed insignificant compared to others. I wasn't on a big stage; I wasn't leading huge initiatives. I was simply managing small projects, organizing schedules, and making sure things ran smoothly for those around me. In the natural, it looked like administrative work, but in the Spirit, it was training. God was showing me that discipline, consistency, and integrity in the "little things" mattered deeply to Him. Over time, those small acts of faithfulness became the foundation for stepping into larger assignments, missions work overseas, teaching in Bible schools, and leading in ways I could have never imagined.

Grace isn't opposed to effort; it's opposed to earning. And when you understand that, discipline stops feeling like a burden and becomes a joy. I no longer see structure, boundaries, and faithfulness as limitations. They're the runway for God's vision to take flight in our lives. Grace is the fuel that makes discipline possible, and discipline, in turn, positions you for God's "well done."

Guard Your Fields

Here in Proverbs 24:30–34 (*ESV*), it paints a vivid picture: "*I passed by the field of a sluggard, by the vineyard of a man lacking sense, and behold, it was all overgrown with thorns; the ground was covered with nettles, and its stone wall was broken down. Then I saw and considered it; I looked and received instruction. A little sleep, a little slumber, a little folding of the hands to rest, and poverty will come upon you like a robber, and want like an armed man.*"

When I first read that, I thought about land and gardens, but then the Lord showed me it's a picture of the heart. Your life is a field. God has entrusted it to you to cultivate, protect, and keep fruitful. But if you neglect it, if you let your priorities slip, the weeds of distraction will take root. It doesn't happen overnight; it's "a little" here and "a little" there. A little compromise in prayer time. A little ignoring what God is prompting you to address. A little choosing busyness over intimacy. Before you know it, the wall is down, and the enemy has easy access.

The way I guard against neglect is intentionally scheduling time with the Lord, not just squeezing Him into the cracks of my day. I rebuilt the walls by guarding my spiritual disciplines: worship, time in the Word, and praying in the Spirit. Slowly, the weeds came out, the soil grew healthy again, and fruit began to appear.

Guarding your field isn't about paranoia; it's about stewardship. It's knowing that the health of your heart will directly affect the harvest of your life. Discipline, empowered by grace, keeps your field fruitful and your wall strong. It's not just about avoiding loss; it's about making sure your life remains ready for God to plant and grow what He desires.

Strengthened by His Deliverance

When you know your position in God's abundance, you stop living like you're fighting to survive and start living like you've already been delivered. That's what David understood when he wrote these words: "*My God in his steadfast love will meet me; God will let me look in triumph on my enemies*" (Ps. 59:10, *ESV*). He wasn't naïve to the danger around him; he knew enemies were real, but he also knew the steadfast love of God was even more real. He could rest because God's love would meet him right where the battle raged and bring him into triumph.

I've had moments in my own life when fear wanted to take over, moments when the situation looked impossible, and my emotions felt anything but victorious. One of those times came when I faced a sudden and intimidating threat overseas. Everything in my natural reasoning wanted to panic, to scramble for a solution. But in that moment, the Holy Spirit reminded me of who I was in Christ and who my God is. I didn't need to match the chaos with my own chaos. I needed to stand still and let His steadfast love meet me. And He did. Just like David, I could look back and see that God didn't just rescue me, He delivered me in such a way that fear lost its hold.

Grace doesn't just save you; it disciplines your trust in His timing. There's a training that happens when you face trials and choose to rest in God's deliverance rather than your own strategies. Each time you watch Him come through, you become less dependent on your own plans and more confident in His perfect timing. That's why David could say, "*For great is your steadfast love toward me; you have delivered my soul from the depths of Sheol*" (Ps. 86:13, *ESV*). He didn't just know God as a rescuer in theory; he had lived through moments that proved God's faithfulness.

When you know your position in God's abundance, you stop living like you're fighting to survive and start living like you've already been delivered.

And here's the beauty: when you live from that place of deliverance, your actions change. You stop rushing ahead of God, trying to force outcomes, and instead begin moving at His pace, knowing that every step is secure. His steadfast love is not just a comfort; it's the strength that allows you to walk in abundance, unshaken by the threats around you.

Fearless in His Care

I love how Psalm 56:8 (*NLT*) says that God keeps track of all our sorrows and collects our tears in His bottle. He knows every step we take, every battle we've faced, and every whisper of fear that has tried to settle in our hearts. This is so personal because God is not distant; He is attentive. When the enemy comes against you, when situations arise that would try to shake you, you can rest in the truth that our God is fully aware and actively working on your behalf. Verse 11 says, "*In God I have put my trust; I will not be afraid. What can man do to me?*" That's not arrogance; that's confidence born from intimacy with Him.

There was a time when I faced a situation that could have paralyzed me with fear. My mind kept running through all the what-ifs, imagining worst-case scenarios. Fear doesn't just cloud your judgment; it can shrink your vision and make you want to retreat. I remember kneeling before the Lord and saying, "God, I can't carry this fear anymore. I give it to You." And in that moment, it wasn't that the circumstances instantly changed; it was that I changed. Fear lost its grip, and in its place came a supernatural boldness. I stood up with a renewed awareness: I am guarded by the One who knows every tear I've cried, who counts each step I take, and who will not abandon me.

His steadfast love is not just a comfort; it's the strength that allows you to walk in abundance, unshaken by the threats around you.

This is the discipline of grace: it trains your heart to choose trust over panic, to walk forward even when every natural instinct tells you to freeze. Grace teaches you to remember that the God who holds the universe also holds your life. He is your protector, your advocate, your refuge. And when you really know that, you can face situations that once seemed impossible without shrinking back. Fear no longer defines your limits; His love and His care do.

Abundance Beyond Imagination

One of my favorite promises in the Word is Ephesians 3:20: "*Now to Him who is able to do exceedingly abundantly above all that we ask or think* [or imagine], *according to the power that works in us.*" This isn't just a nice phrase to put on a coffee mug; it's the reality of what happens when we live in surrender to Him. God's definition of "enough" is so far beyond our imagination that even our biggest dreams look small compared to His plans. His abundance doesn't just meet the need—it surpasses it.

I remember a ministry project we stepped into with what seemed like a clear, reasonable plan. We had budgeted, prayed, and prepared with the best wisdom we had. But God had a bigger picture. As the project unfolded, resources began to pour in from unexpected places. People we didn't even know sowed into the work. Needs we hadn't anticipated were already met before we had the chance to ask. By the time it was complete, we stood in awe because not only was every goal accomplished but we also had an overflow that allowed us to bless other ministries. That's the heart of God: He doesn't just fund the vision; He expands it.

This is what the discipline of grace teaches us: to keep our hearts open to His ways and our faith stretched beyond what we can control. If we cling too tightly to our own limited plans, we can miss the miraculous. But when we surrender our vision and our resources to Him, we position ourselves for a life where His "exceedingly abundantly" becomes our normal. His abundance isn't just a provision; it's an invitation to dream with Him, and watch Him exceed even our most faith-filled requests.

Remembering Builds Resilience

Psalm 78:11 (*ESV*) gives a sobering warning: "*They forgot his works and the wonders that he had shown them.*" The Israelites had seen God split the Red Sea, rain down manna, and bring water from a rock, yet when they faced the next challenge, they doubted Him all over again. Forgetting what God has done is dangerous because it robs us of faith for what He is about to do.

I've learned that resistance often comes right before a breakthrough. And in those moments, the enemy will try to convince you that you're not going to make it and that this time, the mountain is too big. That's when remembering is your lifeline. I think back to a time when God brought miraculous provision in a situation that looked impossible. The doors that opened, the people He brought, and the exact timing, it was all Him. When

I later faced another situation that stirred up fear, I reminded myself: The same God who carried me then will carry me now. That memory became fuel, turning fear into forward motion.

The discipline of grace teaches us to build a habit of remembrance. Keep a journal of His faithfulness. Speak it out loud to your family and friends. Tell your own heart the stories of His goodness until you believe them more than the lie of defeat. Resistance is not a sign of failure but proof you're stepping into something great. And when you remember what He has already done, you face the future not with trembling, but with a bold, unshakable trust.

Your Strength Is in Him

Paul's words in Ephesians 6:10 (*ESV*) are not a suggestion; they're a command: "*Finally, be strong in the Lord and in the strength of his might.*" That's a powerful reminder that your strength does not have to come from your own reserves. Psalm 28:8 reinforces it: "*The Lord is the strength of his people; he is the saving refuge of his anointed.*" This is why when resistance rises and pressure bears down, your source of strength must shift from "what I can do" to "what He has already done."

Grace teaches us to lean on Him as our continual source, not just in emergencies. Discipline says, "I will not try to muscle through on my own, but I will abide in His might." The resistance you feel is not there to defeat you; it's there to push you deeper into dependence on Him. And in that place, you'll discover that His strength is not only enough, but you will find it's overflowing.

Equipped for Every Good Work

Paul reminded the Corinthian church that in Christ they had been enriched in every way, in all speech and all knowledge, because the testimony about Christ was confirmed among them. That means when you belong to Him, you're not stepping into assignments empty-handed. His Spirit fills you with the words you need to say, the wisdom you need to lead, and the insight you need to navigate challenges.

Resistance is not a sign of failure but proof you're stepping into something great.

It's not about having a good memory or polished presentation; it's about being a living vessel for His truth. Every time we see lives touched, it reminds us that it is His equipping, not yours, that is making the difference.

That is why when you understand your position in God's abundance, you stop looking at your lack and start drawing from His supply. Discipline in grace means showing up faithfully, prepared to obey, trusting that God's Spirit has already equipped you for the good works He's called you to. And here's the best part—you'll often find yourself doing things you never imagined, with fruit you couldn't have produced on your own.

Strength to Endure All Seasons

Paul's words in Philippians 4:13 are more than just a motivational slogan. When he said, "*I can do all things through Christ who strengthens me*," he was speaking from a life that had known both abundance and lack. His contentment wasn't tied to his circumstances; it was anchored in the unchanging strength of Christ.

I've walked through both ends of that spectrum. There were seasons when life meant counting every dollar, stretching meals, and trusting God for what seemed like the smallest necessities. And there have been other seasons where provision flowed in such abundance that we could give generously, plant into new works, and fund kingdom projects far beyond our budget. The grace for one season was the same grace for the other because my source wasn't the bank account, the donors, or the ministry's plans. My source was, and is, Christ.

Resistance in any season, whether it comes in the form of scarcity or the pressures of managing abundance, is an opportunity to lean deeper into His strength. Remember to keep showing up, keep believing, and keep your heart steady, because the One who called you is also the One who equips you to endure. And as you remain anchored in Him, you'll discover that both the lean seasons and the overflowing ones are simply different backdrops for His faithfulness to be displayed.

Faithful in the Little, Ruler over Much

When Jesus told the parable of the talents, He painted a clear picture of how the kingdom measures success. It wasn't about who had the most to start with; it was about what each servant did with what they had. In Matthew 25:21, the master says, "*Well* done, *good and faithful servant; you were faithful over a few things, I will make you ruler over many things. Enter into the joy of your lord.*"

Faithfulness is rarely flashy. It's showing up when no one is watching. It's doing the small, hidden assignments with the same diligence you would bring to a public platform. In my own life, I've seen God open doors I never could have forced open, but they often came after seasons of simply tending to what was in my hand, whether it felt significant or not.

Discipline isn't about earning God's favor; it's about positioning yourself to steward His gifts well. Every act of obedience, every moment you choose His way over your own convenience, is an investment that heaven takes note of. And the beautiful truth is this: God is not only watching—He's preparing to entrust you with more.

Discipline isn't about earning God's favor; it's about positioning yourself to steward His gifts well.

What I've seen in my walk is that faithfulness in the little is not the warm-up before "real" ministry, purpose, or opportunity; it is the real thing. And when you live that way, promotion in the kingdom doesn't feel like a sudden leap; it feels like the natural next step in the story He's been writing all along.

Reflection

The grace of God is more than a safety net; it's His empowering presence that shapes every moment of your life. Grace teaches you to say yes to the right things and no to the distractions that pull you off course. It builds the discipline to guard your spiritual fields, strengthens you to endure every season, and equips you for assignments you never imagined you could carry.

Remember that God's abundance is not just about resources; it's about His sufficiency in every circumstance. Resistance is not a sign of failure; it's often confirmation that you're pressing into the territory He's called you to occupy. When challenges come, remember your history with Him. Every past deliverance is a deposit that builds your resilience for the next battle.

Every past deliverance is a deposit that builds your resilience for the next battle.

Your part is to stay faithful with what's in your hand today. Steward it well. Nurture intimacy with Him. Lean on His strength instead of your own. You will find that, as you walk in His ways, He opens doors, multiplies your influence, and fills your life with the kind of abundance only heaven can provide.

My Challenge to You

1. Guard Your Field: Identify one area of your life where distractions have crept in. Clear the "weeds" by setting boundaries around your time and attention.
2. Remember His Faithfulness: Write down three times God has come through for you in the past. Keep this list somewhere visible and revisit it when challenges arise.
3. Strengthen Yourself in Him: Begin each day with a moment of surrender, asking the Lord to be your strength for whatever lies ahead.
4. Practice Faithfulness in the Small Things: Choose one small responsibility or commitment this week and give it your very best effort as an act of worship to God.
5. Expect His Abundance: Ask God for one specific thing that feels beyond your capacity and believe Him to exceed your expectations.

Scripture References

Titus 2:11–12
Matthew 25:21
Proverbs 24:30–34
Psalm 59:10
Psalm 86:13
Psalm 56:8–11
Ephesians 3:20
Psalm 78:11
Ephesians 6:10
Psalm 28:8
Philippians 4:13

Chapter Thirteen

Strengthened for the Long Run

Introduction

When you think about running a race, it's not just the start that matters; it's the endurance to reach the finish line. Anyone can run hard for a few steps, but it's those who keep their eyes on the goal, and their hearts anchored in hope who finish strong. The Christian life is a marathon of faith. It's about learning to give your time and energy to what truly matters; staying the course when distractions try to pull you aside and drawing boldness from knowing who you are in Christ.

The truth is, resistance will come. There will be moments when quitting seems easier, when the path ahead feels too steep, or when gratitude seems far away. But God's grace equips us to keep pressing forward, no matter what we face. I want us to explore how discipline and hope work together to sustain us for the long run, how to push past the pull of laziness or discouragement, and how gratitude fuels both endurance and abundance.

This isn't about willpower; it's about Spirit-powered living. When you lean into His strength, you'll discover that every step, whether in plenty or in pressure, becomes part of a race worth running.

Fix Your Focus

I encourage you to start cultivating the kind of endurance that can only be built through a deep relationship with God. We need to learn to set our focus on what truly matters, even when distractions or difficulties try to steal your attention. Here are three ways you can start to fix your focus:

- Give Priority to God's Assignments: Ordering your life around what He says is important, not what clamors for immediate attention.
- Press Forward with Purpose: Building resilience that pushes through resistance, and keeps your heart engaged in the race He's marked out for you.
- Live with a Thankful Heart: Letting gratitude be the fuel that sustains momentum and opens the door for greater abundance.

Every principle we'll explore is grounded in Scripture, tested in the challenges of real life, and empowered by the same grace that saved you. By the end of this chapter, you'll see that endurance isn't just surviving; it's thriving all the way to the finish line.

Gratitude Fuels Your Race

When you're running the race God has marked out for you, gratitude isn't just a polite add-on to your faith; it's the fuel that keeps your spirit strong. Paul writes, *"Give thanks in all circumstances; for this is the will of God in Christ Jesus for you"* (1 Thess. 5:18, *ESV*). Notice, he doesn't say give thanks "for" all circumstances, but in them. Gratitude isn't about pretending every season feels good; it's about recognizing that God is good in every season.

When our hearts choose thankfulness, even in the middle of hardship, something powerful happens. Our perspective shifts. The weight of the trial doesn't feel as heavy because our focus moves from the problem to God, who is my source. That's why Paul also said, *"Rejoice in the Lord always. Again I will say, rejoice!"* (Phil. 4:4). It's not a suggestion; it's a spiritual strategy. Joy and gratitude are companions that carry you forward when everything in the natural says you should quit.

There was a time when I faced constant obstacles in ministry. It seemed like every time I took a step forward, something came against me; whether it was financial challenges, travel delays, or unexpected crises. I could have let frustration take the driver's seat, but the Holy Spirit whispered, "Guard your joy. Keep your heart thankful." I started each morning by writing down three things I was grateful for, not grand sweeping miracles, but simple, tangible blessings: a roof over my head, a message of hope to share, the laughter of a friend. As the days went on, gratitude built a strength inside me that the enemy couldn't touch. My circumstances hadn't changed overnight, but my spirit was alive, my vision was clear, and my feet kept moving forward.

> *Gratitude isn't about pretending every season feels good; it's about recognizing that God is good in every season.*

Gratitude does that; it anchors you to God's faithfulness and fuels the endurance you need to finish strong. It's not weakness; it's a declaration of trust. When you thank God in the middle of the battle, you're proclaiming, "I know how this ends: He wins, and so do I."

Clear the Weeds and Run Freely

When God calls you to run your race, He also calls you to prepare the path. *"Prepare your work outside; get everything ready for yourself in the field, and after that build your house"* (Prov. 24:27, *ESV*). This verse reminds us that spiritual momentum begins with intentional preparation. You can't run freely if your path is overgrown with weeds—distractions, compromises, or unwise habits that slow you down.

In Proverbs 6, Solomon gives a surprising example of diligence that it will take to run our race: *"Go to the ant, O sluggard; consider her ways, and be wise. ... she prepares her bread in summer and gathers her food in harvest"* (Prov. 6:6 and 8, *ESV*). The ant doesn't waste her seasons; she understands timing. When it's time to work, she works wholeheartedly so she's prepared for the future. Spiritually speaking, that's what discipline and preparation do for us: they ensure that when God opens the door, we're ready to walk through it without delay.

When you thank God in the middle of the battle, you're proclaiming, "I know how this ends; He wins, and so do I."

I've had moments when I tried to sprint ahead without first tending my field. The vision was exciting, the opportunities were real, but because I hadn't cleared out the distractions or set my priorities, the pace wasn't sustainable. It's like trying to run a race through tall weeds: you might move forward, but the drag is constant. Every unnecessary commitment, every unaddressed area of compromise, becomes a thorn that catches at your momentum.

I remember a year when the ministry schedule was packed, and my personal time with the Lord had slipped into the leftover margins of my day. Outwardly, I was "running the race," but inwardly, I felt weighed down. The Lord showed me that I had allowed small weeds—the unnecessary meetings, overcommitment, a reluctance to say "no"—to crowd out the clarity and joy I once carried. He led me back to diligence, not just in ministry tasks, but in guarding my spiritual ground. As I removed those weeds, I felt light again, free to move in step with His Spirit.

Clearing the weeds isn't just about cutting away the bad; it's about making space for the good to flourish. When you diligently prepare your field, the race God has called you to becomes a joy, not a burden. And gratitude naturally grows in that kind of soil, because you're no longer expending all your energy on the wrong battles; you're running freely toward the right finish line.

Stay in Pursuit, No Matter What

Paul's words in Philippians stir a holy determination: *"Not that I have already obtained this or am already perfect, but I press on to make it my own, because Christ Jesus has made me his own. Brothers, I do not consider that I have made it on my own. But one thing I do: forgetting what lies behind and straining forward to what lies ahead, I press on toward the goal for the prize of the upward call of God in Christ Jesus"* (Phil. 3:12–13, *ESV*). The Christian life isn't a casual stroll; it's a relentless pursuit. That pursuit is not about striving in the flesh, but it is about fixing our eyes on Jesus, the Author and Finisher of our faith (Heb. 12:2), and refusing to let go, no matter what obstacles come.

I remember one trip overseas where nothing went according to plan. Flights were delayed, ministry meetings were rescheduled, and the enemy tried to use exhaustion to cloud my faith. In the natural, it felt like a week of setbacks. But in the Spirit, God was using every delay to put me in the right place, at the right time, to minister to someone who desperately needed a word of hope. If I had let frustration stop my pursuit, I would have missed the assignment He had woven into the inconvenience.

You see, pursuit is not proven in the easy seasons; it's proven in the ones that require endurance. Every time you press forward when quitting would be easier, you're strengthening the spiritual muscles that will carry you into your next assignment. You're telling heaven, "I trust Your leadership," and you're telling hell, "You can't shake my focus."

The enemy would love for you to stall out in discouragement, replaying the past or obsessing over what hasn't happened yet. But pursuit requires a forward lean. You let go of what's behind, not because it's insignificant, but because what God has ahead is far greater. You lock your eyes on Jesus, His voice, His presence, His joy, and you keep running. That's where His best unfolds, not just in the outcome, but in the transformation that happens along the way.

Boldness Through Revelation

Look at what Paul prayed for believers in Ephesians 1:18 (*NIV*): *"I pray that the eyes of your heart may be enlightened in order that you may know the hope to which he has called you, the riches of his glorious inheritance in his holy people."* True boldness doesn't come from personality type or natural confidence; it comes from seeing something in the Spirit so clearly that no circumstance can intimidate you. When revelation from God's Word pierces your heart, it shifts you from reacting to situations to ruling over them.

Psalm 62:1 (*NIV*) says, *"My soul finds rest in God alone; my salvation comes from him."* This is the bedrock of spiritual boldness, resting so deeply in His truth that you can step into the unknown with absolute peace. The confidence isn't in your ability to control the outcome; it's in knowing who is leading you.

Revelation changes the posture of your heart. It anchors you when the winds of opposition blow, silences the enemy's accusations, and causes you to walk into assignments with a calm, steady assurance, even if your circumstances look chaotic. When you've seen God's plan in the Spirit, it doesn't matter how big the obstacles look in the natural; you know the victory is already written.

Discipline Defeats Hopelessness

Proverbs 12:11 (*ESV*) states, "*Whoever works his land will have plenty of bread, but he who follows worthless pursuits lacks sense.*" Then in Proverbs 13:4 it tells us, "*The soul of the sluggard craves and gets nothing, while the soul of the diligent is richly supplied.*" These verses aren't just about farming or work in the natural; they reveal a spiritual principle. Laziness is often rooted in hopelessness. When you stop believing that your efforts will produce fruit, you stop showing up with diligence, and the effectiveness of your run will be hindered.

You lock your eyes on Jesus, His voice, His presence, His joy, and you keep running.

Hopelessness whispers, "Why try? Nothing will change." But grace answers with, "God is faithful, and He multiplies what you put in His hands." God's grace empowers you to get up, take the next step, and keep moving forward, knowing He is the One who breathes life into your obedience.

I've seen this so clearly in my life. There was a time when the vision God had placed in my heart seemed far bigger than the resources we had. In the natural, I could have sat back and waited until "everything lined up." But the Lord kept reminding me to work the field in front of me—faithfully, consistently, without waiting for perfect conditions. I made small, steady investments of time, prayer, and energy. Doors began to open, relationships formed, and provision started to flow, often from places I never expected.

That's the power of discipline fueled by hope in God's promises. You don't wait until you feel like it. You move because you know God is faithful to finish what He started. Hopelessness looks at what's missing; diligence looks at the One who provides. When you keep showing up with that kind of faith, your soul will indeed be "richly supplied."

Hope Restores Diligence

Sometimes, when you've faced disappointment or endured a long delay, it's tempting to believe the best opportunities have already passed. The enemy loves to whisper, "It's too late. You've missed your chance." But God tells a different story. He says in Joel 2:25, *"I will restore to you the years that the swarming locust has eaten...."* That promise isn't just for someone else—it's for you. He's the redeemer of time, and when He restores, He doesn't just give back what was lost; He multiplies it for His glory.

There were moments in my life when it felt like momentum had been stolen, and times when obedience didn't seem to produce the fruit I had expected. But the Lord reminded me of this promise in Joel and showed me that no act of faithfulness is wasted. Even when it looks like nothing is happening, God is cultivating something below the surface. And when hope is renewed, it fuels a fresh commitment to get back to work in His field.

That's why we need to stay reminded of what Proverbs 20:4 (*ESV*) warns, *"The sluggard does not plow in the autumn; he will seek at harvest and have nothing."* Hopelessness will always tempt us to stop sowing, to put down our plows before the season is over. But when our hope is anchored in the faithfulness of God, we can pick up our tools again and press forward. Diligence born from hope isn't about striving; it's about partnering with our God who restores and redeems every season for His purposes.

When we realize this truth, then hope comes alive again and diligence returns. We recognize that plowing may not be glamorous, but it's what prepares the soil for harvest. God sees every unseen act of obedience. Even if the results aren't immediate, they are inevitable when we're faithful to His call.

You see, hope and diligence are intertwined. Without hope, we stop moving. But when our hope is anchored in God's faithfulness, discipline becomes a joy because we're not just working for today's results, we're sowing into His eternal purposes. We can approach each day differently, thanking Him for the opportunity to sow, confident that in His timing, we will reap a harvest.

Diligence born from hope isn't about striving; it's about partnering with our God who restores and redeems every season for His purposes.

If you feel like you've been in a long season of plowing without seeing much change, don't give up. Ask God to restore hope in your heart.

Your Confidence Is in Him

There's something unshakable about the kind of confidence that comes from knowing God is with you. It's not loud or boastful; it's steady, like a deep river that keeps flowing, no matter what's happening on the surface. Confidence rooted in Him isn't about having all the resources or being the most talented in the room. It's about being fully convinced that His presence goes before you, His strength upholds you, and His wisdom guides your steps.

That's why Philippians 4:13 (*ESV*) means so much to me: *"I can do all things through him who strengthens me."* Paul wasn't promising an easy road;

he was pointing to the secret of endurance in every season, which is leaning on Christ's strength. Psalm 27 echoes this truth when David declares, "The Lord is my light and my salvation, so why should I be afraid? The Lord is the stronghold of my life, so why should I be shaken?" (adapted from Psalm 27:1, *ESV*).

I remember a time when I was invited to share at an outdoor evangelistic event in a foreign country. The weather had turned unexpectedly cold, the sound system was struggling, and the crowd was restless. Everything in the natural said, "This isn't going to work." But as I stood there, I felt the Lord whisper to my heart, "This isn't about your comfort; it's about My Spirit reaching people."

In that moment, I stopped looking at the obstacles and let His peace settle over me. I spoke with clarity, warmth, and joy, not because the conditions improved, but because my confidence wasn't in the setting. It was in Him. And by the time we finished, hearts were touched, and lives were changed.

When you know who is in you, your courage stops rising and falling with your circumstances. Instead, you walk in a steady boldness that's anchored in the God who never leaves your side.

See the Abundance Already Here

One of the most powerful shifts we can make in our walk with God is learning to see what He's already done. Sometimes we're so focused on what we're waiting for that we miss the blessings surrounding us right now. I've learned that when we slow down, remember His faithfulness, and give thanks, our hearts become lighter and our perspective changes. Gratitude doesn't just make us feel better; it opens our eyes to the abundance that is already here.

I think about how Moses reminded Israel of this in Deuteronomy 10:21: *"He* is *your praise and He* is *your God, who has done for you these great and awesome things which your eyes have seen."* Moses was calling the people back to a place of worship by pointing to what God had already done in their midst. It's the same for us; when we recall His goodness, our hearts can't help but lift in praise.

In Psalm 71:17, it says, *"O God, You have taught me from my youth; And to this* day *I declare Your wondrous works."* That verse has always stirred something deep inside me. I can look back over the years, from the early days of ministry when we didn't know how God would provide, to seasons of breakthrough that could only be explained by His hand, and I see His fingerprints all over my life.

I remember a time when everything felt like it was taking longer than I thought it should. I had been praying for a specific breakthrough, and I felt like I was just...waiting. But one morning, as I sat with the Lord, He gently reminded me of all the prayers He had already answered, the doors He had already opened, the protection He had already given, the friendships and ministry opportunities I already had because of Him. In that moment, my heart moved from frustration to gratitude, and gratitude gave me strength to keep running my race.

When we take time to remember what God has done, it's like stopping to catch our breath during a long run; it restores our energy and our focus. We realize that we're not running on empty; we're running on a foundation of His faithfulness. And that is more than enough.

Keep Your Eyes on the Goal

There's something powerful about knowing the finish line is ahead and choosing, no matter what, to run all the way through it. Paul said in 2 Timothy 4:7–8, *"I have fought the good fight, I have finished the race, I have kept the faith. Finally, there is laid up for me the crown of righteousness, which the Lord, the righteous Judge, will give to me on that Day, and not to me only but also to all who have loved His appearing."* Those words should stir something inside us because Paul didn't write them from a place of ease; he wrote them after a lifetime of challenges, resistance, and sacrifice. Yet his eyes were fixed on the reward, not the obstacles.

> *When we take time to remember what God has done, it's like stopping to catch our breath during a long run; it restores our energy and our focus.*

There will be journeys in life where the road ahead feels uncertain, where the path God is leading you down doesn't match your idea of how things "should" go. In those moments, you'll have to remind yourself of Romans 8:28 (*ESV*), which says: *"And we know that for those who love God all things work together for good, for those who are called according to his purpose."* That isn't just a verse we should quote; it's an anchor that keeps us steady when we can't see around the next corner.

When we know that God is weaving every step, every detour, and every setback into His perfect plan, we can keep our focus on the ultimate goal: pleasing Him. Boldness rises in us when we remember that the race we're running isn't about competing with anyone else; it's about staying faithful to the Lord who called us. When our eyes are locked on Him, no twist or turn in the road can shake our confidence in how this race will end.

Why Endurance Is Important

When God gives us a vision, it is never meant to stop with us. His heart is always generational, always expansive, always reaching further than our lifetime. This is why endurance is important; the vision He plants in us carries the power to shape nations and impact generations yet to be born.

I've seen this firsthand with the call to start a Bible school. When we first began in Russia, I could not have imagined that the seed planted there would multiply into schools across Europe, Asia, Africa, and beyond. What started in one city grew into a ripple effect, touching nations I had never even set foot in. That's the nature of God's vision; it carries His eternal DNA, and it multiplies far beyond what you and I could ever orchestrate.

Paul captured this in Philippians 3:12–14 (*NIV*) when he said, "*Not that I have already obtained all this, or have already arrived at my goal, but I press on to take hold of that for which Christ Jesus took hold of me ... I press on toward the goal to win the prize for which God has called me heavenward in Christ Jesus.*" Paul's life was not about short-term success; it was about stewarding a heavenly call that would echo through the ages. The same is true for us: our vision is not just about our assignment today; it's about the legacy we leave tomorrow.

The psalmist reminds us: "*From everlasting to everlasting the Lord's love is with those who fear him, and his righteousness with their children's children—with those who keep His covenant and remember to obey His precepts*" (Ps. 103:17–18, *NIV*). God's love is generational. He is not only thinking about us, He's thinking about our children, and their children after them. When we walk in obedience to the vision He gives, we are laying down a pathway of faithfulness for those who will come after us.

Psalm 45:16–17 (*NIV*) gives us this picture: "*Your sons will take the place of your fathers; you will make them princes throughout the land. I will perpetuate your memory through all generations; therefore the nations will praise you for ever and ever.*" That's the promise of legacy: when we partner with God, our obedience doesn't die with us. It multiplies into the lives of others, shaping leaders, birthing movements, and carrying His glory into nations we may never personally visit.

I often think of Romans 9:17 (*NIV*), where God said to Pharaoh, "*I raised you up for this very purpose, that I might display my power in you and that my name might be proclaimed in all the earth.*" Whether we realize it or not, our obedience makes room for God's name to be declared in the earth. The vision He entrusts to us is not about our platform or reputation; it's about His glory being revealed in the nations.

Live with eternity in mind. Don't settle for temporary gain or short-term success. We need to lift our eyes to see that our vision is part of a much bigger story. We are writing history with God, and generations yet unborn will walk in the fruit of your obedience.

Gratitude Is the Language of Victory

One of the most freeing truths I've learned is that gratitude changes everything; it's the language of victory. In Psalm 32:8 (*ESV*), it says, "*I will instruct you and teach you in the way you should go; I will counsel you with my eye upon you.*" No matter what season we're in, that verse reminds us that God's guidance is constant. He's not scrambling to figure out our future; He already sees it and is walking us through it step by step.

Paul captured the heart of this when he said in Philippians 4:12 that he had learned to be content in whatever state he was in, whether well-fed or hungry, living in plenty or in want. I've been in times when resources were so tight I had to pray for the next meal, and I've been in seasons where God's provision overflowed beyond what I could have imagined. In both, I learned that gratitude wasn't dependent on the size of my bank account or the ease of my circumstances; it was a choice to keep my eyes on our God, who never changes.

The vision He entrusts to us is not about our platform or reputation; it's about His glory being revealed in the nations.

Gratitude is powerful because it keeps our hearts from being ruled by lack or excess as we run our race. It keeps us present to see God's goodness right where we are, not just where we hope to be. When we thank Him in lean seasons, we are declaring that our trust is in Him, not in our situation. When we thank Him in abundance, we are acknowledging that every good gift comes from His hand. Gratitude turns our attention away from what's missing and onto the victory we already have in Christ.

Reflection

Running the race God has set before us isn't about quick bursts of inspiration; it's about staying faithful for the long run. We've seen how gratitude keeps our hearts strong, how diligence clears away distractions, how hope restores what was lost, and how boldness arises from revelation and not circumstance. We've talked about pressing forward when the path feels uphill, drawing confidence from His strength, and keeping our eyes fixed on the goal.

Being strengthened for the long run means learning to live from a place of deep connection with Him, where gratitude isn't just an occasional response but the steady rhythm of our hearts. It's choosing to prepare our fields, even when results aren't immediate. It's trusting that God is restoring time, opportunity, and strength we thought were gone. It's finishing each lap with the assurance that He is both our starting point and our finish line.

The long run requires endurance, and endurance is built one choice at a time.

The long run requires endurance, and endurance is built one choice at a time. Every time we choose gratitude over grumbling, focus over distraction, diligence over passivity, we're building spiritual muscle for the race ahead. And we're not running alone. The same God who called us is the One who strengthens us to finish well. His instruction will never run dry. His Spirit will never leave us. His grace will never fail to meet us at our point of need.

So keep running. Keep trusting. Keep your heart anchored in His goodness. Because when we live strengthened by His grace, the long run becomes not just possible, it becomes joyful.

My Challenge to You

- Start Each Morning with Gratitude: Before you check your phone or look at your to-do list, take a moment to thank God for three specific things. Gratitude sets your pace for the day.
- Clear Your "Spiritual Field": Identify one distraction, habit, or time-waster that's slowing you down, and intentionally set it aside for a time every day. Even one small change can create space for fresh momentum.
- Keep Your Eyes on the Goal: Write down one scripture from this chapter that strengthens your heart and keep it where you'll see it throughout the day. Let it remind you why you're running.
- Press Forward When It Gets Hard: When you feel weary, stop and pray, "Lord, You are my strength for the long run." Invite His power to carry you, not just your own effort.
- Celebrate the Wins, Big or Small: At the end of the day, thank God for one way He showed His faithfulness, even if it was simply giving you the grace to take the next step.

Scripture References

1 Thessalonians 5:18
Philippians 4:4
Proverbs 24:27
Proverbs 6:6–8

Philippians 3:12–13
Hebrews 12:2
Ephesians 1:18
Psalm 62:1
Proverbs 12:11
Proverbs 13:4
Joel 2:25
Proverbs 20:4
Philippians 4:13
Psalm 27:1 (paraphrased)
Deuteronomy 10:21
Psalm 71:17
2 Timothy 4:7–8
Romans 8:28
Philippians 3:12–14
Psalm 103:17–18
Psalm 45:16–17
Romans 9:17
Psalm 32:8
Philippians 4:12

In Closing

When I think about the life God has called us to, I don't picture a calendar crammed with meetings, a to-do list a mile long, or even a ministry that looks impressive to the world. What I see is fruit that lasts. Fruit that remains long after the moment is gone, long after we've left the room, long after we've taken our last breath. That's the kind of life Jesus spoke of when He said, "*You did not choose Me, but I chose you and appointed you* that *you should go and bear fruit, and* that *your fruit should remain*" (John 15:16).

So much of the world's definition of success is tied to productivity, image, or accumulation. But God's idea of fruitfulness is so different. It's not about being busy; it's about being rooted. It's not about doing more; it's about abiding more. When we learn to manage our time from the place of intimacy with Him, we discover that our schedules stop owning us. Instead, our days are shaped by His priorities, His wisdom, and His grace.

I've learned over the years that every season of life carries its own distractions. In ministry, in work, in family, in leadership, I've faced opportunities to overextend myself and lose focus. But I've also seen how God's wisdom protects, how His pruning shapes, and how His Spirit empowers me to stay on the path He has designed. Fruitfulness isn't about what I can make happen; it's about what I allow Him to cultivate in me.

And here's the beautiful thing: when you and I walk in God's vision for our lives, the fruit goes far beyond us. It touches generations. It shifts cultures. It multiplies in ways we could never orchestrate. Abundance, in God's economy, is not measured in possessions but in eternal impact. This is the kind of fruit that can't be stolen, can't be burned up, and can't be lost.

Final Challenge To You

As you close this book, I don't want these truths to remain on the page; I want them alive in your everyday walk with God. In this next season, I encourage you to begin introducing these challenges into your time with the Lord. Don't try to do them all at once; instead, invite the Holy Spirit to highlight where to begin. Take one step, and then another, and let Him lead you into fruit that lasts.

Here are some practical ways to walk it out:

Abide in His Presence

- Pause and Abide: Set aside one intentional block of time where you simply sit with God—no agenda, no list. Just be with Him.
- Be Still in His Love: Silence distractions and let Him remind you daily that you are deeply loved.
- Abide Before You Act: Before beginning any task, whisper: "Lord, flow through me." Let His presence set the tone for your day.

Journal Prompt:

What do I hear the Lord saying when I pause and simply sit with Him?

____

____

____

____

Guard and Grow the Word

- Guard the Word: Write down one scripture the Holy Spirit highlights. Keep it visible and return to it often.
- Evaluate Your Fruit: Ask yourself, "Is what I'm doing producing eternal fruit or just temporary results?" Allow Him to realign your focus.

Journal Prompt:

Which verse is God highlighting to me right now, and how does it speak to my current season?

___

___

___

___

Live from Rest, Not Striving

- Choose Rest over Striving: When you feel pressure to "do more," stop and cast that care on the Lord. Rest becomes your weapon.
- Surrender Small Worries: When needs arise, resist panic. Pray, trust Him to provide, and watch for His unexpected answers.

Journal Prompt:

Where in my life do I need to replace striving with trust?

___

___

___

___

Think Legacy and Identity

- Think Generationally: Ask God, "Who will my obedience today impact tomorrow?" Pray for your family, friends, and even nations.
- Think Legacy: Share one truth from this journey with someone else. Fruit multiplies when you pass it on.
- Declare Your Identity: Each morning, speak:
    - o "I am loved."
    - o "I am chosen."
    - o "I am anointed and highly favored."

Journal Prompt:

Who in my life is God calling me to intentionally impact with His love and truth?

____

____

____

____

Endure in His Strength

- Commit to Endurance: Identify one area where you feel weary. Ask the Spirit to renew your strength and hold to this promise: "*The one who calls* [me] *is faithful, and he will do it*" (1 Thess. 5:24, *NIV*).

Journal Prompt:

Where do I need fresh strength and endurance from the Lord today?

____

____

____

Remember: This is not about adding more to your to-do list. It's about walking in divine order, resting in His love, stewarding His Word, living from His abundance, and carrying His vision into the world. Your next season is not about survival; it's about overflow.

About the Author

Carrie Pickett has been a believer for over forty years and sensed God's call to be a missionary and Bible teacher from a young age. She has ministered in more than thirty-five nations and spent sixteen years as a full-time missionary in Russia after graduating from Charis Bible College. It was there that she met her husband, Mike Pickett, who was also serving as a missionary.

Together, Mike and Carrie launched and built Andrew Wommack Ministries and Charis Bible College across Russia, impacting sixteen Russian-speaking nations. They currently serve as the Executive Vice Presidents of Andrew Wommack Ministries and Charis Bible College International.

Carrie is the Director of the Woodland Park campus in Colorado and one of the primary instructors at Charis, equipping the next generation of ministers for global impact. She is also a visionary within the Gospel Truth Network, where she hosts the daily program *Life Foundations* and co-hosts *Andrew's Classics* alongside Andrew Wommack and her husband. In addition, she contributes to numerous other programs for the expanding global network.

Writing and developing new teaching materials to support conferences, leadership training, and worldwide outreach is a central passion of her ministry.

In the midst of her leadership and teaching roles, Carrie treasures her calling as a wife and mother. She and Mike travel extensively with their two children, who are growing up immersed in ministry and missions.

Contact Information

CarriePickett.com
719-635-1111
info@gtntv.com

Andrew Wommack Ministries, Inc.
PO Box 3333
Colorado Springs, CO 80934-3333
info@awmi.net
awmi.net

Helpline: 719-635-1111 (available 24/7)

Charis Bible College
info@charisbiblecollege.org
844-360-9577
CharisBibleCollege.org

For international offices
visit **awmi.net/contact-us**.

Connect with us on social media.